Doing Autoethnography

CW00690267

Doing Autoethnography

Foreword by Carolyn Ellis and Arthur P. Bochner

Edited by

Sandra L. Pensoneau-Conway, Tony E. Adams and Derek M. Bolen

SENSE PUBLISHERS
ROTTERDAM / BOSTON / TAIPEI

A C.I.P. record for this book is available from the Library of Congress.

ISBN 978-94-6351-156-8 (paperback)
ISBN 978-94-6351-157-5 (hardback)
ISBN 978-94-6351-158-2 (e-book)

Published by: Sense Publishers,
P.O. Box 21858,
3001 AW Rotterdam,
The Netherlands
https://www.sensepublishers.com/

All chapters in this book have undergone peer review.

Printed on acid-free paper

All rights reserved © 2017 Sense Publishers

No part of this work may be reproduced, stored in a retrieval system, or transmitted in any form or by any means, electronic, mechanical, photocopying, microfilming, recording or otherwise, without written permission from the Publisher, with the exception of any material supplied specifically for the purpose of being entered and executed on a computer system, for exclusive use by the purchaser of the work.

TABLE OF CONTENTS

TABLE OF CONTENTS

CAROLYN ELLIS AND ARTHUR P. BOCHNER

FOREWORD

In this book, twenty-two writers take up the challenge of doing autoethnography. They treat their own lived-through experiences as primary data and sites of moral responsibility. They invite you, their readers, to come away with an appreciation of what it felt like to live through what happened and to make sense of it. They reveal themselves to themselves, and to you, seeking a perspective on their experience that neither they nor you had before they did autoethnography. As auto-ethnographers, these writers integrate emotional, spiritual, and moral parts of themselves with the intellectual and analytical in order to hold on to the personal connection to their experience that inspired them to do autoethnography in the first place. They eschew the conventions of disinterested and impartial analysis, choosing instead to point their inquiries toward "acts of meaning" associated with the lived processes of creating and managing identity, making sense of lived experiences, and communicating it to others.

You, their readers, play an important role in their pursuit of doing autoethnography. After all, the truths of autoethnography exist between story teller and story reader. These writers want you to engage with their struggles with adversity, to empathize with the too often heartbreaking feelings of stigma and marginalization, to identify with the difficulties they experience in finding words to express pain and disruption meaningfully, and to want to do something yourself to assist fellow sufferers. In other words, they want you to interact with their stories, using all the senses available to you, feeling each story's tensions, experiencing their dilemmas or contradictions, and living in the reality of the story for a time. They want you to take what they have done and engage with it, allowing yourselves, perhaps even forcing yourselves, to consider the ways in which their stories relate to your life and to find in this connection some truth about yourself. This is the gift they offer you in what they have done. What will keep the conversation going is your willingness and conscientiousness to enter into dialogue with these stories, maintaining an openness to "otherness" and a dedication to social justice, ethics, and moral imagination. As we like to say to our students, autoethnography is not a spectator sport.

Unlike much of the writing one finds across and within the social sciences, you should find these stories a pleasure to read. These writers are determined to communicate with you rather than simply to impress you with their intellect or theoretical acumen. They care about how you may react and engage with their stories. They write in a revealing and passionate way because they are seeking connection, desiring to evoke something deep in your guts and your heart that will allow one consciousness to reach another, yours to theirs.

We heard a number of these stories when they were first presented at the *Doing Autoethnography* Conferences. If you're like us, you will find it difficult to put the book down, once you start it. Many of these stories will take you into the depths of suffering in the human experience, including mental illness, divorce, abuse, male rape, male violence, ambiguous loss, stigmatized bodies, brain injury, learning disability, physical illness, dislocation, and the secrets we keep about the associated pain. Though authors do not eschew their pain, they don't dwell there; instead, they enact resistance, adaptation, and resilience as they write to uncover for themselves what these experiences mean and forge connections to many of you who may have felt similar disruptions in your lives. You will realize that you are not alone and neither are they. You will journey with them in their search for sexual, racial, ethnic, and gendered identities, at home and work. You will be taken into relationships between partners, colleagues, siblings, mothers and sons, fathers and daughters, teachers and students, counselors and clients.

We were delighted to experience the ways in which these writers, many of them new to autoethnography, introduced and experimented with novel modes of expressing and performing lived experiences and concentrated on new frontiers of inquiry including materiality, new media, and technology. As you move through the pages of these stories, you will be accompanied by autoethnographers struggling to hold onto a story yet realizing that sometimes the right thing to do is to let it go. And, you will become involved in—and sometimes share through your own life and work—the breathtaking moral and ethical issues that arise as authors seek to unveil their experiences yet stay acutely alert to the dangers and responsibilities they hold to intimate others and to the groups, families, and organizations implicated in their work and their lives.

Thanks to Derek for spearheading the *Doing Autoethnography* Conferences for five years. He handled the ice storms and electrical outages with grace and class, allowing the conferences themselves to take center stage and prosper, providing a safe space for new and old scholars to gather, to share, to learn, and to celebrate autoethnography together. Thanks to Sandy, Tony, and Derek for gathering and editing these papers and making them accessible to a wider audience. We look forward to future conferences and eagerly anticipate the next volume. This volume brings us joy and security about the future of autoethnography as embodied by the young talent and loving hearts of these writers.

Carolyn Ellis and Arthur P. Bochner
Franklin, NC (in the middle of nature)

ACKNOWLEDGMENTS

We are grateful to the contributors of this collection—without them, this book would not exist. Their enthusiasm, responsiveness, and patience have been treasured. We would also like to thank Peter de Liefde and Michel Lokhorst for their support, as well as the opportunity to publish with Sense Publishers.

SANDRA L. PENSONEAU-CONWAY, TONY E. ADAMS, AND
DEREK M. BOLEN

1. DOING AUTOETHNOGRAPHY

I sit in the classroom-turned-conference room on the first floor of Manoogian Hall
at Wayne State University, taking in an evocative narration of the power of music
in autoethnography. As the presenter drums, and my closed eyes take me far from
Detroit, Michigan (United States), I notice a definite change in the atmosphere. All
goes quiet, a momentary and collective feeling of confusion. The lights have gone
out in the building. It may be the middle of the day, but it's also a wintry
November afternoon. Outside the door's window, I notice what seem to be
conference assistants moving swiftly one direction, then another, likely wondering
what happened and how to remedy it. Our little collective in our first floor room
remedies it on our own—the presenter keeps drumming, we return to closing our
eyes, and take in the magic that is autoethnography.

* * *

In 2010, (then graduate student) Derek Bolen had a vision: to create *Doing
Autoethnography*, the first conference that focused solely on autoethnographic
principles and practices.[1] *Doing Autoethnography* would tap into a burgeoning
interest in, and build upon a rich history of, conferences foregrounding
ethnographic and qualitative research, specifically the *Ethnographic Alternatives*
Conference hosted by Art Bochner and Carolyn Ellis (2000) and the annual
International Congress of Qualitative Inquiry, which Norman Denzin started in
2005.[2] Derek's vision was a success: the *Doing Autoethnography* Conference has
occurred five times (2011, 2013, 2014, 2015, 2016).

Across the five conferences, thousands of attendees from more than ten
countries have attended hundreds of presentations, more than a dozen workshops,
and multiple keynote addresses. While some attendees participated in one
conference, others have attended all five. There have been many publications
connected to conference discussions and presentations,[3] and, as of this writing, the
Doing Autoethnography Facebook page has more than 800 members.

Uniquely, Derek sought to create generative space for those newer to
autoethnography. Such a personal and identifiable method of research certainly
brings with it a host of anxieties associated with the revelation of personal
experience, reliving one's past, the craft of writing, confrontation of struggles, and
so on. And so, in the beginning, and aside from workshop presenters and keynote
speakers, conference attendees were largely limited to graduate and undergraduate

S. L. Pensoneau-Conway et al.(Eds.), Doing Autoethnography, 1–5.
© 2017 Sense Publishers. All rights reserved.

students. In that first conference held in November 2011 at Wayne State University in Detroit, attendees found support in one another. Derek certainly aimed high, and achieved it.

In addition to the unique focus of the conference, Derek's organization also merits praise. Every year, the conference has been free; there were never any submission or registration fees, and all programming was open for general admission. Most years, Derek even secured on-campus lodging available for a nominal cost, and sometimes the sessions had free food and coffee. Although adequate funding is increasingly difficult to secure for such an event, we hope that future *Doing Autoethnography* Conferences can meet such impeccable standards.

Yet, there have been some hurdles. In 2011, all of the power went out in the building where the presentations were held. But the attendees pushed through, sitting in darkness as the presenters used cell-phone lights to present their work. In 2014 and 2015, there were ice storms, cancelled flights, and dangerous roadways. Across the years, there have been a few fussy attendees, as well as fiery disagreements about the use and significance of personal experience in research. These hurdles aside, each conference has been infused with passion and support.

After the fifth *Doing Autoethnography* Conference (2016), the three of us decided to assemble a collection of essays that would capture the essence of the first five years of the conference. We submitted a proposal to Sense Publishers, which, as this book demonstrates, was positively received. We then had the difficult task of determining who to include. We began by scanning all five years of the programs. Given that the three of us assisted with every conference, as well as attended many of the presentations and workshops, we had a good sense about which presentations would be critical chapters. We also sought to include chapters by those who attended the conference multiple years and chapters based on presentations that generated large audiences and important conversations.

This collection offers original chapters that made it through the selection process, as well as through multiple revisions. Together, they address many overlapping themes: identity norms and negotiations; issues tied to race, gender, sexuality, size, citizenship, and dis/ability; exclusion and belonging; oppression, injustice, and assault; barriers to learning/education; and living in/with complicated relationships. The chapters show autoethnography in practice, and interrogate autoethnography ethically, theoretically, relationally, and methodologically. Some provide clear resolutions; others seemingly provide none. Some authors highlight conventionally positive aspects of experience; others dwell in what might be understood as relational darkness. Some experiences likely resonate with many readers; others likely feel unique, unusual, exceptional. These chapters also pose questions to readers: What is the role of resolution in an autoethnographic story? How does a positive-negative dichotomy function in autoethnography? How does autoethnography invite identification in the midst of storying both the familiar and the strange?

We envision multiple uses of this book. It should appeal to attendees of the annual *Doing Autoethnography* Conferences, as well as people interested in, but who could not attend, the conferences. This book could be used as a primary text in undergraduate and graduate courses about autoethnographic research and personal narrative, or as a supplemental text in courses about writing and/or qualitative research. (Given the short length of the chapters, each could serve as a model for a final course project.) This book could also serve as a resource for new and established researchers who have an interest in autoethnography.

As demonstrated by the *Doing Autoethnography* Conference and this collection, autoethnography has amassed a significant following. Courses devoted to autoethnography are taught at many colleges and universities, and scholars from numerous disciplines use autoethnography in their research.[4] Numerous books, edited collections, and special journal issues foreground autoethnographic practice,[5] and prominent texts about qualitative research include chapters about the method.[6] We look forward to many more years of *Doing Autoethnography* and to assembling the next collection of essays from conferences yet to occur.

NOTES

[1] Autoethnographers use personal experience to describe—and sometimes critique—cultural beliefs, experiences, practices, and identities. They engage in rigorous self-reflection in order to identify and interrogate intersections between self and society, as well as show "people in the process of figuring out what to do, how to live, and the meaning of their struggles" (Bochner & Ellis, 2006, p. 111). For comprehensive accounts of autoethnography, see Adams, Holman Jones, and Ellis (2015), Bochner and Ellis (2016), and Holman Jones, Adams, and Ellis (2013).

[2] In form, we intended for this book to resemble past conference collections such as *Ethnographically Speaking: Autoethnography, Literature, and Aesthetics* (Bochner & Ellis, 2002) and *Contemporary British Autoethnography* (Short, Turner, & Grant, 2013).

[3] Publications with ties to presentations at *Doing Autoethnography* include Adams (2012), Crouse-Dick (2013), Doshi (2014), Hopkins (2015), Ivey (2015), Meyer (2015), Pensoneau-Conway, Bolen, Toyosaki, Rudick, and Bolen (2014), Purnell (2014), Smith (2015) and Toyosaki and Pensoneau-Conway (2013).

[4] Scholars in numerous disciplines have used autoethnography including, but not limited to, accounting (Haynes, 2017), nursing (Sealy, 2012), music (Bartlett & Ellis, 2009), criminology (Sollund, 2017), physical cultural studies (Smith, 2017), media studies (Dhoest, 2014), anthropology (Toor, 2017), human resources (Sambrook, 2016), communication (Bochner, 2014), and sport management (Cooper, Grenier, & Macaulay, 2017).

[5] Numerous books (e.g., Adams, Holman Jones, & Ellis, 2015; Bochner, 2014; Boylorn, 2017; Denzin, 2013; Ellis, 2004; Spry, 2016), edited collections (e.g., Boylorn & Orbe, 2014; Short, Turner, & Grant, 2013; Wyatt & Adams, 2014), and special issues (e.g., Adams & Bolen, 2017; Berry & Clair, 2011; Manning & Adams, 2015) foreground autoethnographic practices.

[6] Qualitative research methods texts with chapters about autoethnography include Denzin and Lincoln (2000, 2005, 2011, 2017), Leavy (2014), and Lapan, Quartroli and Reimer (2012).

REFERENCES

Adams, T. E. (2012). The joys of autoethnography: Possibilities for communication research. *Qualitative Communication Research*, *1*, 181–194. doi: 10.1525/qcr.2012.1.2.181

Adams, T. E., & Bolen, D. M. (Eds.) (2017). Queer autoethnography [Forum]. *QED: Journal in GLBTQ Worldmaking*, *4*(1).

Adams, T. E., Holman Jones, S., & Ellis, C. (2015). *Autoethnography*. Oxford, UK: Oxford University Press.

Bartleet, B.-L., & Ellis, C. (Eds.). (2009). *Music autoethnographies: Making autoethnography sing/making music personal*. Bowen Hills: QLD Australian Academic Press.

Berry, K., & Clair, R. P. (2011). Special issue: The call of ethnographic reflexivity: Narrating the self's presence in ethnography. *Cultural Studies ↔ Critical Methodologies, 11*(2).

Bochner, A. P. (2014). *Coming to narrative: A personal history of paradigm change in the human sciences*. Walnut Creek, CA: Left Coast Press.

Bochner, A. P., & Ellis, C. (2016). *Evocative autoethnography: Writing lives and telling stories*. New York, NY: Routledge.

Bochner, A. P., & Ellis, C. S. (2006). Communication as autoethnography. In G. J. Shepherd, J. St. John, & T. Striphas (Eds.), *Communication as ... Perspectives on theory* (pp. 110–122). Thousand Oaks, CA: Sage.

Boylorn, R. M. (2017). *Sweetwater: Black women and narratives of resilience* (revised edition). New York, NY: Peter Lang.

Boylorn, R. M., & Orbe, M. P. (Eds.). (2014). *Critical autoethnography: Intersecting cultural identities in everyday life*. Walnut Creek, CA: Left Coast Press.

Cooper, J. N., Grenier, R. S., & Macaulay, C. (2017). Autoethnography as a critical approach in sport management: Current applications and directions for future research. *Sport Management Review, 20*(1), 43–54. doi: 10.1016/j.smr.2016.07.003

Crouse-Dick, C. E. (2013). (In)fertile encounters: An autoethnography. In K. Fast & R. Epp Buller (Eds.), *Mothering Mennonite* (pp. 195–214). Bradford, Ontario: Demeter Press.

Denzin, N. K. (2013). *Interpretive autoethnography*. Thousand Oaks, CA: Sage.

Denzin, N. K., & Lincoln, Y. S. Lincoln (Eds.). (2000). *Handbook of qualitative research* (2nd ed.). Thousand Oaks, CA: Sage.

Denzin, N. K., & Lincoln, Y. S. (Eds.). (2005). *The Sage handbook of qualitative research* (3rd ed.). Thousand Oaks, CA: Sage.

Denzin, N. K., & Lincoln, Y. S. (Eds.). (2011). *The Sage handbook of qualitative research* (4th ed.). Thousand Oaks, CA: Sage.

Denzin, N. K., & Lincoln, Y. S. (Eds.). (2017). *The Sage handbook of qualitative research* (5th ed.). Thousand Oaks, CA: Sage.

Dhoest, A. (2014). "If you asked me ... ": Exploring autoethnography as a means to critically assess and advance audience research. In F. Zeller, C. Ponte, & B. O'Neill (Eds.), *Revitalising audience research: Innovations in European audience research* (pp. 29–43). New York, NY: Routledge.

Doshi, M. J. (2014). Help(less): An autoethnography about caring for my mother with terminal cancer. *Health Communication, 29*, 840–842. doi: http://dx.doi.org/10.1080/10410236.2013.809502

Ellis, C. (2004). *The ethnographic I: A methodological novel about autoethnography*. Walnut Creek, CA: AltaMira Press.

Haynes, K. (2017). Autoethnography in accounting research. In Z. Hoque, L. D. Parker, M. A. Covaleski, & K. Haynes (Eds.), *The Routledge companion to qualitative accounting research methods* (pp. 215–230). New York, NY: Routledge.

Holman Jones, S., Adams, T. E., & Ellis, C. (Eds.). (2013). *Handbook of autoethnography*. Walnut Creek, CA: Routledge.

Hopkins, J. B. (2015). Coming "home": An autoethnographic exploration of Third Culture Kid transition. *Qualitative Inquiry, 21*, 812–820. https://doi.org/10.1177/1077800415574909

Ivey, C. L. (2015). Glossary (not) for non-ADHD partners. *Departures in Critical Qualitative Research, 4*, 99–116. doi: 10.1525/dcqr.2015.4.4.99

Lapan, S. D., Quartaroli, M. T., & Riemer, F. J. (2012). *Qualitative research: An introduction to methods and designs*. San Francisco, CA: Jossey-Bass.

Leavy, P. (2014). *The Oxford handbook of qualitative research*. Oxford, England: Oxford University Press.

Manning, J., & Adams, T. E. (Eds.). (2015). Connecting the personal and the popular: Autoethnography and popular culture. *The Popular Culture Journal, 3*.

Pensoneau-Conway, S. L., Bolen, D. M., Toyosaki, S., Rudick, C. K., & Bolen, E. K. (2014). Self, relationship, positionality, and politics: A community autoethnographic inquiry into collaborative writing. *Cultural Studies ⇔ Critical Methodologies, 14*(4), 312–323. doi: 10.1177/153270861430302

Purnell, D. F. (2014). My brother's keeper. In E. D. Miller (Ed.), *Stories of complicated grief: A critical anthology* (pp. 304–314). Washington, DC: NASW Press.

Meyer, M. D. E. (2015). On the identity politics of pregnancy: An autoethnographic journey through in/of reproductive time. In R. E. Silverman & J. Baglia (Eds.), *Communicating pregnancy loss: Narrative as a method for change* (pp. 135–150). New York, NY: Peter Lang.

Sambrook, S. (2016). Autoethnography: A novel way to study HRM. In K. Townsend, R. Loudoun, & D. Lewin (Eds.), *Handbook of qualitative research methods on human resource management: Innovative techniques* (pp. 42–57). Cheltenham, England: Edward Elgar.

Sealy, P. A. (2012). Autoethnography: Reflective journaling and meditation to cope with life-threatening breast cancer. *Clinical Journal of Oncology Nursing, 16*, 38–41.

Short, N. P., Turner, L., & Grant, A. (Eds.). (2013). *Contemporary British autoethnography.* Rotterdam, the Netherlands: Sense Publishers.

Smith, B. (2017). Narrative inquiry and autoethnography. In M. Silk, D. Andrews, & H. Thorpe (Eds.), *Handbook of physical cultural studies* (pp. 505–514). London, England: Routledge.

Smith, C. (2015). (Re)imagining "normal" movement: Dystonia, the chronic illness disrupting my life. *Departures in Critical Qualitative Research, 4*(3), 92–107. doi: 10.1525/dcqr.2015.4.3.92

Sollund, R. (2017). Doing green, critical criminology with an auto-ethnographic, feminist approach. *Critical Criminology, 25*(2), 245–260. doi: 10.1007/s10612-017-9361-z

Spry, T. (2016). *Autoethnography and the other: Unsettling power through utopian performatives.* New York, NY: Routledge.

Toor, R. (2017, April 23). Scholars talk writing: Ruth Behar. *The Chronicle of Higher Education.* Retrieved from http://www.chronicle.com/article/Scholars-Talk-Writing-Ruth/239847

Toyosaki, S., & Pensoneau-Conway, S. L. (2013). Autoethnography as a praxis of social justice: Three ontological contexts. In S. Holman Jones, T. E. Adams, & C. Ellis (Eds.), *Handbook of autoethnography* (pp. 557–575). Walnut Creek, CA: Left Coast Press.

Wyatt. J. & Adams, T. E. (Eds.). (2014). *On (writing) families: Autoethnographies of presence and absence, love and loss.* Rotterdam, the Netherlands: Sense Publishers.

Sandra L. Pensoneau-Conway
Department of Communication Studies
Southern Illinois University Carbondale

Tony E. Adams
Department of Communication
Bradley University

Derek M. Bolen
Queer Scholar/Activist
Director of the Doing Autoethnography *Conference*

ROBIN M. BOYLORN

2. BITTER SWEET(WATER)

Autoethnography, Relational Ethics, and the Possible
Perpetuation of Stereotypes

I was honored to give a preconference lecture for the fourth annual Doing Autoethnography conference (2014). At the time, my first book, *Sweetwater: Black Women and Narratives of Resilience* (Boylorn, 2013a), had recently won some prestigious awards, and I was anxious to talk about the process of *doing* that "ethnographic autoethnography" (Chris Poulos, personal communication, May 23, 2014). I was also interested in reflecting on the consequences of potential mischaracterization and misappropriation of rural black women, as a result of the work. Because black women are routinely misrecognized as tropes or controlling images, I wrote *Sweetwater* to push against those images. However, the process of doing autoethnography is not limited to our good intentions.

In the lecture, I wanted to hone in on what it meant and might mean to do harmful autoethnography, particularly when you are a member of a marginalized group whose story is offered as generalizable. How is telling a representative story problematic? What happens when our stories can be used against us?

Accordingly, *Sweetwater* was an achingly beautiful tribute to my community, but it could also be read as an indictment of it. In 2016 I began working on a revised edition of *Sweetwater* (2017), which offers a new framing to the stories, a response to critiques and reviews, excerpts from a *Sweetwater* forum, and an opportunity to re-engage how writing *Sweetwater* was a bittersweet experience.

In the following lecture, I wrestled, for the first time publicly, with what it means to write an autoethnography about black women that exposed them, and me, as equally stereotypical and extraordinary. I reckon with the ways that they are implicated by my telling of a story that is ours, not just mine. As a black woman autoethnographer, I am always concerned about the possible perpetuation of stereotypes in my stories, and I struggle with what it means to tell these stories (Boylorn, 2014). The lecture transcribed below engages those questions, introduces my theorization of blackgirl (one word) autoethnography (Boylorn, 2016a), and discusses ethical engagement that rescues secrets while preserving relationships.

* * *

I would like to thank Derek Bolen for the invitation and opportunity to participate in the preconference tonight. I also want to thank each of you who made an effort

S. L. Pensoneau-Conway et al. (Eds.), Doing Autoethnography, 7–17.
© *2017 Sense Publishers. All rights reserved.*

to be here on the eve of the fourth Doing Autoethnography conference. And as I tend to do, I want to recognize those whose work, vision, mentorship, friendship, love, guidance, and support have made my blackgirl autoethnographic life possible. Those folk include colleagues, former teachers, co-writers, editors, mentors, family members, black woman warriors, allies, friends, and my mama, to name a few. In particular I want to acknowledge Bud Goodall, Carolyn Ellis, Art Bochner, Stacy Holman Jones, Tony Adams, Chris Poulos, Mary Weems, Mark Orbe, Marsha Houston, Bryant Alexander, Cynthia Dillard, and the writers in this room, those I have already read and those I will yet read. Thank you for making space for my words and filling this space with your presence.

I stand on the shoulders of giants and my work follows a legacy of folk who didn't have the platform, or the education, or the opportunity, or the microphone that I do. I endeavor to always use my place and space to acknowledge whose I am and where I come from. So to that end I thank my family, my rural roots, and the women of Sweetwater who selflessly and generously shared stories about their lives, helping me re-imagine my own. To the Crunk Feminist Collective, I am grateful to join my voice in a symphony of others doing the work and literally, so many times, putting our lives on the line, our business in the street, our reputations on the forefront, our vulnerabilities in the air, our anger on display, our sadness on the threshold, our weakness on the windowsill, our hearts at the open door. My work would be meaningless without witnesses.

The title of my lecture tonight, *BitterSweet(water): Autoethnography, Relational Ethics and the Possible Perpetuation of Stereotypes,* is based on my first baby, *Sweetwater: Black Women and Narratives of Resilience*, a project conceived of 10 years before it was born, based on my thesis *Finding Voice: African American Women in the New American South*, and my dissertation *Southern Black Women: Their Lived Realities*. Sweetwater is a commentary on my autoethnographic life's work, which began with my very first autoethnography, called Working-class Black Girl. I presented it in 2002, at a small regional conference not unlike this. I was terrified to be sharing my story to strangers, none of whom were calling themselves autoethnographers. And, as is oftentimes the case, I was the only blackgirl in the room. My voice and legs shook as I stood in front of a podium, reading words out loud that had only previously been read by my professor. It was an autobiographic confession of my lived life and the ways my race, gender, and class were interconnected, shaping my life and experience. I worried about how I would be seen, and more so, how other blackgirl women would be seen, after I put all of our business in the street. As the saying goes, wherever you go, there you are. And there I was, truthtelling for the first time in public and feeling free.

Audience members thanked me for allowing them access to an experience they were unfamiliar with, for trusting them with my truth, for being my bare boned blackgirl self. The panel moderator, stunned to silence, remarked, "that was a beautiful piece of literature." I didn't know if her response was a compliment or criticism, but I was grateful for the opportunity to share parts of my life that I had always kept secret.

My blackgirlness (one word, no space) has always centered and situated my autoethnographies, even before I knew I was writing autoethnography. I can't tell a story without my blackgirlness coming out, in my language or way with words, in my culturally-centered situatedness, in my consciousness and intentionalities, and in the signals and clues I leave for readers who share my blackgirl standpoint or background. But still, I am protective of my inner blackgirl, and sometimes concerned about the implications of blackgirl storytelling and the ways I inevitably participate in the perpetuation of stereotypes. This was uniquely the case with Sweetwater, because I was not just telling my own story, but generalizing by telling the stories of a community of women, who would invariably come to represent each other and me.

In this process I have realized that intention, however well meaning, does not always dictate reception. I can't protect myself or other black women from the ways my stories might reinforce misguided mischaracterizations of race, gender, and class. But that is one, of a few things, I want to talk through with you tonight. In tonight's lecture, I am going to talk about *Sweetwater*, I'm going to talk about blackgirls (no space) and blackgirl autoethnography, and I'm going to talk about what happens when the stories we tell, tell stories (read: lies) on us.

Sweetwater was my contribution to the academy, in order to create and situate narratives that were largely absent during my own education, and a contribution to my community, a location that was the center of my world and the place of possibility that surrounded my transitions through blackgirlhood. *Sweetwater* is the beginning of an ongoing narrative I continue to tell in individual autoethnographies and will extend in a forthcoming book project, *Blackgirl Blue(s),* where I will more explicitly detail blackgirl autoethnography.

I want/ed *Sweetwater* to push against assumptions about black women. I wanted *Sweetwater* to humanize them, to challenge one-dimensional representations of them, to prove mythic and stereotypical tropes are incapable of capturing our essence, to offer a counter-narrative to fictional accounts of our lives, and to offer stories that were not prescriptive or rigid, but rather nuanced and fluid. That was my intention. I know black women to be brilliant, masterful, resilient, resistant, and brave. But I also know black women to be self-righteous, mean-spirited, indignant, head strong and a little ratchet. If *Sweetwater* was going to represent the lives I witnessed, the life I live(d), the stories I collected, and the themes that emerged, then I was faced with the conundrum of writing a story that was ethnographic and autoethnographic, and that resisted and embodied stereotypes.

In the conclusion of *Sweetwater* I reflected on why I felt an autoethnography about rural black women was important, but also why I felt it was somewhat problematic. In addition to the possibility of participants recognizing each other's stories in the final manuscript (Tolich, 2004), I was also concerned about how they would respond to the representations I developed, namely those that were stereotypical. In order to write a story that was ethically responsible I knew I would have to embrace stereotypes as well as challenge them, especially those parts that I found to be close to the truth. This meant exposing the positive and negative aspects of rural black women's lives. Since I knew that so many of the issues I would be bringing to light about rural black women were stereotypical, I feared what those declarations of lived experience might mean—for them and for me.

When I endeavored to write *Sweetwater* I committed to writing a story that was accessible to the participants who took part in the research while simultaneously being evocative and provocative for the reader (Adams, Holman Jones & Ellis, 2015; Goodall, 2000). My intention was to bring voice and intentionality to the representations of rural black women and their lives, which have routinely been marginalized, silenced, and overlooked (McLaurin, 2001). It is/was important to me that readers experience some kind of resonance with the story, the place, and/or the characters. In many ways, as Bud Goodall taught me, that is the call of good ethnographic storytelling (Boylorn, 2016b; Goodall, 2004, 2005).

METHOD

I conducted interviews, transcribed and thematized them, created a chronological timeline, translated the interviews to stories, and modeled my autoethnography accordingly (focusing on and responding to the same themes and topics that emerged from the interviews). I wanted to tell a parallel narrative that represented what it was like to live in Sweetwater in the 20th century, over three generations.

In many ways the storytelling part was somewhat instinctive. I utilized storytelling techniques to create scene and setting, and then situated the narratives I wrote about/around the emergent themes.

I interviewed nine women several times over the course of two years, where I spent summers, holidays, and special occasions in the town (including church services, family gatherings, parties, and Sunday dinners). I compiled over 30 hours of audio taped interviews, but spent several hundred hours observing, discussing, and interacting with women in the community to gather data.

As much as possible I preserved the voices and language of participants, attempting to capture the rhythm of their voices, the cadence of their moods, and the feelings evoked through their re-telling, both in my observations of them and my observations of my observations of them. Each story that is included in *Sweetwater* is intentional and some things were intentionally left out. I want to talk briefly about what I left out and why.

There were three ways I had to intentionally consider ethics when writing *Sweetwater*: 1) relational ethics and ethical considerations when writing about intimate others (Ellis, 2007); 2) ethical considerations when you are a member of a marginalized group and must be mindful about existing representations and stereotypes that you are contributing and/or responding to; and 3) the ethical considerations as an insider of the community being researched.

My specific concerns were related to representations of black women, representations of rurality, personal relationships I had with participants, and my insecurity about disguising the identity of interviewees within the community:

- Representations of black women. I did not want to reinforce existing, racist stereotypes of black women. (I will say more about those stereotypes and why they are so dangerous.)

- Representations of rural places/rurality. There are stereotypes of rural folk being backward, poor, and non-progressive. I struggled with wanting to present rurality as a distinct and unique experience and way of life without creating caricatures of my participants.
- I had personal relationships with participants and other anonymous members of my community who I interviewed and observed. I felt comfortable ensuring external confidentiality for some participants, because people outside the community would not know who they were, but people within the community would be automatically identifiable because of their biological relationship to me.
- The community members I interviewed also had relationships with each other, so while I could ensure outsiders would not recognize them, I could not guarantee internal confidentiality because they would likely recognize each other and the stories shared.

STEREOTYPES OF BLACK WOMEN

Regarding representations and my concern for contributing to and/or reinforcing stereotypical representations of black women, I struggled with the fine line between telling a narrative with verisimilitude and telling a narrative that could be used against rural black women as evidence of their inferiority. To address this, I acknowledge my concerns, I acknowledge the fact that some of these stories, women, and their actions are stereotypical, being explicit about my intention to make them three-dimensional, not one-dimensional characters. I was fully committed to offering authentic representations of them, acknowledging if/when those representations may be problematic, but also explaining that black women don't necessarily see themselves in the same way that outsiders/non-black women see them. Black women often embrace and celebrate the unique aspects of their lives that are characteristically black, stereotype or not.

In *Black Feminist Thought*, Patricia Hill Collins (2009) discusses the ways Black women are generally pigeon-holed according to any one or combination of specific stereotypes, including but not limited to the mammy, matriarch, jezebel, sapphire, and Black lady. Today these stereotypes include "educated bitches" or "bad Black mothers." These stereotypes, sometimes based on characters, are common "controlling images" (Collins, 2009; Harris-Perry, 2011) used to represent black womanhood.

The mammy stereotype conjures images of slavery and the Black woman. She often cared for White children at the expense of her own. This character is rhetorically constructed as big bodied, intimidating, matronly, asexual, and nurturing. In contrast, the matriarch character is situated as a failed mammy because of her rejection of willing subjugation. The matriarch is often blamed for the plights of the Black family and community. Matriarchs are seen as "overly aggressive, unfeminine women" who "allegedly emasculate their lovers and husbands" because of her place as head of the household (Collins, 2009, p. 83).

11

The historical Jezebel image is related to Black women's presumed hypersexuality and lack of sexual agency during slavery. Jezebel was seen as a temptress and seductress whose indiscriminate sexual appetite condoned slave-master rape (Yarbrough & Bennett, 1999). Modern representations of the Jezebel are the hoochie and welfare queen (Collins, 2009). These representations express a deviant female sexuality wherein Black women have insatiable sexual appetites. Promiscuity and fertility are dominant traits of the Jezebel.

The Sapphire image combines stereotypes of the sassy mammy and the angry Black woman. The Sapphire is considered rude, loud, malicious, stubborn, and overbearing (Bell-Scott, 2015; Boylorn, 2014). She is an antagonizing verbal emasculator who continuously berates and nags Black men. She is both offensive and easily offended, and aggressively defends herself or speaks her mind. Sapphire is often represented as uneducated and unsophisticated.

The Black lady is a class-specific image of the "middle-class professional Black woman" (Collins, 2009, p. 88) who is independently successful and educated. This stereotype is a unique mix of the modern mammy and the matriarch due to her work ethic and dedication to work above family. The Black lady's obsession with her own success is usually at the expense of her domestic pursuits. Often she is unmarried and childless.

Generally these black woman stereotypes dictate how black women are characterized and read (Collins, 2009; Harris-Perry, 2011). The women in *Sweetwater* can be read as the embodiment of any number of these stereotypes at different points of their lives. While the women I interviewed may not be familiar with the theoretical implications of the mammy, matriarch, Jezebel, Sapphire and black lady, they are aware of the descriptions and definitions associated with the characters, and therefore themselves, and would respond to them with both resistance and acceptance.

In *Sister Citizen: Shame, Stereotypes and Black Women in America*, Melissa Harris-Perry (2011) discusses a post-World War II cognitive psychology research experiment she refers to as the "crooked room" to explain how black women's perceptions and presentations are sometimes consistent with problematic stereotypes. In the experiment, individuals were placed in a crooked room and asked to align themselves vertically. Linking the findings to black women's perception Harris-Perry explains,

> When they confront race and gender stereotypes, black women are standing in a crooked room, and they have to figure out which way is up. Bombarded with warped images of their humanity, some black women tilt and bend themselves to fit the distortion. (p. 29)

This misperception explains why many times black women, consciously and unconsciously, knowingly and unknowingly reinforce stereotypes through their experiences and life choices. In many ways the stereotypes box them into their circumstances, which are always intersectional, and then punish them for not having the means to find a way out.

ETHICAL STRATEGIES

The other two ethical concerns, around my relationships with others (in my family and community) and their relationships with each other, are linked to relational ethics. I had to act in a manner that protected and prioritized interpersonal relationships. While I was confident I could keep participants from being recognizable outside of the community, I was less sure I could protect their anonymity within the community, especially when there was some overlap between the stories being told and/or the stories that were well known in the community or family. I did not want to compromise my relationships so that I would not be able to go back home, nor did I want the women I interviewed to experience dis-ease in the community they still resided in. I used two specific strategies to help ensure anonymity among participants: 1) I collapsed characters so that their likeness, actions, and experiences would be indistinguishable; and 2) I used pseudonyms and fictionalization, both as a tactic of storytelling and in an effort to disguise the lives and experiences of some participants.

INSIDER ETHICS

Still, there were insider ethics beyond me writing about black women as a black woman. As a member of the community (an insider) I had access to and memories of stories that may not have been shared through interview and archival research. If/when I decided to tell a story I knew as a former community member, I had to think about whether or not the person implicated in the story would be comfortable with me sharing it. Although I had no way of knowing if their exclusion had been intentional or circumstantial, I had to decide which stories and/or details to keep and which to leave out. I made this determination on a case-by-case basis.

A second ethical dilemma I faced was linked to my ability to "pass" in the space. I was a researcher, but most everyone recognized me as just Robin, Bettina's daughter, Gert's granddaughter. There were times when I was acting as a "researcher" but being seen and interacted with as a family or community member. This means that some things may have been shared with me in confidence or "off the record" when I was recording them as data. This is/was especially true when as a researcher I interacted with participants informally (without tape recording). Again, this revelation came to me post-data compilation, so I wasn't as conscious of the dualism while I was conducting the research and could not therefore confirm their understanding that I was never not "researching."

A third ethical dilemma dealt with inner-intersectionality and absences. In other words, who was not being outwardly represented in the community and narratives and why. So, for example, while it was not uncommon for black women in the story to be genderqueer in their behaviors and presentations, masculinity being common in working-class communities, there was an absence of mention of lesbians, transwomen, women with disabilities not attributed to their age, women who were non-Christian, etc. I felt that their invisibility was not indicative of their absence, but rather the ways they are not mentioned or remembered because they have been pushed past the margins of the margins. For this reason, I created the characters Sweetie Pie and Peewee in a prelude between the two parts of the book. Sweetie Pie and Peewee are lovers and friends, but whose relationship is misinterpreted as platonic and/or ignored altogether in the community.

BLACKGIRL AUTOETHNOGRAPHY

Now, I want to shift to talk about the ways I theorize the lives of black woman as a black woman who is also an autoethnographer. In order to best analyze the stories and lived experiences of black women, it is important to simultaneously theorize what it means to be a black woman in a racist, anti-black, misogynistic culture that plagues black women with oppressions, discriminations, and stereotypes.

One way I have decided to respond to and/or resist the possibility of perpetuating stereotypes is by embracing them, or rather embracing the fact that stereotypes of black women are parts of me and sometimes provide predictability because of circumstances beyond my control. Some of them are negative, others delicious. Many of them are problematic, most of them are flat-out wrong, but some of them are recognizable, and I absorb both into my writing and analysis.

I write blackgirl (one word) auto/ethnography because it speaks to the two-ness and one-ness of my raced and gendered identity that is ever present in my work, alongside my class background. I am never only black or only girl/woman, but always both/and at the same time and that colors and situates my lived experience. I see blackgirl and black (space) girl as distinct and not the same, so I merge the words to make them touch on paper the way they touch in my everyday existence. I do it knowing that by impulse folk will want to separate those words in an effort to be "right," or right wrongs, but being a blackgirl (one word) means something specific and carries with it the meanings and microaggressions blackgirls live with every day. In the context of my life, my feminism, my politics, my lived experience, my autoethnography, I put the two words together so that when you see them, hear them, think about them, read them, and write them, you see the connectedness of those pieces of me, of those pieces in me and my story.

Blackgirl.
So that the words look the way they sound on my tongue.
    Blackgirl,
    not
    black
    (then)
    Girl.
    There is no pause in my identity.
    Blackgirl,
    not
    black
    (space)
    girl.

There is no space left in me.
Blackgirl
(no space)
Because there is no protection between my race and sex.
Because I am never seen or experienced as black by itself or girl without race.
(Boylorn, 2016a, p. 49)

Blackgirl autoethnography is blackened (Boylorn, 2013b), in that it centers and makes claims about particular, but shared, experiences of women of color, but it also troubles traditional (white, male, heterosexual) ways of knowing and being in the world by embracing the tenets of autoethnography (Ellis, Adams, & Bochner, 2011) which resist singular representations of experience or research. Blackgirl autoethnography also embraces the impulse to critique, theorize, and analyze our lives as we live and reflect on them.

Black women are beautiful.
And sassy.
And strong.
And needy.
And belligerent.
And mean.
And hateful.
And hopeful.
And loving.
And protective.
And forgiving.
They are all of these things and more.
We are all of these things and more.

In *Sweetwater* and the stories that center my personal lived experience, I attempt to show blackgirlness in all its majesty, rough edges and all.

In *Sweetwater*, some of the themes that emerged from grounded theory analysis included 1) the prevalence of domestic violence; 2) problematic relationships between men and women (gender performances); 3) an absence of queer representation; 4) class consciousness (or lack thereof); 5) God (as a waymaker, provider, healer, protector); and 6) relationships between women (mother-daughter, sister-sister, bff, intergenerational).

* * *

The final thing I want to talk about is what's missing from the story.

There were several stories that I wrote that didn't make it to the final version of the book manuscript, some of which didn't make it to the final draft of the dissertation version. The reasons for particular exclusions varied, but included

- speculations that I could not or did not confirm (for example, the potential prevalence of sexual abuse and child molestation);
- motherlessness having similar emotional consequences as fatherlessness;

- a detailed story of spousal abuse, based on an interview with a woman who witnessed the abuse of her mother as a child.

None of those three stories made it to a final version for a few reasons.

1) I didn't tell the molestation story because while I suspected it frequently occurred in the community, no interviews substantiated my suspicions, and I didn't feel it was appropriate to ask outright;

2) The character of Twiggy lost her mother as a young child, and I was curious about the impact growing up a motherless child had on her relationships with her children. While I had some content from interviews with Twiggy that could have worked as an independent story chapter it would have required me to push the timeline of the book back, focusing on her childhood instead of her children's childhoods, and it felt too complicated to accomplish. I couldn't make it work, logistically, as a flashback, and decided that the additional research that would be required was not worth it.

3) Because of the emotional toll that particular interview had on the participant and my commitment to an ethic of care, I left it out because I worried it might be triggering to the participant. Instead, I abbreviated the violence depicted in that story in a general description of intimate partner violence in the community.

A lot of the decisions I made about what to include in the final iteration of *Sweetwater* had a lot to do with my concerns about representation, but more to do with my commitment to relational care. As qualitative researchers in general, and autoethnographic researchers in particular, it is our responsibility to make the best decisions possible for each individual project. It is also important that we consider our identity politics and how they frame and fracture the stories we tell.

WHAT THIS PROJECT REINFORCED ABOUT AUTO/ETHNOGRAPHIC ETHICS

Auto/ethnographic methods are powerful opportunities to story lived experiences and capture cultural phenomenon, but it is important that auto/ethnographers continually be self-aware and self-reflexive about the ethical ramifications of their work, and the reality that ethics span not only the relationships between researcher and researched, but also the larger community when the content of stories can be used against us. It is also important to consider that auto/ethnographic ethics don't end just because we complete the research. We must reckon with the choices we make and their ongoing costs. It is irresponsible and unprofessional to enter a space/"the field," disrupt it with our presence, and leave without giving it a second thought. It is equally irresponsible and unprofessional to tell stories that may have cultural consequences without considering, understanding, and responding to those consequences. It made writing *Sweetwater* bittersweet, but worth it.

Sweetwater has left me with more questions than answers. I am challenged to consider the implication and responsibility of insider research. I am also cognizant of how important it is to reflect on the process of writing throughout the writing process. The goal of my work is social justice, cultural understanding, visibility for the invisible, and creation of the world I want to see. At the end of the day, if the work we do does not make an impact, and does not leave the world better than how we found it, what's the point in doing it? And further, if we do work that does more harm than good, is it work that we should be doing?

REFERENCES

Adams, T. E., Holman Jones, S., & Ellis, C. (2015). *Autoethnography: Understanding qualitative research*. New York, NY: Oxford University Press.

Bell-Scott, P. (2015). Debunking Sapphire: Toward a non-racist and non-sexist social science. In A. Hull, P. Bell-Scott, & B. Smith (Eds.), *All the women are white, all the blacks are men, but some of us are brave: Black women's studies* (2nd ed.). New York, NY: Feminist Press. (Original work published 1982)

Boylorn, R. M. (2013a). *Sweetwater: Black women and narratives of resilience*. New York, NY: Peter Lang.

Boylorn, R. M. (2013b). "Sit with your legs closed" and other sayin's from my childhood. In S. Holman Jones, T. Adams & C. Ellis (Eds.), *The handbook of autoethnography* (pp. 173–185). Walnut Creek, CA: Left Coast Press.

Boylorn, R. M. (2014). A story & a stereotype: An angry and strong auto/ethnography of race, class, and gender. In R. M. Boylorn & M. P. Orbe (Eds.), *Critical autoethnography: Intersecting cultural identities in everyday life* (pp. 129–143). Walnut Creek, CA: Left Coast Press.

Boylorn, R. M. (2016a). On being at home with myself: Blackgirl autoethnography as research praxis. *International Review of Qualitative Research, 9*, 44–58. doi: 10.1525/irqr.2016.9.1.44.

Boylorn, R. M. (2016b). The Good(all) effect: Answering the call of narrative ethnography. *Qualitative Inquiry, 22*, 2–16. doi: 10.1177/1077800415603400

Boylorn, R. M. (2017). *Sweetwater: Black women and narratives of resilience* (revised edition). New York, NY: Peter Lang.

Collins, P. H. (2009). *Black feminist thought: Knowledge, consciousness, and the politics of empowerment*. New York, NY: Routledge. (Original work published 1991)

Ellis, C. (2007). Telling secrets, revealing lives: Relational ethics in research with intimate others. *Qualitative Inquiry, 13*, 3–29. doi: 10.1177/1077800406294947

Ellis, C., Adams, T. E., & Bochner, A. P. (2011). Autoethnography: An overview. *Historical Social Research, 36*(4), 273–290.

Goodall, H. L. (2000). *Writing the new ethnography*. Lanham, MD: AltaMira.

Goodall, H. L. (2004). Narrative ethnography as applied communication research. *Journal of Applied Communication Research, 32*, 185–194. doi: 10.1080/0090988042000240130

Goodall, H. L. (2005). Narrative inheritance: A nuclear family with toxic secrets. *Qualitative Inquiry, 11*, 492–513. doi: 10.1177/1077800405276769

Harris-Perry, M. V. (2011). *Sister citizen: Shame, stereotypes, and Black women in America*. New Haven, CT: Yale University Press.

McLaurin, I. (2001). Theorizing a black feminist self in anthropology: Toward an autoethnographic approach. In I. McLaurin (Ed.), *Black feminist anthropology: Theory, politics, praxis, and poetics* (pp. 49–76). New Brunswick, NJ: Rutgers University Press.

Tolich, M. (2004). Internal confidentiality: When confidentiality assurances fail relational informants. *Qualitative Sociology, 27*, 101–106.

Yarbrough, M., & Bennett, C. (1999). Cassandra and the Sistahs: The peculiar treatment of African American women in the myth of women as liars. *Journal of Gender, Race and Justice, 3*, 625–657.

Robin M. Boylorn
Department of Communication Studies
University of Alabama

KEITH BERRY

3. THE CONSUMED SELF

Understanding the Stories I Cannot Have

I am sitting at my office desk writing emails to former students whose stories I would like to include in my book (Berry, 2016). The book uses autoethnography and personal narrative to examine youth bullying and identity from a relational communication perspective. In particular, I focus on symbolically negotiated interactions, relationships, and identities produced in bullying performances.[1] The basis for this book is a research study I conducted in conjunction with the students enrolled in an undergraduate interpersonal communication course I just finished teaching. For their final projects students wrote vulnerable stories that conveyed their lived experience with bullying from middle school and/or high school. Their stories, as well as mine, and reflections on our processes of writing them, serve as focal points in the book.[2] One student, Renee, and I have already exchanged several emails.[3] Because her story focuses on the death of a family member, she has expressed concerns. In her last email she declines to participate in the study. I write her this response:

Dear Renee:

Thank you for letting me know of your decision. I will miss not being able to include your story. As I mentioned to you at the end of the semester and in our recent emails, the account of your cousin's suicide that resulted from his being bullied is powerful, and heart breaking. I cannot imagine what this loss must feel like for you and your family. You have my sincere admiration for being able to muster the strength necessary to write the story. It is a testament to his life. Your being comfortable is my first and foremost concern, so I respect your decision not to participate. If you should happen to change your mind, and I hope you might, do not hesitate to write or call me. I would be honored to include your story in my research.

Warmly,
Keith

I never again hear from Renee, but her story continues to trouble me. While autoethnography is known for its openness in imaginative concept and form (Bochner & Ellis, 2016; Ellis & Bochner, 2000), writing and telling reflexive stories is not "anything goes" inquiry and comes with relational dangers and

S. L. Pensoneau-Conway et al. (Eds.), Doing Autoethnography, 19–27.
© 2017 Sense Publishers. All rights reserved.

pitfalls. No story or book is worth risking harm to others, especially to people we hold close to us (Ellis, 2007), which, for me, includes some students. Nevertheless, in my email to Renee I omitted important information. Missing are details that speak to the deeper ways her story, and my being unable to include it, makes me react—ways of thinking and feeling that are, to me, real and important, but also controversial and risky. Noticing the ways I am holding on to her story, I decide to write her another email.

Dear Renee:

I cannot stop thinking about you and your story. I stay up late at night thinking about what happened to your cousin. Now when I see bullying stories on the news or the Internet, I think of his suicide. I must admit: your story has consumed me and I do not understand how to make sense of what I am feeling.

Once I graded your story, I knew I had to have it as part of my study. Reading about the depths of pain and suffering that your cousin was made to endure from being bullied made the hairs on the back of my neck stand up. Frankly your story excites me. I feel as though a book with bullying stories must have at least one suicide story, if it is to be a "good" book, right? What will not having such a story do to the book's "credibility"? At the same time, I want to include a suicide story so that readers can understand how deep the despair from bullying can be. I need your story, and sometimes it feels as though I need it badly … too badly.

I also feel this way about other students' stories. There's this one student who … I'm sure you remember his story from class … wrote about the boys who horribly bullied him in high school for being gay and "out." Over the course of a semester these boys repeatedly called him "ugly duckling" and "fish face." They even would tell him he has "a mouth that is perfectly made for sucking dick." The horrors he must have felt when hearing these words, and experiencing this violence! He has never responded to my invitation for the study, and no matter how hard I try I cannot stop thinking of him. I object to what the boys called him and feel sad about the misery their words instigated for him. But I also want that story. I don't have any other story like it, and the graphic language, as horrible as it is, is … perfect.

Renee, at times I feel obsessed with these stories. They have an allure that makes them difficult to resist. I feel close to them and am struggling to let them go. I am disappointed by not being able to have some of them. In fact, not being able to include them makes me want them even more. I crave these stories, and as hard as I try, I cannot stop thinking about them.

Maybe I have already gone too far in what I have shared with you, but there is more to say. Craving disturbing stories like these, and in these particular ways, also feels, to me, to be dirty, embarrassing, and shameful. What type of person becomes so obsessed with and excited by such hardship? Who gets disappointed when learning "good stories" are not available? What does it mean to want to "have" and "use" people's stories? What gives me the right?

I should end this note here. Concerned by how I might look, I have drafted and redrafted this email many times. I feel like I am pressuring you, and that is the last thing I want to do.

I hope you understand. And if by some chance you should change your mind, I am still open to including your story.

Unsettled,
Keith

I never send this email to Renee.[4]

* * *

This story conveys one of the most dynamic experiences I've lived through when "doing autoethnography." The rawness of emotion and thought conjures up, for me, important meta-methodological questions including: How do I appear in this story to readers, and what is at stake with their appraisal? To what extent will (or should) I expose myself—deep longings and attachments I feel—to readers when seeking to tell evocative stories? While each of these questions merits consideration, in this chapter I am primarily interested in the *reactions I personally had* when working through the loss of Renee's story, and others like hers.

In much of my research I have used autoethnography to investigate complicated cultural and methodological problems (see, for example, Berry, 2006, 2007, 2012, 2016), and I have often closely explored reflexivity (see Berry, 2013; Berry & Clair, 2011). This work has entailed using stories to confront painful thoughts and feelings, mine and others', and to disclose intimate details about how I perform, and who I am, to others. In fact, most of the research I've conducted has confounded me in some way, sometimes leading me to undesirable outcomes. This is to say, I am not a stranger to the personal challenges tied up with being reflexive and grappling with the uncertainty that makes storytelling both challenging and exciting. Still, working through the loss of Renee's story allures me in ways that feel different and worthy of further reflection. The loss rendered me living with a *consumed self*, a way of being that was fixated on her story in significant ways. Thus, I ask: What does it mean to become *consumed* by stories I cannot "have"? Put differently, what are the social conditions that make this performance of the consumed self possible, or even necessary?

In what follows I reflect on these questions by focusing on three interrelated issues: bullying's status today as a prominent and life-shaping cultural and interactional symbol; my personal connection to the problem of bullying; and the relationship between my consuming response to the loss of her story and what I see as more mindful ways I perform in the liminal situations of everyday life. I convey these ideas to underscore the complexities involved with performing reflexivity in these deeply personal and intimate ways, especially in autoethnographic research and writing.[5]

SATURATED BULLYING SELVES

Cultural discourse on bullying makes this performance of the consumed self possible. Bullying is a prominent issue across diverse contexts in U.S. cultural life. Whether appearing as "breaking news" on cable news stations, "shared" posts on Facebook or Twitter, or anti-bullying policies instituted by schools, stories of the latest tragic episode of bullying, its consequences, and calls to reform the problem, abound. These stories are echoed by significant events in popular culture and politics, such as television programs (*Glee*) and documentaries (*Bully*), and first of their kind governmental events and initiatives (e.g., U.S. President Obama's "White House Conference on Bullying Prevention" in 2011). By immersing oneself in today's cultural life, one is invited to learn and talk about bullying in ways that stress and underscore how this problem is meaningful and consequential.

Moments of my lived experience in interpersonal communication amplify the ways bullying matters. Bullying is an issue *du jour* in everyday social interaction. I am thinking specifically of communicating *about* bullying. From the moment I told others I was studying and writing a book on bullying, most people affirmed how "important" and "needed" the project was to them and society. People usually would follow this affirmation by sharing with me (without my asking, I should note) a memory from when *they were bullied* in their youth. Some have even shared their worries about being bullied today. For instance, Addison, my six year old niece, reported to me on the telephone that she hopes her new eye glasses—the first pair she's ever worn—"don't get her bullied" when she "wears them to school for the first time." Indeed, folks who I know, and strangers to me, young and old, have had something to say about the problem and how it needs to be stopped before it is too late.

Suicide that results from bullying served as a potent symbol within these cultural and relational experiences. News that youth have killed themselves, or have tried to do so, and whether or not one knows the youth in question, often has served as a primary focal point. Further, that *youth* are engaged in suicide, or suicidal ideation or other self-harming practices, matters even more, and rightfully so. Youth are especially vulnerable, more shapeable, and ostensibly less equipped to handle such intense emotional and psychological problems. Nevertheless, the issue of suicide as a response to being bullied serves as a consistent worry and provides a routine character to the ongoing story of our engagement with bullying.

Concerning my response to Renee's story, the potency of youth suicide as a bullying symbol makes possible my performances of the consumed self. The consistent emphasis of suicide I experienced culturally and interpersonally over time led me to expect that a story of someone who took their life would be in my book. It *needed to be in my book*. I came to identify closely with this aspect of the problem. As I suggest in my email to Renee, I wanted my book to contribute to cultural responses that would help to keep youth safe, or at least safer. Further, given the prominence of discourse on suicide, the likelihood that I would not "have" a story of this type prompted me to feel as though my research efforts would be incomplete, or that my book and any other research I published on the topic, would not be "good" or "credible."

LOOKING INTO THE MIRROR

I have a personal relationship to bullying that shapes the ways I perform as consumed. Indeed, I have a bullying past (see Berry, 2016). Others bullied me in my youth, and I bullied others. I also witnessed friends being bullied in unconscionable and violent ways. Sometimes I reported them to teachers. More often I served as a bystander who knew what was going on, but never mentioned it to teachers. Granted, Renee's story is not explicitly about me. The same goes for the story about the boy who endured homophobic bullying. Still, phenomenologically speaking I am most certainly "in" them. That is, I feel a deep resonance with those stories, and in ways that activate memories from my past and lead me to think and feel about bullying. This reaction impacts the feelings of being consumed and obsessed that I convey in my second email.

Renee's story about her cousin takes me back to the ways in which my being bullied meant enduring repeated and cruel jokes and intimidation tactics; to how my body, that is, my objectionable not-masculine-enough body, provided bullies with an attractive target at which to shoot their relational daggers; to how I often lived in silence in my youth in regards to being bullied and to feeling "different" in general, a way of coping that may have allowed me to not have to think about and feel the pain I experienced, but also kept me from receiving the support I needed form others; and to how my coping techniques tended only to keep me moving and remain afloat, rather than feeling better, emboldened, and thriving. In these ways, Renee's story was at once hers, but also a reflection and reminder of mine. Indeed, I was consumed by her story and unable to dislodge myself from its storyline.

In these ways "consumed" serves as a descriptor that points to dynamic and complex feelings that are at play when dealing with the loss of Renee's story.

Consumed:
… I was remembering the prevalence of bullying in my youth, and how miserable being bullied made me feel.
… I was feeling angry about the unnecessary cruelty that allows bullying to happen and become impactful.
… I was encountering outrage over the reality that, still today, youth are subjected to the corrosive nature of bullying, to the point where people like Renee's cousin, likely seeing no other possibility for relief, must kill themselves.
… Renee's story led me to re-live the pain of my bullying stories and the despair and uncertainty that being bullied made me to feel.
… I was feeling that, if I was able to include Renee's story, I could help to keep youth alive.

This story, and the loss, consumed me and brought to my attention the ways I had once lived, the ways I wanted to live, and the ways I longed to help others live.

AWARENESS INTERRUPTED

Over the last twenty years, I have committed myself to learning about and practicing mindfulness. I aim to make it a central part of my everyday life. My experiences with Renee's story spun me in quixotic ways. So much so that mindfulness provides an additional way in which to explore my performances, to better understand how my responses within this experience were and were not mindful.

I draw on Eastern perspectives to mindfulness to inform my practice (see Batchelor, 1997; Chödrön, 2002; Kornfield, 1993). These approaches frame mindfulness as an ongoing process of trying to live with full awareness in the present moment, using breathing as a constant centering and steadying point. It entails working directly and deeply with one's pain and suffering to learn about ourselves, others, and the world, all of which are interconnected dimensions of lived experience. Further, being mindful means coming to terms with the impermanence of all beings and things—as folk wisdom on mindfulness would suggest, "the only constant is change"—and the ways human beings tend to struggle as a result of our working to find firm ground within groundless experiences. Too much striving, desiring, or attachment instigates further suffering. Underlying these aspects is the call in mindfulness to live, and learn, gently and even humorously, and with compassion for self and others.

On one level, my responses to losing Renee's story feel, to me, mindful. For instance, I engaged with the rush of difficult thoughts and feelings directly, and didn't avoid or deny these responses. I was present to them. In addition, my inclusion of this story about Renee in my book, as well as my writing this current new chapter, speaks to a mindfulness practice: I stayed with this experience of hardship, to learn about how I related, and am still relating, as well I put myself on the line vulnerably, by sharing this story and reflexive process publically, so that others, too, might experience this process in ways that are meaningful to their lived experience.[6] Also, recall I wanted to include Renee's story in my book because I felt it would make for a better book on bullying, which, in turn, might help others. Thus, compassion is also at the heart of these performances. Taken together, performing in these ways serves as a continuation of the mindfulness practice that has served me well for many years.

On another level, my consumed response lacks mindfulness, and demonstrates mindlessness. Take, for instance, the ways my story shows me holding on to Renee's story, to the point that I felt obsessed with including it in my research, indeed, to the point of needing to "have" it, to the point where I inadvertently began to objectify Renee, her story, and for that matter, her deceased cousin.[7] My inability to let go, in part, results from Renee's perfectly understandable decision to not give me permission to use her story, which created an experience of groundlessness that I needed to reconcile. While I didn't presume I would be able to include *her* story, I did presume I would have a story that conveyed suicide resulting from bullying. I found myself hooked on her story, and this loss swept me over and knocked me down, leaving me wanting and even needing her story, worrying about not being able to use it, and striving to make sense of it all. In turn, my responses to the ways I was reacting were not very mindful either: *What type of person becomes so obsessed with and excited by such hardship? Who gets so disappointed when learning "good stories" are not available? What does it mean to want to "have" and "use" people's stories? What gives me the right?* Rather than trying to respond with compassion and understanding to the ways I was suffering, I showed self-judgment and shame. As a result, trying to reconcile this situation in these ways intensified, rather than alleviated, the dis-ease I felt.

Working reflexively in these ways—coming into contact with my being consumed in the experience of loss, and struggling through those feelings in the storytelling process—created the conditions for a "breaching" response (Garfinkel, 1967). That is, the experience disrupted the "common sense" or status quo ways of performing to which I had grown accustomed in this research project. It required me to re-consider the assumptions and expectations that I had taken for granted concerning bullying research and what my book would include (or not). Even more, it challenged me to re-assess what I understood about my subjectivity, who I was as a person. *Why these reactions now? Who am I? How do I get back to "normal"?* Prior to this experience, I understood that I struggled with mindfulness. Most people I know do. After all, it is a life-long practice. Yet, this level of wanting and attachment was particularly strange to me. In these ways, while the loss of Renee's story prevented me from sharing her story with others through my book, or from addressing bullying and suicide in the particular ways for which her account would have allowed, it also allowed me to come to understand myself more fully and intimately, even if those ways felt ugly and unwanted at the time.

As I emerge from this consuming experience, now feeling better over time about how I handled this situation, I would not change much about how I performed. I *do* wish I could have been better to myself through the experience. I could have worked to minimize some of the self-judgment and anxiety stemming from feeling obsessed with Renee's story. However, mindfully working through the experience has served to remind me that there will likely always be aspects of who autoethnographers are, or are not, that come into being within the reflexive practices fueling autoethnography. It will be helpful to stay open to them, and even brace ourselves for the ones that may feel overpowering. Further, although time and experience may allow autoethnographers to become more comfortable with the process, and efficient with being vulnerable and putting ourselves on the line, there are likely always new ways of learning about ourselves and others, and more humane and compassionate ways to share our vulnerabilities and the vulnerabilities of others. It will be helpful, here, to remember there probably will come that extra-ordinary research moment, like that one story that we cannot "have," that will take us into experiences that are deeper and darker than those we have been ready for and needed to face before. May we stay open and be well within that reflexive learning process.[8]

25

NOTES

[1] I use "performance" in this chapter to mean the constitutive sense of the term; that is, to signal performing or a making and remaking of selves.

[2] This research study has been approved (Pro00014179) by the Institutional Review Board at the University of South Florida.

[3] "Renee" is a pseudonym that I use to help protect the identity of this student. Also, I have worked in other ways to mask or camouflage identities for Renee and the other student I mention in this chapter.

[4] I cannot think of any circumstance under which I would actually send an email like this to Renee. However, what if I *had* sent it to her? What is at stake? I suspect that answering this question entails considering related ethical issues, both in terms of research protocol and teaching philosophy. Concerning teaching, this issue begs the question: What is "too much information," who makes such a decision, and to whose benefit and at whose expense? Further engaging with these and related questions extends beyond the scope of my chapter.

[5] I examine the issues comprising this chapter by using a hermeneutic phenomenological orientation. This entails, at least, focusing on the ways lived experience, mine and others, or aspects of our *lifeworld* (everyday reality), create the possible, and sometimes necessary, conditions through which people constitute, or make and remake, human understanding. It also entails investigating lived experience as a temporal phenomenon: people constitute meaning by drawing on experiences from our past, lived present, and anticipated future. Overall, this phenomenological approach pursues correlative, not causal, understanding, and assumes that the understanding discerned here is contingent, uncertain, and subject to multiple interpretations.

[6] My book (Berry, 2016) includes five "methodological dilemmas," vignettes that convey and examine challenges inherent to using autoethnography (with students) to study bullying.

[7] Storytellers and their stories are special beyond words. Both need to be treated with great care. Their specialness is what makes the presence of objectifying impulses in this experience, feelings I advocate against in my usual research practices, so uncomfortable and curious.

[8] My thanks to Chris Patti (Appalachian State University) for his mindful input during my writing of this chapter.

REFERENCES

Batchelor, S. (1997). *Buddhism without beliefs: A contemporary guide to awakening*. New York, NY: Riverhead Books.

Berry, K. (2006). Implicated audience member seeks understanding in autoethnography: Reexamining the "gift." *International Journal of Qualitative Methods, 15*, 1–12.

Berry, K. (2007). Embracing the catastrophe: Gay body seeks acceptance. *Qualitative Inquiry, 13*, 259–281. doi: 10.1177/1077800406294934

Berry, K. (2012). (Un)covering the gay interculturalist. In N. Bardhan & M. P. Orbe (Eds.), *Identity research and communication: Intercultural reflections and future directions* (pp. 223–237). Lanham, MD: Lexington Books.

Berry, K. (2013). Spinning autoethnographic reflexivity, cultural critique, and negotiating selves. In T. E. Adams, S. Holman Jones, & C. Ellis (Eds.), *The handbook of autoethnography* (pp. 209–227). Walnut Creek, CA: Left Coast Press.

Berry, K. (2016). *Bullied: Tales of torment, identity, and youth*. New York, NY: Routledge.

Berry, K., & Clair, R. P. (2011). Contestation and opportunity in reflexivity: An introduction. *Cultural Studies ⟺ Critical Methodologies, 11*, 95–97. doi: 10.1177/1532708611401326

Bochner, A., & Ellis, C. (2016). *Evocative autoethnography: Writing stories and telling lives*. New York, NY: Routledge.

Chödrön, P. (2002). *When things fall apart: Heart advice for difficult times*. Boston, MA: Shambhala Publications.

Ellis, C. (2007). Telling secrets, revealing lives: Relational ethics in research with intimate others. *Qualitative Inquiry, 13*, 3–29. doi: 10.1177/1077800406294947

Ellis, C., & Bochner, A. P. (2000). Autoethnography, personal narrative, reflexivity: Researcher as subject. In N. Denzin & Y. Lincoln (Eds.), *The handbook of qualitative research* (2nd ed., pp. 733–768). Thousand Oaks, CA: Sage.

Garfinkel, H. (1967). *Studies in ethnomethodology*. Englewood Cliffs, NJ: Prentice-Hall.

Kornfield, K. (1993). *A path with heart: A guide through the perils and promises of spiritual life*. New York, NY: Bantam Books.

Keith Berry
Department of Communication
University of South Florida

KATHRYN THOMPSON

4. PLEASURES AND PARADOXES OF NEW MEDIA

An Autoethnography of a Redditor

Studying information technology and new media feels like navigating a sprawling, organic labyrinth. Flush with seeming contradiction and paradoxes, the social and technical elements of any medium or piece of technology blossom outward while simultaneously folding and refolding in on themselves in a dense, tangled-yet-expansive whorl of self and other, individual and group, human and machine. The approaches to this sociotechnical Gordian knot are as multiple and varied as the area itself, ranging from broad, macro-level theorizations of an "information society" (van Dijk, 2005) or "network society" (Castells, 2010) to meso- and micro-level theorizations of the processes of technological "domestication" and the emergence of "media ideologies" and "idioms of practice" that surround everyday engagement with these technologies (Baym, 2010; Gershon, 2012).

The multiplicity of approaches, theories, and discourses generated on this topic demonstrates the difficulty and complexity of reconciling the multiple tensions and paradoxes that emerge around this topic: between the self and the social, the one and the many, the public and the private. However, autoethnography as a method provides a unique critical traction and scaffolding that makes it ideal for such an undertaking. Reed-Danahay (1997) writes that autoethnography is "a form of self-narrative that places the self within a social context" (p. 9), which is precisely the kind of reflexive, critically informed reconciliation and articulation I would like my work to accomplish.

This chapter is an exploration of my paradoxical encounters with a particular piece of new media technology: the social news site Reddit.com, which is the topic of my dissertation. I will use autoethnographic vignettes to scaffold between my own experiences and larger community and cultural structures, themes, and trends (Ellis & Bochner, 1996) while exploring two paradoxical themes: public/private and self/Other. Far from being unique to the site, these particular areas motivate social and scholarly anxiety and jubilation, caution and celebration.

I will briefly discuss two key shared aspects of these paradoxical relationships before delving into each one. Although the thematic formations that I am examining are, in many ways, uniquely structured, with their own idiosyncrasies and internal logics, I have nevertheless noticed two overall characteristics that they both share. First, despite the fact that each "end" of the paradox may be discursively and ideologically structured as mutually exclusive (for example, the private is defined by what is not public and vice versa), a "pure" instantiation of either pole is nearly impossible. Within my experiences of Reddit in particular and

S. L. Pensoneau-Conway et al. (Eds.), Doing Autoethnography, 29–36.
© *2017 Sense Publishers. All rights reserved.*

new media technology more generally, it seems that the objects and phenomena I examine contain in simultaneity both ends of the paradox, often in complex, nested, shifting relationship to one another.

Second, these "ends" are always-already interwoven and interrelated, not only with each other, but with other discursive formations such as (but not limited to) gender, race, and class. Each "pole" of the paradox has gendered, raced, sexualized, and classed meanings associated with it, meanings that multiply, resonate, and become increasingly complex as they overlap and intersect with each other. These paradoxes become legible as actant threads in a larger networked web of sociotechnical power and meaning.

Throughout this chapter, I will explore my personal experiences with these technologies and paradoxes, with the aim of pulling on these strands, vibrating them, seeing where they connect, branch off, knot together. I aspire towards, to borrow gratefully from Spry (2011), "string theories of pain and privilege, forever woven into fabrics of power/lessness" (p. 15).

VIGNETTE #1: PRIVATE BLOCKAGES, PUBLIC SHAME

It was the end of August 2011, and I was in the two-week process of writing my doctoral qualifying exams. I had just moved into a new place, and my bedroom, which also served as my office, was tiny and cramped. The first week, I would write for as long as I could force myself to, with frequent, anxious, guilty breaks. Both of my housemates were gone on various end-of-summer visits, and I spent the days silently typing, clicking, and scribbling in relative isolation. Even when I did leave the house, I never really left the questions, remaining intensely preoccupied even when removed from my desk. I was always distracted—the exam and my anxiety hung on me like a heavy veil, occluding my face, my vision.

Four days into my two-week exam, during one of my many frantic breaks, I found a trending Reddit thread. It was titled "IAmA guy who hasn't pooped in the month of August yet. Ask me anything about my extreme constipation." The thread included a picture of his swollen abdomen and a recount of his doctor's unsuccessful efforts thus far to relieve his plight, as well as pictures of his bathroom setup (complete with pillows on the floor in front of the toilet, in case he passed out in his effort and fell face-first onto the tile).

The top-rated thread comment was a (pretty clever) metacultural pun echoing the tone of playful skepticism often seen in various contexts across Reddit: "This guy's full of shit." The second-highest comment was a strongly worded plea for the poster to seek emergency hospital care on the grounds of a possible bowel obstruction. Other comments included various (largely humorous) "shit stories," in which other Redditors shared their stories, either their own or someone else's, of gastrointestinal distress, stoppage, and relief.

References to the thread began to appear almost immediately elsewhere on Reddit, and the thread had thousands of responses, both positive and negative. The clamor for updates and follow-up was almost immediate. The next day the Redditor posted a follow-up, which detailed his ER visit and subsequent home experience passing what turned out to be several pounds of fecal matter. This follow-up included links to images, which were every bit as disgusting as I thought they would be. Even in my disgust, however, I rejoiced in his relief, in the end of his stoppage.

In a way, I felt I had experienced his ordeal along with him, and that somehow his experience of dramatic stoppage relieved had broken through my own anxious isolation. Even though those around me didn't (and probably couldn't) fully understand my discomfort, reading the thread made me realize that there was at least one other person in the world, right now, experiencing a similar sort of deeply private blockage and pain. In that knowledge, I felt less alone, and less afraid.

Formally it would appear we were (and continue to be) strangers—neither of us knew the other's name or face. Yet I saw so many similarities between our situations. We both were experiencing painful, shameful stoppages—straining to expel digested, impacted matter, alone, ashamed, and worried in our respective tiny rooms. We carried it inside us always, leaden and aching, even when we ventured out. In both cases there was an element of failure: we had both failed in the timely, typical expulsion of ingested material, and now we carried with us, still, what should have been already and easily jettisoned, processed, eliminated.

Although I think my situation may have made the unfortunate unpooping man's post more salient to me, I was not the only one following his saga with interest. I was one among thousands of people—a public—that spontaneously emerged around this most private of moments. I was fascinated by the multiplicity and simultaneity of elements at work in this moment, elements that appear to be paradoxical, even contradictory.

The post was neither entirely private, nor entirely public. It seemed to vex any explanatory approach that conceptualized of public and private as mutually exclusive opposites. Within the post and my personal engagement with it, public and private continually oscillated, overlapped, intertwined, in a process of de- and re-territorialization (Deleuze & Guattari, 2006/1972). In *A Thousand Plateaus*, Deleuze and Guattari (2006/1972) describe de- and reterritorialization as conjoined, ongoing processes that operate in tandem with one another. De-territorialization, in its broadest sense, describes a process that decontextualizes a set of relations: disarticulating existing connections between elements. Re-territorialization is the subsequent process of re-articulation and re-arranging of these disarticulated elements, always, as Deleuze and Guattari theorize, towards the end of incorporating new power into the system.

In some ways, the Reddit post is intensely concerned with matters generally demarcated as private, and with privacy—the Redditor posted using a "throwaway" account (a new account, often with a novelty name related to the account's purpose: this Redditor's was "nopooshallpass") so as not to establish linkage with an established Reddit identity. Although the images linked in the thread represent private sights (and sites)—a swollen belly, the interior of a residential bathroom, a former piece of kitchenware-turned-shit-receptacle (for weighing purposes)—they are produced with an awareness of their publicness. The Redditor's face doesn't appear in these photographs; he posts these images under a (double) pseudonym.

And yet, despite the deeply personal and private subject matter of the post and the images, they are always already public.

This is not, however, a simple matter of transformation—of the private being converted into the public through the application of visibility. These categories are muddled as soon as they are invoked—at every turn, the very meanings of "public" and "private" are called into question. Traditional understandings of "public" encompass that which is openly available and visible, while "private" demarcates the personal, that which is not openly shared. While many elements of the thread were decidedly public—a large audience paying close attention, clamoring for details and updates, the ordeal of nopooshallpass still remained distinctly private and always embodied. There is a publicness in his private moments—but simultaneously the private is re-cordoned off from within this new publicity. These boundaries are never fixed, but are always contingent and shifting, moving across and through images, discourses, and ideologies.

My relationship to the thread and the ordeal of the unfortunate unpooping man further complicates these questions of public and private. The publicness of Reddit enabled me to access this most private of moments—making me feel less alone in my private (and seemingly unrelated) struggle. Yet I encountered, read, and followed this thread anonymously and in private, taking solace in the presence of an imagined public at the same time that I connected with the potential isolation of this particular, private, embodied, even shameful experience. I felt, in some ways, a strange intimacy with him—yet this was an intimacy cultivated alone, (relatively) anonymously. These boundaries were layered strata, folded in on one another. In this particular instance, Reddit was a conduit that cut through them, providing a network of both technical and social micro-channels that facilitated the exchange of this public/private information.

However, it is important and necessary to interrogate, within this example, the ways in which the boundaries afforded by new media technology are circumscribed and contextualized by larger systems of power and social meaning. The questions of public and private are never simply theoretical distinctions, as feminist, queer, critical race, and other scholars of difference point out. Far from being a neutral space of open visibility, scholars such as Namaste (2006), Munoz (1999), Halberstam (2005), and Stryker (2008) have all argued that public spaces and discourses are gendered, sexualized, and racialized in particular ways. What is demarcated as "public" (and, subsequently, what is deemed "private") is always already imbricated with larger cultural discourses about difference—about the kind of subjects that are assumed and entitled to occupy, move through, and speak in "public" spaces. The freedom to post details about his body in this nebulous "public" that the unfortunate unpooping man enjoyed was at least partially based on the fact that he was white and male (a fact not stated outright, but inferred and then confirmed through posted photographs). Thus the "universality" of his post— the "everybody" in "everybody poops"—was emphasized and abstracted. This is not always the case within Reddit, however—there is something peculiar and slippery about whiteness and maleness that enables it to take on different mantles, occupy categories of subjectivity without having that foray into that particular identity or status more globally. In other words, what I have observed in this example and through Reddit is precisely what Dyer (1997) has critiqued about whiteness—its ability to consider itself as both universal and particular, global and local simultaneously.

VIGNETTE #2: THE NEOLIBERAL TRAIL MIX OF DIFFERENCE AND SAMENESS

Browsing Reddit feels a lot like eating, and I find myself using food metaphors when I try to describe the experience. Perhaps I'm taking my cue from the word used to describe this kind of new media content delivery—after all, it is called a "feed." I think it's more than that, though. It's the rhythm of consumption, the day in and day out-ness of it, the variety (of different flavors, textures) within sameness (it's all food). I browse the site in the morning after I wake up, and it feels like the sugary cereal of my Internet breakfast. Sure, I consume other content—school and personal email, Facebook—but Reddit is usually the last thing I "eat," and the thing that feels more pleasurable than the others.

I often have a generous helping of Reddit over my lunch break, eating at my keyboard, clicking links, consuming content as I chew. I also have "snacks," nibbling on the site throughout the day—a link here or there on my phone as I'm waiting for the bus, or for a class to start. I usually check the site when I get home from work, and will often browse to "wind down" at night, before I go to sleep. The numbers beside the posts keep ticking up—50, 100, 200—and I often will keep clicking ahead, numb with the rhythm of consumption. My continual clicking, "just one more page, and then I'll go to bed" can feel mechanical, like eating an entire bag of potato chips. One crispy, salty link goes down one after another, me barely chewing, until my greasy fingers scrape the cellophane at the bottom of the bag—an endeavor made even more perilous to my sleep as Reddit's "bag" is essentially bottomless.

And what I'm eating, day in and day out, isn't really structured anything like a meal. Reddit's "feed" structure displays a "frontpage" with highly rated comments from all subreddits, meaning, by default, content is organized by popularity, not by theme. The resulting "meals" are more like a continuous flow of trail mix, made by someone with a particularly generous definition of what counts as such. It's all little unrelated pieces, all my interests and affinities mashed together: a link to a tragic news story will follow a link to an adorable photoset of baby otters which is next to some teenager's sweet coming-out story (posted in the little queer subreddits I subscribe to), next to an live question-answer session by a celebrity. In this feed structure, small micro-communities I've joined—distinct but somewhat disjointable elements of my identity, such as the subreddits r/vegan, r/bisexual, r/polyamory—mix and match with content in which I'm much more broadly (and sometimes incorrectly) interpellated, often into a larger, more generalized identity: Reddit user. This process of parallel and simultaneous hailing produce these micro-moments of sameness and difference, a repeating reiteration, variations on a theme. But this theme is one in which difference can become flattened—where all content, regardless of context, starts to appear as equivalent. The elements of my identity that might have politicized elements to them mix freely with hobbies and favorite media texts in a layered but disordered stream.

In some ways, this was incredibly refreshing, and I relished the ability to seek out and join narrower communities of interest, to find people who were the same as me—what we shared was that we were different in the same way. But that seeking, that personalization and customization, does have the effect of creating a "revolving door" of identities which can sometimes be jarring, engendering a rapid shifting of context and modes of address from one link to the next.

There are sometimes unexpected synchronicities, some chocolate in one's peanut butter. The titles or themes will sometimes speak to each other in an unexpected way—a call and response, a thematic grouping. Scrolling through the link titles feels like reading blank verse—lines of text follow, one after another, in a strange yet sometimes poetic stream of crowd-sourced consciousness. But largely, after a while, the variety itself becomes familiar, commonplace—even if the pieces themselves are extraordinary (as Reddit sometimes is). Phenomenologically and visually, it is easy to experience all difference—even in something as quotidian as consumer preference—as collapsed and bracketed, marked roughly equivalent in importance, sublimated under an assumed Same (the all-powerful individual).

This collapsing and bracketing of difference as quirks of the individual dovetails neatly with larger neoliberal discourses and frameworks that claim colorblindness (and, increasingly, blindness to sexual orientation as well). This move disavows the larger social and political context of inequalities that arise from these supposedly individual differences and undercuts justice claims being made by activists and scholars who critique the larger structural sources of inequality and oppression—ways in which, despite all rhetoric to the contrary, we are not all Same, are not all equal in the eyes of the law or power.

Placing the boundary posts between self and Other, us and them, Different and Same, has always been a project deeply imbricated with hegemonic power. Post-colonial, feminist, and critical race scholars (de Beauvoir, 2007/1949; Fanon, 2006/1952; Taussig, 1993) have traced the mechanisms of the hierarchical power structures that mark certain subjects as Other (as different from the unmarked, white, masculine universal/Same). Even as these structures and discourses endeavor to mark the Other as completely subaltern and utterly dissimilar, these scholars examine the complex ways in which the self and the Other are always already intertwined and mutually dependent. Taussig (1993) traces the oscillation between self/Other, and different/Same within anthropological accounts of indigenous peoples in the monograph *Mimesis and Alterity*. He theorizes sameness and difference as inextricably intertwined—not opposite ends of a spectrum, but a constantly fluctuating set of circuits of imitations of imitations—copies without originals. Highlighting this blurring, the messiness of these categories, undermines modern notions of the monolithic, self-evident, unmarked-yet-particular Subject while simultaneously calls attention to material and discursive conditions of inequality in colonial practice and representation.

However, in my experiences with Reddit, it seems as though the current tangled iteration between sameness and difference has taken a different turn—rather than emphasizing and overdetermining these categories, there appears to be a movement towards flattening and disavowing difference, marking it as personal preference that is only trivially relevant. All forms of difference, whether they be racial or sexual identity or the particular brand of media one likes to consume become, to quote an eminent scholar of postmodern subjectivity (I speak, of course, of the Dude from *The Big Lebowski*), just "your opinion, man," a kind of public pluralism that is simultaneously liberating and constraining.

It is in this space of simultaneous limitation and possibility in which I conclude this chapter. This space is one we, as autoethnographers, know well—we plumb the depths of our experiences and responses, diving into a seemingly limitless well of deeply situated particularity, to do the work that we do. Yet when we surface, we become painfully aware of the limitations and situatedness of that knowledge, rich though it is. And perhaps it is in that interstitial space—between self and other, between personal experience and social context—that autoethnography provides us the most critical traction, a concrete means of scaffolding between the local and the global, the micro to the meso to the macro, of reconciling personal, embodied, private experiences with the broadest and most public of structures and ideas. It is precisely this work of tying personal experience to larger social structures that might provide a way out of this neoliberal morass of identity and difference, by showing that far from being just "your opinion, man," there are concrete relationships between one's identity and the material and justice conditions of one's life, relationships dictated by a web of social meaning and power necessarily larger than the individual.

REFERENCES

Baym, N. (2010). *Personal connections in the digital age.* Malden, MA: Polity Press.

Castells, E. (2010). *The rise of the network society* (2nd ed.). Malden, MA: Wiley-Blackwell.

De Beauvoir, S. (2007). *The second sex.* New York, NY: Vintage Books. (Original published in 1949).

Deleuze, G., & Guattari, F. (2006). *A thousand plateaus: Capitalism and schizophrenia.* Minneapolis: University of Minnesota Press. (Original published in 1972).

Dyer, R. (1997). *White: Essays on race and culture.* New York, NY: Routledge.

Ellis, C., & Bochner, A. P. (1996). Introduction: Talking over ethnography. In C. Ellis & A. P. Bochner (Eds.), *Composing ethnography: Alternative forms of qualitative writing* (pp. 13–48). Walnut Creek, CA: AltaMira Press.

Fanon, F. (2006). *Black skin, white masks.* New York, NY: Grove Press. (Original published in 1952)

Gershon, I. (2012). *The breakup 2.0: Disconnecting over new media.* Ithaca, NY: Cornell University Press.

Halberstam, J. (2005). *In a queer time and place: Transgender bodies, subcultural lives.* New York: New York University Press.

Munoz, J. (1999). *Disidentifications: Queers of color and the performance of politics.* Minneapolis: University of Minnesota Press.

Namaste, V. (2006). Genderbashing: Sexuality, gender, and the regulation of public space. In S. Stryker & S. Whittle (Eds.), *The transgender studies reader* (pp. 584–600). New York, NY: Routledge.

Reed-Danahay, D. (1997). *Auto/ethnography: Rewriting the self and the social.* New York, NY: Berg.

Spry, T. (2011). *Body, paper, stage: Writing and performing autoethnography.* Walnut Creek, CA: Left Coast Press.

Stryker, S. (2008). Dungeon intimacies: The poetics of transsexual sadomasochism. *Parallax, 14*(1), 36 17. doi. 10.1000/13031610701781262

Taussig, M. (1993). *Mimesis and alterity: A particular history of the senses.* London, England: Routledge.

van Dijk, J. (2005). *The deepening divide: Inequality in the information society.* Thousand Oaks, CA: Sage.

Kathryn Thompson
Department of Gender Studies
Indiana University

DURELL M. CALLIER, DOMINIQUE C. HILL, AND
HILL L. WATERS

5. CRITICAL COLLABORATIVE PERFORMANCE AUTOETHNOGRAPHY

*Reflecting on Collective Practice, Black Girlhood,
Black Love and Accountability*

In the three years of our public practice, Hill L. Waters (HLW) has put on workshops celebrating Black girls, living in/theorizing from the body, and creating community accountable partnerships; given lectures on social justice as well as social identities and student self-awareness; and written, performed, and directed plays which highlight: Black love; race, gender & sexuality as interwoven systems of oppressions; and healing. An intentional practice of two Black queer identified scholar-artists, HLW continues the work of Saving Our Lives, Hear Our Truths (SOLHOT), a critical arts-based public practice for Black girlhood celebration (Brown, 2009, 2013).

Employing the creative via critical autoethnographic methods, HLW, is an outgrowth of SOLHOT, and serves as a symbolic commitment to collective action, Black love, and social justice. From our practice, which is rooted in SOLHOT's demand for presence, we have learned that dialogue is necessary to healing. Further, the work of each collective illustrates the necessity of healing rooted in the self in relationship to a collective. The intent of this paper is threefold: to introduce and theorize our practice, to map the ways in which our practice contributes to and diverges from current auto/ethnographic practices, and to illuminate the tensions and politics embedded in auto/ethnographic practices which center collective accountability and action.

METHODOLOGICAL GROUNDING

Our collective action, Hill L. Waters, responds to recent turns in the field of critical auto/ethnography and qualitative research. In particular, our practice is rooted in queer love, justice, accountability, and practice, and illuminates the value of collective action in how we produce and enact scholarship as autoethnographers. Through the usage of poetry, reflective co-authored narrative, as well as dialogue, we explore and identify key ingredients, tensions, principles, and risks necessary in the name of creating collaborative and accountable scholarship. Positing accountable collaboration as integral to social transformation and social justice scholarship, we believe that community is necessary, that someone must be present

S. L. Pensoneau-Conway et al. (Eds.), Doing Autoethnography, 37–44.
© *2017 Sense Publishers. All rights reserved.*

to hear our thoughts, and to hold us responsible for not only our words but also our actions. HLW is our practice to hold ourselves accountable, whereas this chapter is an invitation for readers to enter our community of accountability and place into action principles of accountable collaborative scholarship.

As critical auto/ethnographers, our backslash is in alignment with other Black woman scholars who tend to utilize the backslash as a way to signify and testify to the collective embedded within the individual (Mary Weems, personal communication, May 9, 2012; see also Boylorn, 2013). Auto/ethnography articulates a politic committed to more than the lone autoethnographer, but the autoethnographer in community, collaboratively writing a text, speaking with and to a community/multiple intersectional communities' experiences, reflecting them back to that community and illuminating the lived experience, needs, and desires of an ignored people to the rest of society. Thus, to collaborate in the research process is an attempt to collect and represent a more holistic portrait of a given phenomenon and/or culture (Alexander, Moreira & kumar, 2012; Angrosino, 2008; Brown, 2009; Denzin, Lincoln, & Smith, 2008; Durham 2014; Kasl & Yorks, 2010; Richardson & St. Pierre, 2008; Weems, Callier, & Boylorn, 2014; Wyatt, Gale, Russell, Pelias, & Spry, 2011).

Hill L. Waters contributes to and extends these practices, to think about the possibility of collaborative auto/ethnography as an experimental methodological practice, political commitment, and enactment of love, justice, and hope. By offering up our experiences as a means of insertion not to speak for an entire community, but to speak to these experiences, it is our hope that other Black/queer persons will find moments of resonance and recognition within our narratives (Boylorn, 2013). Blending the two—performance and auto/ethnography—this paper seeks to illuminate the possibilities of critical collaborative auto/ethnography which at times utilizes performance to visibly make salient and therefore confront racialized, gendered, and sexed corporeal cartographies (see McKittrick & Woods 2007) as well as provide transformative and subversive enactments of social justice (Denzin & Lincoln, 2008; Spry, 2001). To illustrate our auto/ethnographic practice and the tensions, politics, and possibilities involved in critical collaborative auto/ethnography, we reflect on two of our performances.

CRITICAL REFLECTIONS

Moment I

Seated back-to-back, in a dimly lit room, legs crossed center stage one over the other, we decorate scraps of construction paper. Drawing heart signs, and scribbling out the words, "I love you" as the poem "We Say We Love Each Other I" is recited:

We Say We Love Each Other I[1]

<Create love notes to give to audience members>
DMC & DCH: Love is

DCH: I love you
DMC I love you
DCH: Some simply wanting to
Gain freedom
See each other, clearly,
DMC: visibly
DMC & DCH: as we really are
DMC: Listen intently with our bodies
Continue to love in spite of the lack I feel in your presence
DMC & DCH: love is
DCH: the unknown
DMC: where we think we headed
DCH: something
disconnected

DMC & DCH:
love IS
ourselves
Co-authored
A love poem
to each other
<distribute to audience>
<Walk off>

The moment is over. Lines exchanged, we each glance into the audience. Who needed to know today that they were loved? Who needed to be affirmed in this moment from a stranger?

A manifestation of our commitments and convictions, "We Say We Love Each Other I" is a poem within *Love, Funk and Other Thangs*, our first enacted performance. It deploys dance, poetry, and dialogue to expose the raw, uncut, and complicated realities of Black love and capture the journeys of our quest for community, home, and love. Moreover, *Love, Funk and Other Thangs* disrupts stereotypical understandings of love between and across Black women and men as predicated upon sexual fulfillment and desire. Through juxtaposing our lived experiences with our intention to embody a complicated enactment upon the stage, alternative visions of Black identity and Black love were offered for audience members. Within the performance were four different iterations of the poem, "We Say We Love Each Other." This particular iteration, "We Say We Love Each Other I" came at the top of the show with three clear purposes: 1) introduce the complications of Black love, 2) offer an act of love to audience/witnesses vis a vis love cards, and 3) acknowledge and situate love as a co-authored responsibility.

Moment II

Who do you bring with you?" This was the phrase we asked the audience after performing an elegy in remembrance of Mark Carson, a Black openly gay man who was slain in Greenwich Village in May 2013. We opened the space for the audience, which along with us, HLW, allowed everyone to co-create the space. This was the performative moment to which Saldaña (2006) asks us all to lay witness to, the co-performance Denzin (2003) notes, which occurs in the dialectic between the audience and performer, and a "tactics of intervention" as Conquergood (2002) describes.

The question in this moment of our co-constructed performance was "Who do you want us to know and remember in this moment?" Know and Remember (Brown 2009), a sacred practice within SOLHOT, is a moment in which the girls, homegirls and homeboys create room to remember those individuals and things which are important to us. In doing so, we hold space for those no longer with us, affirm each other, call into collective remembrance, goodness, loss, our ancestors, present kinfolk and loved ones, prayers for someone or something. Knee-deep in exploring the pain enacted against and endured by Black and queer bodies, this moment opened up the possibility to hold the space and acknowledge death. Moreover, our sacred practice of Know and Remember, shared collectively during the performance, allotted us room to collectively name those who have transitioned early, suffered chronically, and/or experienced brutal violence of multiple iterations (i.e., physical, mental, spiritual, emotional, financial, etc.). It was also a moment for us to recall not only "Seaside Shore Sorrows," the elegy poem which illuminated the precarity of Black queer life through the remembrance of Mark Carson (Leland, 2013), the dangers of living a life in a body marked as Black and queer but to also remember that "some of us did not die." The two pieces, "Seaside Shore Sorrows" and "Still Here/Some of Us Did Not Die," were enacted one after the other. And now we were charged with holding the weight of the moment.

"Who do you want us to know and remember in this moment?" The audience answered, "my brother who died of cancer a few years ago," "my mentor Baba Asa Hillard," "my two parents." Tears welled up in some of their eyes as these names and ideas left their mouths and entered into our collective care; we weren't simply co-creating a performance together, but also embodying healing and care.

Soon, it was time to move into another section of the performance. If the Black queer body is more than the scene/seen of pain, what else does/can it experience? Pleasure certainly had to be a possibility, and so we made sure it was incorporated in the show. To know and remember those no longer with us did not foreclose the possibilities of our pleasure. Surely, these were interrelated, if some of those we called into the space did indeed provide meaningful connections to our erotic (see Lorde 1993). We deploy the erotic similar to Lorde in that it serves as a resource for creativity, a tool for manifesting. In turning toward this conceptualization, the question shifts: "What brings you pleasure, what is your P principle?" Some answered, "sleep," "chocolate," sex," "conversation," "laughter," and "joy." After reveling in the Black queer body as a site of pleasure and naming pleasure-filled things, we stand face-to-face and this dialogue ensues:

DCH: who are you loving
DMC: how are you loving
DCH: that is the question
DMC: who are you healing
DCH: how are you healing
DMC: that is the work
DCH: loving
DMC: healing
DCH: the work

The above excerpt is a co-constructed poem, "The Challenge," which is in a larger performance entitled, *Bodies on Display: An Exploration of Love, Intimacy, Violence and the Black Queer Body*, which engages reflexive narrative and poetry, created jointly, dance as well as dialogue, to explore the interwoven relationships of race, gender, and sexuality. Set as a live-art installation, this performance is cast as a living museum where our bodies—via poetry, movement, and a series of visual images—are intentionally displayed to render the Black queer body as the seen—the "epidermalization of Blackness the inscription of meaning onto skin color" (p. 1), and the scene—the spectacular event created when discursive imaginings of Blackness create (deleterious) material realities (Young, 2010). These artistic mediums endeavor to illuminate historic and contemporary moments of anti-Black violence and anti-queer violence and their imprints on our Black queer bodies. By deploying arts-based modes of inquiry to offer up our literal bodies and narratives, our bodies serve as interpolators to mono-causal framing, which often ignore the intersections of Blackness and queerness.

CONCLUSION

Both of the above poems emanate from a similar process of what Laurel Richardson (1994) calls "writing as inquiry" and what we name as co-constructing the site. Black feminist Katherine McKittrick (2006), in her book *Demonic Grounds*, discusses the body as both the site of injury and pain as well as the sight of possibility and healing. In this case, our initial writings serve as performative sites of re-memory—individual and collective, injury, and truth. From these stream of consciousness writings of our personal experiences as well as social, cultural and historical realities, we then generate poetic manifestations, which layer these data. As epiphanic moments, "We Say We Love Each Other I" and "The Challenge" embody pivotal shifts in the performance as well as our practice.

In *Love, Funk and Other Thangs,* "We Say We Love Each Other I" begins the conversation around love between Black men and women, generally. At the end of this grappling with different constructions of what love is and what it means when we, Black men and women, say we love each other, is an implicit call to action.

41

More specifically, there is a framing of love as something mutually created. The call to action, then, is to identify how we once configured love, to own our part in this architecture, and accept responsibility by taking on the task of re-imagining it. In the case of our practice, this moment demanded that we reconsider how our love manifests in our friendship and collective practice that is Hill L. Waters. Since then, we tell each other "I love you" more, hug more, and mind the needs—expressed verbally but more so not expressed—more.

Whereas "The Challenge," in *Bodies on Display*, demonstrates the crux of our work, love and healing. As a performance, *Bodies on Display* highlights alternative entryways into the narratives of marginalized individuals/communities, while creating pathways to enact justice (Brown, 2013; Carlson 1996; Denzin 2003; hooks 1990; Leavy, 2010; Madison & Hamera 2006; Spry, 2011). By placing our bodies on display we invited and employed witnesses to see the subject of interest (i.e., Black queer bodies) and to trouble, disrupt, and confront, along with us, understandings of the intersections of art, justice, love, violence, Blackness, and queerness. In moving through the section of *Pain*—what is done to the Black queer body—and moving to the section on *Pleasure*—what this body does/experiences that is life giving, affirming and sustaining—we moved from trauma to agency.

"The Challenge" sets forth a challenge and admonishment to those of us who recognize our turning to auto/ethnography, to "save our names" a la Robin Boylorn (personal communication, 2012), or to demarcate a space for "change, a reconsideration" as Holman Jones, Adams, and Ellis (2016) illuminate, a means to make research more accessible and to fulfill the social justice aspects and commitments of critical autoethnography. Our work foregrounds love and healing and is precisely the type of lovemaking that engenders revolutionary loving and healing labor. To do this work we privilege epistemological orientations, asking "who" and "how" we are loving, in both material and discursive ways, by asking not only who we extend love towards, but how we call attention to the need to interrogate the type and utility of the love we offer. Therefore, when considering how we enact love, we mean how are we valuing others' knowledge, truths, growth, and dismantling those forces which decrease their life chances and opportunities but to also consider the space in which healing takes place as pedagogy, as a research program, and in our professional obligations.

To do this work—of centering and mobilizing love, of engendering healing, and collectively carrying the struggle and experience of being differentially marked as Black and queer—is a radical act. To labor in the name of love, love that does not require submission and conquest sexually or otherwise, is a queer act. Moreover, to do this work under increased surveillance and policing of Black and queer bodies, an insurgence of anti-Black racism, anti-queer antagonisms and death is to stage claims to citizenship, expressions of (self) love, and imagine possibilities for an unpoliced, breathing, alive, and free Black queer life.

NOTE

[1] The form of the script takes on poetic sensibilities. See Brown (2013), Durham (2008), Muller and Jordan (1995), Pendergast, Leggo, and Sameshima (2009), and Weems et al. (2009).

REFERENCES

Alexander, B. K., Moreira, C., & kumar, h. s. (2012). Resisting (resistance) stories a tri-autoethnographic exploration of father narratives across shades of difference. *Qualitative Inquiry*, *18*, 121–133. doi: 10.1177/1077800411429087

Angrosino, M. (2008). Recontextualizing observation: Ethnography, pedagogy, and the prospects for a progressive political agenda. In N. Denzin & Y. Lincoln (Eds.), *Collecting and interpreting qualitative materials* (pp. 161–184). Thousand Oaks, CA: Sage.

Boylorn, R. M. (2013). *Sweetwater: Black women and narratives of resilience*. New York, NY: Peter Lang.

Brown, R. N. (2009). *Black girlhood celebration: Towards a hip hop feminist pedagogy*. New York, NY: Peter Lang.

Brown, R. N. (2013). *Hear our truths: The creative potential of Black girlhood*. Urbana: University of Illinois Press.

Carlson, M. (1996). *Performance: A critical introduction*. New York, NY: Routledge.

Conquergood, D. (2002). Performance studies: Interventions and radical research. *The Drama Review*, *46*, 145–156. doi:10.1162/105420402320980550

Denzin, N. K. (2003). *Performance ethnography: Critical pedagogy and the politics of culture*. Thousand Oaks, CA: Sage.

Denzin, N. K., & Lincoln, Y. S. (Eds.). (2008). *Collecting and interpreting qualitative materials* (Vol. 3). Thousand Oaks, CA: Sage.

Denzin, N. K., Lincoln, Y. S., & Smith, L. T. (Eds.). (2008). *Handbook of critical indigenous methodologies*. Thousand Oaks, CA: Sage.

Durham, A. (2014). *At home with hip hop feminism: Performances in communication and culture*. New York, NY. Peter Lang.

Durham, A. S. (2008). Between us: A bio-poem. *Meridians: Feminism, race, transnationalism, 8*(2), 177–182.

Holman Jones, S., Adams, T. E., & Ellis, C. (Eds.). (2016). *Handbook of autoethnography*. New York, NY: Routledge.

hooks, b. (1990). *Yearning: Race gender, and cultural politics*. Boston, MA: South End Press.

Kasl, E., & Yorks, L. (2010). "Whose inquiry is this anyway?" Money, power, reports and collaborative inquiry. *Adult Education Quarterly, 60*, 315–338. doi: 10.1177/0741713609347367

Leavy, P. (2010). *Method meets art: Arts-based research practice*. New York, NY: The Guilford Press.

Leland, J. (2013, May 29). Man killed in the Village is remembered as outgoing and private. *The New York Times*. Retrieved from http:\\www.nytimes.com\2013\05\30\nyregion\mark-carson-gay-man-killed-in-greenwich-village-is-remembered.html?_r=0

Lorde, A. (1993). The uses of the erotic: The erotic as power. In H. Abelove, M. A. Barale', & D. M. Halperin (Eds.), *The lesbian and gay studies reader* (pp. 339–343). New York, NY: Routledge.

Madison, S. D., & Hamera, J. (2006). Introduction: Performance studies at the intersections. In S. D. Madison & J. Hamera (Eds.), *The Sage handbook of performance studies* (pp. xi–xxv). Thousand Oaks, CA: Sage.

McKittrick, K. (2006). *Demonic grounds: Black women and the cartographies of struggle*. Minneapolis: University of Minnesota Press.

McKittrick, K., & Woods, C.A. (Eds.). (2007). *Black geographies and the politics of place*. Cambridge, MA: South End Press.

Muller, L., & Jordan, J. (1995). *June Jordan's poetry for the people: A revolutionary blueprint.* Florence, KY: Taylor & Francis.

Prendergast, M., Leggo, C., & Sameshima, P. (2009). Poetic inquiry. *Educational Insights, 13*(3), 743–744.

Richardson, L. (1994). Writing: A method of inquiry. In N. K. Denzin & Y. S. Lincoln (Eds.), *Handbook of qualitative research* (pp. 516–529). Thousand Oaks, CA: Sage.

Richardson, L., & St. Pierre, E. A. (2008). Recontextualizing observation: Ethnography, pedagogy, and the prospects for a progressive political agenda. In N. K. Denzin & Y. S. Lincoln (Eds.), *Collecting and interpreting qualitative materials* (pp. 161–184). Thousand Oaks, CA: Sage.

Saldaña, J. (2006). This is not a performance text. *Qualitative Inquiry, 12*(6), 1091–1098. doi: 10.1177/1077800406293239

Spry, T. (2001). Performing autoethnography: An embodied methodological praxis. *Qualitative inquiry, 7*, 706–732. doi: 10.1177/107780040100700605

Spry, T. (2011). *Body, paper, stage: Writing and performing autoethnography.* Walnut Creek, CA: Left Coast Press.

Weems, M. E., Callier, D. M., & Boylorn, R. M. (2014). Love, peace, and sooooooul: The fire this time writers' group. *Cultural Studies ⟺ Critical Methodologies, 14*, 333–337. doi: 10.1177/1532708614530304

Weems, M. E., White, C. J., McHatton, P. A., Shelley, C., Bond, T., Brown, R. N., Melina, L., Scheidt, L. A., Goode, J., De Carteret, P., & Wyatt, J. (2009). Heartbeats exploring the power of qualitative research expressed as autoethnographic performance texts. *Qualitative Inquiry, 15*(5), 843–858. doi: 10.1177/1077800409333155

Wyatt, J., Gale, K., Russell, L., Pelias, R. J., & Spry, T. (2011). How writing touches: An intimate scholarly collaboration. *International Review of Qualitative Research, 4*, 253–277.

Young, H. (2010). *Embodying Black experience: Stillness, critical memory, and the Black body.* Ann Arbor, MI: University of Michigan Press.

Durell M. Callier
Miami University

Dominique C. Hill
Amherst College

Hill L. Waters

JOHN MARC CUELLAR

6. MARRIAGE OR MIRAGE?

The Breakdown of a Break-up

She enters the church, adorned in white. I'm nervous, but excited, my face slightly pale. In front of family and friends, we share this moment. We are to be united as one, one happy couple. The pastor begins the service and the ceremony begins. He quickly asks:

"Do you take this bride to be your lawfully wedded wife, to have and to hold, from this day forward, for better, for worse, for richer, for poorer, in sickness and in health, until death do you part?"

"I do," I respond.

He asks her the same.

She looks at me, smiles, and says back, "I do."

TRUE MOTIVATIONS

I drive into the garage and stop the car, silencing the musical stylings of Clint Black who sings about a goodbye he swore would never materialize. We both, my wife and I, make it to the door at the same time, me after retrieving the leftovers of our dinner from the back seat and her after struggling to get past all the clutter on her side of the garage. I place the leftovers on the kitchen table as she insists that our decision to dine at Joe's Italian restaurant was a good choice. Then, she does it again. She leans over, kisses me on the cheek, and whispers that she thinks we should try to procreate again. I feared this. I thought it would be a relaxing evening, both of us satisfied with a nice meal and the possibility of drifting off to sleep while watching TV. It was not to be. Yet again, I am asked to perform what seems like my nightly duty in hopes that she will become pregnant with our first child. We both want this child, but I am beginning to feel exhausted by the constant suggestion of sex. I am not performing as the hypersexual notion of an immensely masculine guy when I whine and faintly say, "Again?"

"In order to get pregnant, you have to keep trying. You have to do it as much as it takes," she insists.

"Okay," I concede. I throw in a demand. "But only once tonight," I say, remembering that on the previous night she gave me a thirty-minute break before insisting that we try it again.

"Good," she says, before disappearing into the bedroom. "I'll get ready," she hollers from a distance.

S. L. Pensoneau-Conway et al. (Eds.), Doing Autoethnography, 45–53.
© *2017 Sense Publishers. All rights reserved.*

I prepare myself mentally, but realize that I am going to need some more stimulation. It would be hard to perform this act without being *hard*, so I try to relax and find motivation. I turn to the TV. I'm sure something on television will help me with this dilemma. I start switching channels.

Animal Planet: No. As much as I find chimpanzees cute, I don't find the sexual stimulation I need on a countdown program of the world's most extreme tool-users.

TV Land: No. If anything, Lucy's whining and mischievous antics are a turnoff. I love Lucy, but she just doesn't do it for me.

The Home Shopping Network: I am interested in the new Nikon camera for sale, the one with the zoom lens. Yet, it's doing nothing for my sexual stimulation, so I change the channel again.

HBO: I hear the bluesy strumming of the guitar chords, warning me of bad things to come, and I know I'm on the right channel.

It's the second episode of HBO's *True Blood*, entitled "The First Taste" (Ball, Harris, & Winant, 2008), and there's a character who has caught my attention. This character has my ideal body type. To me, he's aesthetically pleasing, both facially and physically. My male gaze objectifies the physical specimen on the screen (Mulvey, 2009). Yet, as gratifying as the gorgeous specimen before me is, I am still not fully aroused. I am in need of something more.

I watch Tara Thornton brush off a romantic suitor at a party by pretending that her ex-partner is a psychotic, jealous type, when all of a sudden I see bodies thrusting against each other, crashing against the dresser mirror. I stare at a perfectly fit, well-rounded backside and, as if by magic, I am ready to perform my sexual duty.

"I hope you're ready. I'm coming in now," I yell from the living room. I did not think I would be able to perform again tonight, but I found my inspiration. I enter the bedroom and we begin. It's easy. It's intense. It's enjoyable.

When we finish, she goes into the bathroom to clean off and I turn on the television in the bedroom. I turn it to HBO and watch the rest of the episode. I learn the name of the character and immediately go to the computer in our spare bedroom to google search the name of the actor.

I just had sex with my wife. I have performed my hetero-masculine duties. I am proud of my hypersexual abilities. It's as if John Wayne himself should be congratulating me and saying, "Way to go, Pilgrim." Instead, I know the reality. I know why I got hot. I know his name. I might have just had sex with my wife, but it was *True Blood*'s Jason Stackhouse, played by Ryan Kwanten, who helped me do it. What would John Wayne think of that?

* * *

Marriage, in western society, is established as the end state for romantic relationships, the ultimate dream. The goal is for two betrothed lovers to join together in what Foucault (1976/1990) calls a "deployment of alliance" (p. 106). Warner (1999) speaks of a hierarchy when differentiating between good and bad sexual relations, stating that society privileges certain discourses. These discourses, including procreation, sex in pairs, relationships, partners of the same generation, and private acts of sex, among others, are situated on the favored side of the hierarchical structure. Most of these acts are traditionally thought of as behaviors that a man and a woman engage in while combined as one: husband and wife, a married couple. But life doesn't always flow harmoniously with the constructs of social consciousness. Sometimes, a marriage is not met with society's notion of success. It fails to extend to the "happily ever after" of fairytale endings. When a marriage ends, one must ask: Was it ever worth the effort? Was it true love? Was it real? Or was it not really a marriage after all? Is a marriage that does not achieve the socially constructed notion of success truly a marriage or is it just something that seemed to be present, but never truly was—a mirage?

The good and the bad, sickness and health, the best and the worst ... Are these complete opposites or dialectical tensions that necessitate the other, false dichotomies that inform one another? These discursive struggles are in concert together. As Baxter (2011) notes, "it is the interplay of competing discourses where the action sits—the interplay of discourses is how meanings are made" (p. 18). The discourses "interpenetrate" one another. When I am desiring to be connected with my relational other, I also simultaneously have yearnings toward autonomy. Which discourse is centered over the other is dependent upon temporal circumstances, particular instances. A marriage is made up of these moments. Never fully one or the other, a marriage is both: the good and the bad.

I echo the sentiments of Adams, Holman Jones, and Ellis (2015) and come to autoethnography with multiple ways of doing research: utilizing my personal experience, demonstrating my own sense-making process, maintaining reflexivity throughout my engagement in research, using my own particular insider knowledge, critiquing cultural norms, and seeking a response from you—the audience (p. 26). Autoethnography is more than merely a detached personal story, disconnected from social and interpersonal connections and devoid of personal responsibility. When doing autoethnography, instead, I interrogate the relationship between myself, the writer, and the audience in a continuous reflexive process, a process Berry (2013) names "spinning reflexivity." Through its ability to reach multiple readers, autoethnography has the potential to inspire cultural change (Boylorn, 2014). Bruner (2002) claims, "we are so adept at narrative that it seems almost as natural as language itself" (p. 3). That is the gift of autoethnography—its ability to bridge the gap between author and reader, self and other, the personal and the cultural (Ellis & Bochner, 2000).

I first came to autoethnography through a reading assigned in a master's level course that was written by my advisor. Bolen (2014) demonstrated to me how to story one's personal experience—particularly his autoethnographic account of aesthetic moments in a father-son relationship—in a meaningful and informing way. Drawing upon such influences, like Vickers (2007), I use autoethnography as a methodological tool to retrospectively make sense of my experiences. This story, my story, comes from my own personal experience. As somebody who identifies as gay and lived through a heterosexual marital relationship that resulted in divorce, I come from the standpoint of an insider. This is equivalent with

Goffman's (1963) description of those who know from personal experience what living with a stigma is like (p. 20). My autoethnographic account critiques the dominant cultural discourse that values sex merely for its reproductive value and situates sexual relationships as normalized only through heterosexual relationships between husband and wife (Foucault, 1976/1990; Warner, 1999).

BLUE LIGHTS

I hold onto her hand. I am confident enough as a driver to steer the car with one hand while maintaining my hold of her hand with the other. As we drive, festive displays emerge before us. Mostly following the same cookie-cutter formula, these houses typically display clear icicle lights, as that has been the trend for the past few years. One by one, each follows the lead of the other—icicle lights, icicle lights, and even more icicle lights. But then it appears. One house disrupts the monotony. One house calls to mind the festive displays of yesteryear.

I pull her hand close to my lips and give it a kiss. "Blue lights," I utter. I hear her chuckle. We drive for several minutes before I repeat this game again. Each time I see a house lit up by multi-colored lights, or even rarer, whenever I see a house lit by nothing but blue Christmas lights, I kiss her hand and say the same thing, "blue lights." We've been playing this game for a few years now and it has become expected. As synonymous as egg nog and mistletoe, "blue lights" has begun to represent Christmas. It is a warm reminder of my affection for her. We pass another block and more icicle lights illuminate our path. Then, there all alone, situated between the strings of clear, bright lights is another house that defies the trend. I see the colorful display, pull her hand close to my lips again, and repeat these words, expressing my love for her, "blue lights." I kiss her hand and drive on.

* * *

My friend is thirsty. I counted on this. If beer is available a mile away, he can reliably be expected to consume as much alcohol as his linebacker-sized frame can hold. He can knock 'em down. And on this night, that's what I was hoping for. He declined the chance to join our other friend on a journey into Temptations, a popular strip club on Bourbon Street. Instead, he wanted to walk the street with me. I, however, had other plans. I had desires and nothing was going to keep me from following through with the plans that I made for my last night in New Orleans.

"Look, it's those big beer containers you were looking for," I call out. He falls for my trick. He asks me to wait for him and goes to the back of the line. I wait for a bit and then, following the course of action I had planned the moment he attempted to ruin my agenda for the night, I dash off and disappear into the crowd. He loses sight of me and I am on my way to the Rainbow Room.

I had seen the Rainbow Room on our previous trips to Bourbon Street. Rather, I had seen the guy who they sent out to lure other men into the strip club. Almost identical each night, the guy is young, cute, impressively built, and shirtless—there for lustful eyes to objectify so that the business inside can free sexed-up tourists of their hard earned cash. On the previous night, the guy outside the Rainbow Room did it for me. Perhaps it was the combination of rippling abs and a boyish grin, but whatever it was, it did the trick. Here I was, now ready to enter the doors of this uniquely advertised strip club.

Several minutes into my experience at the Rainbow Room, I am ready to leave. I have enjoyed the sights, but as a married man, that is about all I should be doing on this night of adventure, lust, and drunken debauchery. Then, he appears. The DJ introduces him onto the stage, using the stage name White Lightning. "Day N' Nite" by Kid Cudi (Mescudi & Omishore, 2008) pounds on the speakers and he steps up, immediately throwing off his shirt. Blue lights shine on his chiseled body. I'm intrigued. I decide to stay a bit longer. He does his act for a bit, when I decide to partake in the customs of such an establishment. I dig deep into my pocket and produce a dollar bill. I'm embarrassed. I've never done this before, but this is my last chance. It's my last night in New Orleans. I go up to the stage and sit down. He immediately notices me and moves closer toward me, releasing his grip from the pole and shoving his crotch closer and closer to my face. He then slides his boxer briefs down, creating an opening for me to dispense my money. I slide the dollar down into his boxer briefs and he thanks me by gyrating in front of me for several minutes. Part of me thinks this should be the time that I consider myself lucky for having finally experienced the gratifying touch of an attractive male body and head toward the door. Yet, I haven't had enough. I produce another dollar bill. This happens two times and on the third, I realize I am out of money. I look into my wallet and see that I only have a twenty-dollar bill left. Hesitant, I give in. I display my money and he heads toward me again.

After the show, I sit back and take in the experience. I decide to finish the beer I just ordered and plan on leaving when it's finished. My friend continues to text me. He is concerned that he cannot find me. Our other friend, enjoying the offerings at Temptations, could care less about my whereabouts. I take another sip of my Miller Lite and he materializes before my eyes.

"Hey, thanks for that up there," he tells me and then continues, "We have a VIP room upstairs. Would you be interested in going up there with me, alone?"

My heart begins to pound. I think of my wife and look at the bag of souvenir t-shirts I bought for my kids. Against what might be considered my better judgment, I agree to his offer. I head to the bar, ready to withdraw several twenties from the conveniently-placed ATM. I follow him up the spiral stairway and he takes me on a tour of the space upstairs. He shows me into the room where we are to be alone. It is lit by a warm, blue tint. He closes the door and takes off his shirt again. I sit on a couch and gaze my eyes upon his chiseled body. The blue lights brighten up what until now I had only fantasized about.

A DIFFERENT PLACE

In my apartment in Athens, Ohio, I am far removed from my hometown in west Texas. Almost a year into my PhD program, this new "reality" is now somewhat normal. I have a routine. I go to class. I study literature. I write a little. I study literature. I prepare to teach my Public Speaking course. I study literature. I study so much literature that past pleasures, such as sleep, nourishment, and relaxation seem like sacred gifts now, to be enjoyed only in the rarest of occasions. Twenty minutes into my reading, I decide to take a break. I pick up my cell phone, search dating apps, look at social networking activity, and decide to make a phone call. I touch the phone icon on my iPhone 6 and head toward favorites. I press my wife's name and wait for her voice to resonate.

"Hello," she answers.

"Hey, what are you doing?" I ask.

"Nothing much. I'm just getting things ready for tomorrow." I know what this means. It is a weeknight and that means she is getting our oldest ready for school. It is a common routine: My wife bathes our children, preparing our daughter for her first grade class in the morning. Then, either her, in person, or I, via FaceTime, read a story to our two children before bedtime.

"How are the kids?" I ask.

"They're good. They're currently playing in the living room." She pauses. There is a long silence before she continues. "I saw the lawyer today and paid her the money you sent."

"Oh yeah?" I nonchalantly reply. This has been a long-running act. My wife will threaten or say something to try to make me jealous. Despite knowing my sexuality, she seems insistent upon trying to make things work out between us.

She speaks again. "Yeah. The divorce will be final in 60 days."

I continue the conversation, but I do not even know where I am anymore. Did I just hear her correctly? I am caught off guard. This is something I saw coming, but yet didn't ever think would happen. I manage to finish the conversation, perhaps by instinct. When she hangs up, I think about what just happened.

Divorced in 60 days. I didn't think it would ever come to this. All of a sudden, I think about the magnitude of what this means. Who will be affected? What will I tell my friends and family? How will we go about sharing the responsibility of raising two kids, paying a mortgage, and managing our shared income? This is a place I never thought I would be, thousands of miles away and headed for divorce. I think about what she said again: "divorced in 60 days." Time was passing by. Before long, I'd be unmarried. We had been together for so long. Despite all the things that made it necessary for the dissolution of our marriage to take place, I still never thought I would hear those words. I think again and ask what I cannot answer: How did we get here?

MESSINESS

I have been dreading this moment all summer long. Though ready to embark on a new journey in Ohio, I am not ready to leave my home. I am certainly not ready to leave my children. In preparation, two days before, I aimed for the best day of our lives. I did all the things the kids loved doing. It was near perfection. The following day, I spent the entire day at home with the kids. I wanted it to be our time, just me and them. However, today has finally arrived. I can't delay it any longer. I have just a few days to drive to Athens, Ohio, a weekend to get ready for my teaching academy, and no time left to delay the inevitable.

"Okay. It's time now. I have to go baby," I tell my daughter. Though I have two children, my son appears to be too young to understand the gravity of the moment. My daughter, however, fully understands. She too has been dreading this moment. She clings on to me. "No daddy. Don't go," she says with urgency.

I think of the night before when I took her outside, holding her in my arms, and asked her to look at the stars above us. I promised her that whenever she looked up at the stars, I would also be looking at the same stars. I had seen something like this on the animated movie *An American Tale* (Barker et al., 1986). The night sky is to be what will always remind me of my precious little girl. I promised this to her. I think of this promise and remind her again that I will always be with her. I add that I will call her every night and talk to her on the iPad through FaceTime.

This is of little comfort to a six-year-old whose daddy is about to leave to get his doctorate in another state. "No daddy. Don't go," she pleads again. I hold onto her for longer than the time I have available. The longer I delay, the later I will arrive in Athens and I have to be there by Friday. It is Wednesday afternoon. I look to my wife and she nods her head to notify me that I should go now.

I try to hand my daughter over to my wife. She begins to scream out in anguish. "No daddy, no. Don't go." She is crying. Immediately, we all begin to cry, realizing that this is actually goodbye. My daughter clings onto me. It is a struggle to get loose from her grip. When I do, the sight of her in complete sorrow urges me to return to her. I cannot leave her. What kind of a monster would break a six-year-old's heart? This is so unnecessary. I do not understand what led me to do this. Yet, I feel there is no turning back. With no job other than the one promised to me in Ohio and with a lease signed, I must make the move.

I attempt it again. Each time, the screaming gets worse and worse. I can't stand to think about what I am doing. I want to be gone so that this moment can be over with, yet I want to stay here forever. I don't know how I manage to do it, but one last time I break free from her grip and hand her over to her mother. Tears well up in my eyes as I turn around, listening to her pleas for me to stay. Until the day I die, I feel that this will be the worst thing I ever do. When I held her for the first time, I never dreamed I would one day leave my little girl. "Daddy, don't go!" she begged over and over again. Somehow, life got messy and I did things I never thought I would do. Somehow, I left.

* * *

My understanding of marriage positioned the phenomenon as a false dichotomy. I held an either-or ideology. If marriage was not successful, it was like a mirage. It appeared to be something it was not. In my mind, it was either fully an institution of commitment, with both parties fully satisfied and rendered complete by the other, or it was simply nonexistent. It appeared out of nowhere and then vanished, a shimmering illusion brought about by the trickery of the sunlight. My initial interpretation of my marital relationship, after the divorce, involved the judgment of failure, dissatisfaction, and deficiency. Yet, in hindsight, new interpretations emerged from a reframing of my relationship. I began to take a dialogical perspective, one in which I saw perceived dichotomies—competing discourses—as continuously "mutually conditioning and mutually opposing" (Rawlins, 2007, p. 58). These discourses are interdependent, completing one another in a process "whereby the unified meaning of the whole is structured and revealed" (Bakhtin, 1981, p. 262). As such, I saw where moments of difficulty rendered moments of joy possible within such an interpersonal bond. What seemed liked finality only became through the realization of a new beginning. Perhaps the marriage was not a mirage after all. Perhaps, with a dialogic perspective, it was exactly what it was meant to be, a joyful union between two people who cared about each other in mutually gratifying ways.

BOTH OF US—BOTH/AND

EnI look up at the stars and I know we will always be together, despite the miles between us. That moment will never leave my memory, even if it only returns as a fragmented reconstruction of the events of that day. Somehow, life got messy. Divorce is messy. Now divorced, I still wonder how I ever got here. We were so happy on that day, June 30, when we vowed to live the rest of our lives together. We were so happy when our first-born entered this world. We were always so happy. What went wrong?

Maybe happiness is never fully available. Maybe happiness is only something that comes in connection with sorrow. The interplay of these competing discourses brings meaning to each, favoring one discourse during one moment and another during the next. Neither ever completely goes away. When I simultaneously want to leave to pursue a dream in academia and to seek a fulfilling relationship with someone of my desires, I also wish to stay. I want to stay with my kids. I want to stay home. I even want to stay with her. We've been together for so long. I do love her. I do, in my own way. But life got messy. Things got messy.

Power is a characteristic of competing discourses. At any given moment, "some discourses are typically more dominant or more central than other more marginalized discourses" (Baxter, 2011, p. 18). At times, I was more connected to my wife. Other times, I wanted to stray away. Maybe marriage can be more than the socially constructed notion of a husband and a wife. Maybe it can transcend beyond linear limitations. Maybe when a marriage ends, it still goes on, in its own way. A marriage can get messy. As such, our understanding of what a marriage means is also messy. It truly is defined by both, simultaneously: happiness and sorrow, sickness and health. My marriage came and disappeared in what seemed like an instant, but the memories I hold onto continue to story my marriage as something that moves forward, something in the process of becoming. I believe my marriage was not a mirage. I believe, in its own way, it was a marriage. I believe. I honor. I trust.

I do.

REFERENCES

Adams, T. E., Holman Jones, S., & Ellis, C. (2015). *Autoethnography: Understanding qualitative research*. New York, NY: Oxford University Press.

Bakhtin, M. M. (1981). *The dialogic imagination* (M. Holquist, Ed.; C. Emerson & M. Holquist, Trans.). Austin: University of Texas Press.

Ball, A., Harris, C. (Writers), & Winant, S. (Director). (2008). The first taste [Television series episode]. In A. Ball, B. Buckner, B. Dunn, C. Jokanovich, N. Oliver, C. D. Trussell, ... A. Woo (Producers). *True blood*. Hollywood, CA: Your Face Goes Here Entertainment.

Barker, K., Bluth, D., Goldman, G., Kennedy, K., Kirschner, D., Marshall, F., ... Spielberg, S. (Producers), & Bluth, D. (Director). (1986). *An American tail* [Motion picture]. United States: Universal Pictures.

Baxter, L. A. (2011). *Voicing relationships: A dialogic perspective*. Thousand Oaks, CA: Sage.

Berry, K. (2013). Spinning autoethnographic reflexivity, cultural critique, and negotiating selves. In S. Holman Jones, T. E. Adams, & C. Ellis (Eds.), *Handbook of autoethnography* (pp. 209–227). Walnut Creek, CA: Left Coast Press.

Bolen, D. M. (2014). After dinners, in the garage, out of doors, and climbing on rocks: Writing aesthetic moments of father-son. In J. Wyatt & T. E. Adams (Eds.), *On (writing families): Autoethnographies of presence and absence, love and loss* (pp. 141–147). Boston, MA: Sense Publishers.

Boylorn, R. M. (2014). From here to there: How to use auto/ethnography to bridge difference. *International Review of Qualitative Research, 7*(3), 312–326. doi: 10.1525/irqr.2014.7.3.312

Bruner, J. (2002). *Making stories: Law, literature, life*. Cambridge, MA: Harvard University Press.

Ellis, C., & Bochner, A. P. (2000). Autoethnography, personal narrative, reflexivity: Researcher as subject. In N. K. Denzin & Y. S. Lincoln (Eds.), *Handbook of qualitative research* (2nd ed., pp. 733–768). Thousand Oaks, CA: Sage.

Foucault, M. (1990). *The history of sexuality volume 1: An introduction*. (R. Hurley, Trans.) New York, NY: Vintage Books. (Original work published 1976)

Goffman, E. (1963). *Stigma: Notes on the management of spoiled identity*. New York, NY: Simon & Schuster.

Mescudi, S., & Omishore, O. (2008). Day 'n' nite [Recorded by Kid Cudi]. On *A kid named Cudi* [CD]. Brooklyn, NY: Headbanga Studios.

Mulvey, L. (2009). *Visual and other pleasures* (2nd ed.). New York, NY: Palgrave Macmillan.

Rawlins, W. K. (2007). Living scholarship: A field report. *Communication Methods and Measures, 1*(1), 55–63. doi: 10.1080/19312450709336662

Vickers, M. H. (2007). Autoethnography as sensemaking: A story of bullying. *Culture and Organization, 13*(3), 223–237. doi: 10.1080/14759550701486555

Warner, M. (1999). *The trouble with normal: Sex, politics, and the ethics of queer life*. Cambridge, MA: Harvard University Press.

John Marc Cuellar
Department of Communication
Ohio University

ALLISON UPSHAW

7. MY BODY KNOWS THINGS

This Black Woman's Storied Theory in Performative Autoethnography

INCITING INCIDENT [TO BE SUNG/READ ALOUD]

My body knows things
My body knows things
My body knows things

I was 3 or 4 years old the first time I felt a man's penis. It belonged to my cousin, Jack. I think he was about 17 at the time. I loved him because he played with me, and to an only child that is everything. His mom and my mama are sisters. That year when Aunt Mary came to visit, Jack came too. I followed him everywhere. He let me ride on his back. I was too big for Mama to do that anymore. When no other adult would play with me, he would take me outside. He was (is) family.

My body knows things
My body knows things
My body knows things

INTRODUCTION

Early abuse at the hands of an older male cousin situated my body as the site of my wounding. My inability to make meaning of a sexual experience at the age of three became my trauma. In therapy off and on for years, I have worked on healing the story behind the wound, but never has anyone suggested that my body needed healing as the site of that wound. They, the professionals who I have sought help from over the years, never told me that my body knows things, and I was not listening to my body's voice.

My body knows things
My body knows things
My body knows things

This written account of early childhood sexual abuse at the hands of an older relative is a textual representation of a performative autoethnographic piece by the same name. In this text, I *braid* together an Afrocentric framing of my story, performative autoethnography, and dance. The intersectionality of my identities as

S. L. Pensoneau-Conway et al. (Eds.), Doing Autoethnography, 55–65.
© 2017 Sense Publishers. All rights reserved.

Black female, autoethnographic scholar, and arts-based researcher twist *under/over, under/over, under/over* repeatedly. Each strand gathers wisps of edges (concepts, theories, writers, and artist-scholars along the periphery), thickening and strengthening the strand and therefore the braid.

My position as an African American graduate student on a predominately white campus (PWI) compels me to create academic space for my identity, with all of its intersections, throughout my work. Braiding as a metaphorical progression facilitates a practical visual for my process, while also reflecting my cultural narrative as a Black woman in an alien environment. Performative autoethnography allows me to draw upon my training and experience as a professional performer, while testing the affordance of various arts-based research methods. In this case, I felt dance was the most appropriate method for an embodied inquiry.

CULTURAL REPRESENTATION/MEANING MAKING

Braiding as a hair styling technique can be simple and complex. It is an unyielding marker of African American female identity, as well as a ritual of bonding and reaffirmation among Black women. This concept evokes strong images of my identity as an African American female and solidifies my sense of belonging. This intersectional self-representation is an important part of my meaning making as a new member of academia. Oscar winning actress Lupita Nyong'o says, "Braiding tells a story" (Wagoner, 2014). I take my place as griot (storyteller) recounting my narrative by braiding performative autoethnography, dance, and Black feminist theory. The reader's engagement with this performative writing closes off the end of the braid and keeps it from unraveling. The readers' interpretations carve out an artistic third space (Leavy, 2014) where making meaning comes not just from the words on the page, but by active and critical engagement.

PERFORMATIVE AUTOETHNOGRAPHY: STRAND ONE

Autoethnography is a research, writing, and storied method of self-analysis that connects the personal, cultural, social, and political (Ellis, 2004). It is a self-reflexive form of research (Marechal, 2010); a qualitative method combing ethnography and autobiography (Pace, 2012); and a form of self-narrative that places self in a social context (Reed-Danahay, 2006).

Performative autoethnography privileges the body as the site of the story and allows for reintegration of mind and body in the personal narrative (Spry, 2001). It grounds me through my access of prior, embodied knowledge (Denzin, 2003; Oikarinen-Jabai, 2003; Spry, 2001). Writing performatively attempts to draw my reader into the socio-emotional context of my story, without which it is impossible to find common ground (Auslander, 2008; Denzin, 2014; Pollock, 1998). Like autoethnography, performative writing is evocative. It is doing, not describing (Pollock, 1998), and to quote Dorothy Allison (1994), "some things must be felt to be understood" (p. 14).

Writing performatively initiates reclamation of my body's place in research (Langellier & Peterson, 2006), and allows an aesthetic and sensory voice to be heard. With increasing purpose in my growth as a performing academician, I twist strands of autoethnographic performance (Spry, 2001) and performative writing (Pollock, 1998). This chapter serves as a written performance for those who will never have the opportunity to see it performed.

This is a script of sorts. It began as images playing out as memory. Through the performative writing of my personal stories, I choose to give my body to the narrative both internally and externally by connecting the inquiry, process, and product. This chapter is for:

– those who will never hear the childlike voice in my head singing, *My Body Knows Things.*
– those who will never see my physical movements in exploration.
– those who cannot touch the tears I may shed in real time.

This narrative voices what my body/mind has internalized. It is my voice encouraging others to rise, and join in the meaning making process. It is my narrative performed that speaks truths for others who have not yet found their own voice (Langellier & Peterson, 2006).

My body knows things
My body knows things
My body knows things

DANCE AS INQUIRY: STRAND TWO

Movement, as an elicitation technique, is difficult to find in the literature of embodied therapies, creative arts therapies, dance therapy, qualitative research methods, arts-based research methods, or emerging methods. In developing the concept of *movement elicitation*, I turn to documented work in photo and music elicitation methods, and by studying the choreography practices of Bill T. Jones, (Jones & Grubin, 1997). Jones' work, with text as the basis for creating movement phrases, provided me with specific ways of drawing forth my body's memories and giving them voice.

Elicitation is a qualitative data collection technique, the most common of which is *photo elicitation*. Photo elicitation uses visual images (photos, videos, paintings, collages, etc.) in the participant interview and the evoked response to the visual image is recorded and later analyzed (Bignante, 2010). This process relies on the body's visceral response to images, since the part of the brain that processes visual information is much older than the part that processes language (Harper, 2002). Interviews that utilize this method often inspired deeper and nuanced responses from the participants (Collier, 1957; Collier & Collier, 1986).

Music elicitation is almost always analyzed in relation to the emotions that are evoked from sound (Allett, 2010; Robinson, 2005). Those sounds and emotions are then linked by the participants to particular experiences, people, places, and things. Bresler (2005) and Leavy (2014) see music's power as an elicitation tool in an embodied practice that crosses the line between the mind-body dichotomy. This practice of using sounds to connect embodied knowledge that the conscious self may not have access to led me directly to the concept of movement as an another way of reclaiming my life's story. In my exploration of movement as an inquiry process, I regained access to very different pieces of my life narrative. Pieces that were not accessible to me through visual or aural techniques. **My Body Knows Things** was originally written as a dramatic monologue. I then used that text in collaboration with composer, Dana Rice, to create a sung version of my story. Both versions provided a type of catharsis for emotions I thought long buried and resolved, but I felt as if there might be more.

Sitting on the floor of the small dance studio diligently trying to avoid my reflection as best I could while facing a wall of mirrors; I plugged the external speakers into my laptop and turned the volume high. I listened, with my eyes closed, to the sound of the piano. The lyrics danced in my head as an antithesis to dancing sugarplums. A sudden need to draw had me pulling out my little black Moleskin notebook and colored pencils. I listened to the melody, drawing what I thought were random shapes. I needed to dance, but I did not want to know what I might have forgotten. I looked at what I had drawn. It was a picture of his boxers, with the little purple designs all over the white background. Putting the notebook down carefully, I stood. Stretching the unused muscles in my legs, I tried to remember how Bill T. Jones began his process. Letting the music play, hearing my words in my head, I started to move.

> He took my hand
> my little brown hand
> into his pants
> my innocent hand

As I moved, I remembered the heat of my cousin's body, the smooth feel of his penis against his course pubic hair. I could see the white boxers with faint purple designs as if faded by too many washings. I did not remember these details in my earlier arts-based processes. Only when I involved my entire body in conjunction with my mind was I able to unlock those details.

> *My body knows things*
> *My body knows things*
> *My body knows things*

BLACK FEMINISM: STRAND THREE

In the oral tradition of the African griot, I stand in my role as storyteller, praise singer, musician, historian, and poet (Hale, 2007). In the written tradition of U.S. Americans, I write this story for Western history to see and acknowledge this black girl's story, "cause don't nothing move white folks like paper" (African American folk saying). I come from a long line of storytellers, and storysingers, from oral traditions that use words, music, song, and body to engage, to praise, to rebuke, to admonish, to teach, and to " sing a black girl's song" (Shange, 1977). I come from a long line of African American women, Black women who have stood, and still stand, in the face of oppression and abuse. Some of these Black women have written songs, poems, dissertations, blogs, and articles, while some have remained silent. I raise my voice to join those who speak out, and I raise my voice to speak for those who remain silent while choking on stories yet untold.

In direct opposition to acceptance of what others have called me, I name myself from the intersectionality (Crenshaw, 1989) of my storied lives. I am African American, female, and riding the line between poverty and middle class. The overlapping of my racialized, gendered, and classed selves informs my work as artist-scholar. From my racialized self, I bring a history of oral tradition (Hale, 2007) that has thrived through the middle passage, slavery (Yetman, 2001), Jim Crow (Chare, Gavins, & Korstad, 2013), and the appropriation of that tradition in the halls of academia. From my gendered self comes an innate affinity for, connection with, and understanding of other. Lastly, from my classed self, I offer stories as a lived practice of personal emancipation, locating itself within a larger tradition of silenced black female voices.

When the void that was white feminism's lack of response to the issues of race and class grew too great for women of color to ignore, they chose to create their own space. In this space, black female voices spoke a formal articulation of Black feminism. However, black feminism has always existed in unrecognized forms through our mothers', grandmothers', and sisters' sacrifices (Hull, Bell-Scott, & Smith, 1982). Our female ancestors might not call their actions feminist, but they would call them survival. Every slave woman who survived the middle passage participated in an act of resistance against those who thought her life worthless. Every enslaved woman who did what she felt was necessary to keep her family safe, performed a feminist act of survival for all those under her care. Black feminism thrived in the lyrics of our great songstresses: International Sweethearts of Rhythm (*Jump Children*), Bessie Smith (*You Been a Good Ol' Wagon*), Erykah Badu (*Bag Lady*), Beyoncé (*Lemonade*), Lauren Hill (*Black Rage*) and others (Hill Collins, 2008). The Combahee River Collective (Hull, Bell-Scott, & Smith, 1982) intentionally formed around addressing the intersecting oppressions of race and gender, and specifically articulated a position for Black women.

One of the foundational tenets of black feminism is the right to self-definition (Hill Collins, 2000). "You can't tell my story 'cause you ain't lived my story" (Savoy, 2016). Black women wear labels from outsiders who never attempt to become insiders. That outsider gaze labels us as *mammies* if we chose not to hold innocent children responsible for the sins of their parents, and *matriarchs* when we stand as head of families after our men leave (Hill-Collins, 2000, 2008). It calls us *jezebel* when we own our sexuality, and *sapphire* when we stand up for ourselves refusing to take what everyone thinks they can dish out just because we are black (Hill-Collins, 2000, 2008). Given that everyone felt such freedom in deciding who we, black women, will be, and what we will be called makes it imperative that black feminists name themselves and tell their stories (Hill Collins, 2000, 2008).

PERFORMATIVE AUTOETHNOGRAPHY: STRAND ONE

I do not consider autoethnography as solely a component of arts-based research. I believe that I live in a performative artistic paradigm. A paradigm that exists outside of both qualitative and quantitative knowing (Haseman, 2006). Therefore any self-study with which I engage becomes arts-based by default. Self-reflection is often an integral part of any artistic process. It is therefore not a stretch to connect the practices of autoethnography (and even narrative inquiry) with the use of arts in the research process (Prendergast, 2014). Although I think of autoethnography as a tool of qualitative research that can be arts-based or not, Leavy (2014) definitely includes autoethnography as an artistic research practice. The practices of autoethnography and arts-based research have much in common.

Unlike other qualitative researchers, performative artist-scholars initiate the research puzzle (Clandinin & Connelly, 2004; Mason, 2002) from a vastly different perspective. Practice as research or arts-based research scholars do not usually start with a specific problem. They start with an "excitable interest that can't be contained" (Haseman, 2006). Performative researchers are not interested in translating their work into more standard forms of representation. As a performative autoethnographer, I find this to be true as well. My writings and performances are not about solving complex, interdisciplinary problems. They are about making meaning for me, allowing others to share in my process and perhaps make meaning for themselves along the way. At the very least, whether I am in my role as autoethnographer, or artist-scholar (or both), I am attempting to lay my practice/process bare so that others might see a connection between us. When that happens, I am no longer the "stranger." You too are no longer the "stranger" and we can move closer to mutual respect and acknowledgement (Shabatay, 1991).

When you study yourself and understand yourself as a knower, you can trace knowing from experience to intellectual understanding. When artists practice research, the focus is process driven rather than product driven. That change in focus is something that is very difficult to accept in a results-oriented society such as that we currently inhabit (Prior, 2013). Arts–based researchers and autoethnographers do not write to simply experience catharsis, although catharsis is often a byproduct of both processes (Prendergast, 2014). Instead, they write (dance, sing, draw, paint, take pictures, act, etc.) to process their thoughts, to examine their perspective to evoke connections, and to move others to action.

Leavy (2014) sees the arts in research as a way to create, or carve out a "third space" of meaning making. Performative autoethnography also carves out a "third space." Like the arts, it situates the researcher/artist in the midst of what is known, as they struggle their way to, and through, that which is unknown. It pulls the actual practice that is the research process to center stage, and demands that it be acknowledged. It reveals all that is usually hidden in the research process when practice is the object of study and not the method (Haseman, 2006).

The challenge with using methods that are themselves marginalized and nominally accepted when you are a marginalized group, is that it is even more difficult to be considered a serious scholar. I have always been on the outside, even within my own community. I have always lived in liminal spaces between acceptance and rejection. The fact that I am drawn to methods that will reinforce that status, while helping others to understand it, is not surprising nor is it something that I fear.

DANCE AS INQUIRY: STRAND TWO

How did I use dance as my inquiry process? I recorded the words before I drove to the dance studio, but I had no idea what to expect. I had already written a monologue and a song about this situation, I could not imagine that moving my body would tell me anything I did not already know. I connected the speakers to the laptop and moved everything over to the side. I hated that wall of mirrors that reflected the dance space. To be accurate, I hated seeing the reflection of my body in the mirrors that lined the wall. I pushed play and walked to the center of the floor. Unconsciously, I closed my eyes as soon as I heard the words, my words …

> *My body knows things*
> *My body knows things*
> *My body knows things*

Movement: Breathe. I breathe deeply as the opening sentence washes over me, catapulting me back in time.
Memory: It's hot under the cover with my older cousin.
Movement: My body sucks in on itself quickly, bending me in half. Breathe.
Memory: His hot body curves around my three year old self.
Movement: Arms tuck into my core. Breathe.
Memory: I feel something hard pressing into my bottom.
Movement: Sway from side to side holding the bent position. Breathe.
Memory: He pulls my hand behind me and puts it on top of his penis, over the boxers.

> *My body knows things*
> *My body knows things*
> *My body knows things*

Movement: Leading with my right shoulder, twist my torso to the left with my left arm slowly distending toward the ceiling. Breathe.
Memory: He rubs my hand over the outside of his boxers.
Movement: Stretch a little past comfortable and quickly return to original position. Breathe.
Memory: He pulls my hand through the flap on his boxers. I feel the softness of his skin and the heat pouring off his body.

Movement: Rise with both arms extending to the side (like a yawn) and left foot rises from the floor in a flexed position, spine curved, right leg bent. Breathe.
Memory: He jumps out of bed and runs out of the room. The adults laugh and tease him about waiting so long before going to the bathroom. I'm very quiet, and they think I'm asleep.
Movement: Plant left foot on floor. Spin to the right for three full turns. Breathe.
Memory: It's winter, but it's hot in here.

I hated remembering. It was all I could do not to shut down completely. I have always remembered what happened, but I did not know I remembered all those details and feelings. My soul aches for the loss of trust and innocence that follows me even now, some forty-six years later. My spirit weeps inconsolably as the memories continue.

My body knows things
My body knows things
My body knows things

BLACK FEMINISM: STRAND THREE

The thing that hath been, it is that which shall be, and that which is done is that which shall be done: and there is no new thing under the sun. (Ecclesiastes 1:9, King James Version)

The sexualization of young female bodies is not new. That it is more prevalent when applied to young black and brown female bodies is also not something that should shock us. Black girls are perceived as "womanish" if they sit with their legs open. They are "fast" when they make fashion choices considered too "old" for them. Elementary age girls wearing extensions/weaves, acrylic nails, and lip gloss are "asking for trouble."

Black women's stories cannot be authentic without discussing the sexualization of black girl bodies in the media, early sexual behavior by choice (Walker, 1995), and sexualization by our own communities. Old women sitting on front porches whisper about how "fass" young girls are as they walk by. Old men grunting and laughing, watching … always watching. Coming into black/brown sexuality, becoming "grown" is often a proud moment for young black/brown girls (Bowen, 2013; Shange, 1977; Walker, 1995). But what if it's not consensual, this sexual reading and representation of our young bodies? What if you are too young to read? To write? To dress yourself well, or to talk clearly? What then?

Who tells those stories to the old women whispering about you as you walk by? Who tells those stories to them, when often your knowledge comes at the hands of their husbands, and sons? When do black women get to tell their stories about black men who do worse things than leave them with children to feed and no job? When will the stories that black women tell about being molested by those we trust not be thrown back in our faces with reprimands to "stop airing dirty laundry before white folk"? Lorde (1984) admonishes us to remember our responsibility to fight against dehumanization from the inside as well as the outside. She says we must question why we as Black sisters are so willing to destroy each other, even our young girls.

Harris-Perry (2011) describes an experiment in which people, placed in a crooked room, had to stand straight. Some, going by the crooked things in the room, thought themselves upright when they were off vertically by as much as 35 degrees. Others, in spite of their crooked surroundings, managed to find the right side up and maintain it against what looked wrong. Before I could go to school, I was introduced to a "crooked room" that housed my sexuality. In that room, I learned shame. I didn't know what to call it then, but I know now. I feel it as I write this experience "airing dirty laundry in front of white folks." Even though Mama addressed the perpetrator immediately and banned him from our house, even though my grandmother stood with one daughter against the other daughter's son and his abuse of me, even though many positive things and feelings comprised my childhood, shame still became an insidious part of my identity … and Jack … he was (is still) family.

Proud/Shamed
Proud of where I am
Shamed of where I've been
They never look past my outer shell
They never hear the silent death knell.

Victim/Victor
Victim of a crooked room
Victor struggling to stay upright
They'll never acknowledge what it takes
They'll never know what's at stake.

Woman/Girl
Woman living alone
Girl singing a lonesome song
Knowledge locked inside myself
Find the key, the song, the shelf.

REFERENCES

Allett, N. (2010). *Sounding out: Using music elicitation in qualitative research.* Realities Working Papers #14: Music elicitation. Manchester, UK.

Allison, D. (1994). *Skin: Talking about sex, class, and literature.* New York, NY: Firebrand Books.

Auslander, P. (2008). *Theory for performance studies: A student's guide.* New York, NY: Routledge.

Bowen, S. (2013, December 6). *Bad fat Black girl.* Retrieved from http://badfatblackgirl.blogspot.com/2013/12/age-consent-from-real-life-fast-ass-girl.html

Bignante, E. (2010, February 24). The use of photo-elicitation in field research. *EchoGeo*. doi:10.4000/echogeo.11622

Bresler, L. (2005). What musicianship can teach educational research. *Music Education Research, 7*, 169 182. doi: 10.1080/14613800500169399

Chare, W., Gavins, R., & Korstad, R. (Eds.). (2013). *Remembering Jim Crow: African Americans tell about life in the segregated South*. New York, NY: The New Press.

Clandinin, D., & Connelly, F. (2004). *Narrative inquiry: Experience and story in qualitative research*. San Francisco, CA: Jossey-Bass.

Collier, J. (1957). Photography in anthropology: A report on two experiments. *American Anthropologist, 59*. doi: 10.1525/aa.1957.59.5.02a00100

Collier, J., & Collier, M. (1986). *Visual anthropology: Photography as a research method*. Albuquerque: University of New Mexico Press.

Crenshaw, K. (1989). Demarginalizing the intersection of race and sex: A black feminist critique of antidiscrimination doctrine, feminist theory, and antiracist politics. *University of Chicago Legal Forum, 1*(8). 139–167.

Denzin, N. (2003). *Performance ethnography: Critical pedagogy and the politics of culture*. Thousand Oaks, CA: Sage.

Denzin, N. (2014). *Interpretive autoethnography* (2nd ed.). Los Angeles, CA: Sage.

Dwyer, S., & Buckle, J. (2009). The space between: On being an insider-outsider in qualitative research. *International Journal of Qualitative Methods, 8*, 54–63. doi: 10.1177/160940690900800105

Ellis, C. (2004). *The ethnographic I: A methodological novel about autoethnography*. Walnut Creek, CA: AltaMira Press.

Hale, T. (2007). *Griots and griottes: Masters of words and music*. Bloomington: Indiana University Press.

Harper, D. (2002). Talking about pictures: A case for photo elicitation. *Visual Studies, 17*. 13–26. doi: 10.1080/14725860220137345

Harris-Perry, M. (2011). *Sister citizen: Shame, stereotypes and Black women in America*. New Haven, CT: Yale University Press.

Haseman, B. (2006). A manifesto for performative research. *Media International Australia, Incorporating Culture & Policy, 118*, 98–106. doi: 10.1177/1329878X0611800113

Hill Collins, P. (2000). *Black feminist thought: Knowledge, consciousness, and the politics of empowerment*. New York, NY: Routledge.

Hill Collins, P. (2008). Learning from the outsider within: The sociological significance of black feminist thought. *Social Problems, 33*(6), S14–S32. doi: 10.2307/800672

Jones, B. T. & Grubin, D. (1997). *Still/Here* [Motion Picture]. United States.

Langellier, K., & Peterson, E. (2006). Shifting contexts in personal narrative performance. In D. M. Hamera (Ed.), *The Sage handbook of performance studies* (pp.151–168). Thousand Oaks, CA: Sage.

Leavy, P. (2014). *Method meets art: Arts based research practice*. New York, NY: The Guilford Press.

Lorde, A. (1984). The master's tools will never dismantle the master's house. In *Sister outsider: Essays and speeches*. Berkeley, CA: Crossing Press.

Marechal, G. (2010). Autoethnography. In A. Mils, G. Durepos, & E. Wiebe (Eds.), *Encyclopedia of case study research* (Vol. 2, pp. 43–45). Thousand Oaks, CA: Sage.

Mason, J. (2002). *Qualitative researching*. London, England: Sage.

Oikarinen-Jabai, H. (2003). Toward performative research: embodied listening to the self/other. *Qualitative Inquiry, 9*, 569–579.

Pace, S. (2012). Writing the self into research: Using grounded theory analytic strategies in autoethnography. In N. McLoughlin & D. L. Brien (Eds.), *TEXT: Creativity: Cognitive, Social, and Cultural Perspectives, 13*, 1–15. http://www.textjournal.com.au/speciss/issue13/Pace.pdf

Pollock, D. (1998). Performing writing. In P. Phelan (Ed.), *The ends of performance* (pp. 73–103). New York: New York University Press.

Prendergast, M. (2014). I contain multitudes: The challenges of self-representation in arts-based educational research. *International Journal of Education & the Arts, 15*(SI 2.2). Retrieved from http://www.ijea.org/v15si2/

Prior, R. W. (2013). Knowing what is known: Accessing craft-based meanings in research by artists. *Journal of Applied Arts & Health , 4*(1), 57–65. doi: 10.1386/jaah.4.1.57_1

Reed-Danahay, D. (2006). Autoethnography. In V. Jupp (Ed.), *The Sage dictionary of social research methods* (pp. 15–16). Thousand Oaks, CA: Sage.

Robinson, J. (2005). *Deeper than reason: Emotion and its role in literature, music, and art.* Oxford, UK: Oxford University Press.

Savoy, C. (2016). You can't tell my story, cause you ain't lived it. Personal communication.

Shabatay, V. (1991). The stranger's story: Who calls and who answers. In C. Witherell & N. Noddings (Eds.), *Stories lives tell: Narrative and dialogue in education* (pp. 136–152). New York, NY: Teachers College Press.

Shange, N. (1977). *For colored girls who have considered suicide/ when the rainbow is enuf.* New York, NY: Scribner Poetry.

Spry, T. (2001). Performing autoethnography: An embodied methodological praxis. *Qualitative Inquiry, 7*, 706–732. doi: 10.1177/107780040100700605

Wagoner, M. (2014, July). *Lupita Nyong'o and friends come together for a braiding party in New York. Vogue.* Retrieved from http://www.vogue.com/article/lupita-nyongo-hair-braiding-video

Walker, R. (1995). Lusting for freedom. In R. Waker (Ed.), *To be real: Telling the truth and changing the face of feminism* (pp. 19–24). New York, NY: Anchor Books.

Yetman, N. (2001). *An introduction to the WPA slave narratives. Born in slavery: Slave narratives from the Federal Writers' Project, 1936–1938.* Library of Congress.

Allison Upshaw
Department of Interdisciplinary Studies
University of Alabama, Tuscaloosa

O. J. DUNCAN

8. LEARNING HOW TO BE A MAN THE HARD WAY

An Exploration into the Dissolution and Reunification of
Masculine Identities

Content warning: Sexual assault.

AT MY DESK: PART ONE

Each time I turn my attention to this piece, my stomach starts to churn. Two decades after a sexual assault I still feel like a sixteen-year-old huddled in the corner sobbing. My hands shake. I struggle to find the words that will show how much my life has changed around a single moment, and the events that transpired afterwards. My heart races and pounds as I struggle to make sense of the treatment I received after a sexual assault, and at how rape culture continues to make that treatment okay. I am stuck in a revolving door between numerous worlds: fear, anger, hate, resentment, loathing, and revulsion.

But I know that I need to write this. I owe it to who I once was, and I owe it to who I want to be. I owe it to myself, and I owe it to the millions of men who struggle with this pain every day. As a man who passes as white and straight, I have the privilege of my voice being heard above many others in society (Scott & Robinson, 2001). From a very young age, I was taught that a white man's voice is more important than voices of women, people of color, and less masculine men (Cheng, 1999). Movies and television always showed a straight white man coming in to take care of problems, and teach valuable lessons. When a straight white man father figure talked, everyone listened. West and Turner (2014) argue that repeated representations on television and the media shape—or cultivate—our cultural realities. In my experience, whenever I start to speak in mixed groups as a straight white man, people listen. In order for things to change, people in power need to speak up and enact the change (Kleiman, Spanierman, & Smith, 2015). My privilege is power. My voice is powerful.

But once I come out as a gay man that voice is easily silenced. Being gay is a large step away from the power of hegemonic masculinity (Bhana & Mayeza, 2016). As a rape victim, that voice is more than silenced; it is ridiculed and torn apart. In this piece I explore the silencing of a rape victim, and the unique hurdles that victims who identify as men go through. The intersection of maleness, victimhood, and sexuality blend together to create an environment where one's

S. L. Pensoneau-Conway et al. (Eds.), Doing Autoethnography, 67–79.
© 2017 Sense Publishers. All rights reserved.

experience is continually invalidated by society. Women seem to be more welcome to speak about and share their stories of sexual assault, while men are told that there is no space for them, and their story is not as important.[1]

AT THE PODIUM: PART ONE

My heart raced as I walked through the desks neatly aligned in the plain white classroom. My stomach sank with each step, the wooden podium signaling my impending doom. Twenty years had gone by and old wounds were already ripped open and bleeding. This presentation felt like digging my fingers into those wounds and twisting them around. But it was too late to stop now. I was almost to the front of the room, twenty sets of eyes boring into the back of my head.

You can do this. I believe in you.[2]

A tiny weak voice in my left ear whispered. He[3] had been silent for so long. Twenty years of brutal silence had been ended by the poem of a young person—just like himself—who had been brave enough to tell their story.

They are you

the voice whispered after watching the video for the fourth time.

My feet were solid lead as I made it to the podium. I fumbled with the computer to find the video I needed to show. Each click of the keys on the keyboard incited another voice in my head to speak up: The voice in my right ear that had guided me for twenty years.

> STOP. YOU KNOW WHAT WILL HAPPEN
> IF YOU DO THIS. YOU KNOW WHAT HAPPENED
> WHEN YOU DIDN'T LISTEN TO ME BEFORE.

I ignored the thundering voice for the first time in twenty years. It was wrong. My hands shook as I pressed play on the video for the class, an earthquake shaking my mind and soul. "When my rapist showed up under the 'people you may know' tab on Facebook, it felt like the closest to a crime scene that I have ever been," flew from the speakers like a meteor, crashing into my head (Kantor, 2015). The words echoed in my head once, twice, twenty times. Mx. Kantor stood in front of an auditorium and told their truth. And they were believed.

LEARNING MANHOOD: PART ONE

An exhausted six-year-old boy ran down the stairs. After helping his aunt move all day, he was ready to pop every tiny piece of the leftover bubble wrap. He approached the pile, his heart racing as his hand outstretched to grab the wrap. His four-year-old cousin pulled the wrap from his hands. She wouldn't give it back to him, his payment for a hard day of work. The boy's brother pulled him aside, brought a cigarette to his lips, and struck a match against the wall. He brought the match to the tip of his cigarette, and inhaled deeply, the tip of the cigarette igniting and burning bright. The smell of cigarette smoke filled the boy's nostrils, as his brother started to talk. A firm hand pressed against his shoulder, the weight of manhood sinking in as the commanding voice started to speak into his right ear. "She's just a little girl. Let her pop the bubbles. It will make her happy. That's what being a man is about. Working to make other people happy. That's what makes *us* happy. You want to be a man, right?"

That sentiment echoed through his head twenty times, over and over again until the words became a voice themselves. The voice of the right side of his brain. The stoic, dark, loud masculine side. His teachers had told his family he was "sensitive," which Dyer and Pidduck (2003) refer to as a code word for "feminine" and "gay" (p. 112). So his family kept working on ways to toughen him up. People often believe that masculinity is the opposite of femininity (Fausto-Sterling, 2000), and his family was no exception. Whenever he did anything feminine, he was told to stop and act "manly." His brother's directive into his right ear was the first time he had been told he had to give up his own happiness. The voices rolled around and collected like a storm in his head as the thundering voice of masculinity.

WHAT YOU WANT DOESN'T MATTER. YOU
NEED TO BE A MAN AND MAKE HER HAPPY.

Later that night he sat at his mother's side sobbing. He didn't understand why he wasn't right. People kept telling him that he needed to act a certain way, and not do what he wanted to do. She leaned in and whispered softly into his left ear. "You are perfect just the way you are. Don't let them make you think you're not perfect. I love you just the way you are." His mother was very loving and affirming, and his heart always swelled with love. Her voice merged with his own, and started to take a counterpoint to the voice that had been echoing in his right ear.

You're perfect just the way you are.

AT MY DESK: PART TWO

Men are socialized from a very young age to believe that they are responsible for the well-being of others in their life (Kimmel, 2004). Their own needs are pushed down, so they can provide for their family and contribute to society. A side effect of this is that the emotional needs of men as a whole are often ridiculed (Locke, 2011). With the exception of anger, men are not allowed to express any emotion, or they risk being labeled feminine (Farrell, 1993). In a patriarchal society, any feminine qualities lead away from dominant hegemonic power. Feminine qualities in men are often met with scorn and attempts to police behavior.

In me, the policing creates voices. They are not physical, nor are they the type of voices present in some forms of schizophrenia. But dissonance about how I should act, and how I wanted to act, became distinct voices in themselves. The earliest memory of these voices was with my brother, but it has continued throughout my life. The voice of how I should act echoed in my ear as he spoke, and remains to this day. Whenever there wasn't a straight man around to police my masculinity, my brain did it on its own. Silencing and shaming my own voice inside.

But there was always a voice to make me feel okay. That voice told me that I was perfect how I was, and that I could do what I wanted. Unfortunately, that voice has never been very strong.

TAKING THE PODIUM: PART TWO

As the video finished, I tried to swallow the lump in my throat. A fist trying to choke the life out of me to prevent me from reading what I had prepared. A phantom smell of cigarette smoke hit my nose, long gone but returning to haunt me again. The bittersweet acrid smell fogged my brain as I closed my eyes and started to speak, "For this assignment, we were supposed to find another poem to compare to the first. I wasn't able to find anything else about the subject, so I wrote my own," I stammered, voice cracking like I was a teenager about to start puberty again. The right side of my brain started screaming, an endless torrent of rage being spewed at me.

STOP THIS RIGHT NOW!
YOU KNOW BETTER THAN
TO TALK ABOUT THIS!

Then the voice in my left ear chimed in,

Just keep breathing.
You want this. You need this.
Everything will be okay.

That night I was really dumb
A naïve 17 year old
I told him I was gay
I was tired
It didn't seem like a bad idea
Saying it out loud lifted me up
Like ten tons of weight were lifted off my chest
He wasn't the first I told
But he was the last for a long time

LEARNING MANHOOD: PART TWO

The smell of cigarette smoke hit his nose from downstairs. He looked out of the window as the sun finally dipped below the set of apartments across from him. He slipped the CD into the player and felt the broken button slightly dig into his flesh as he hit play. "La la la la la la la la la" poured out of the speakers. The upbeat music of the Spice Girls relaxed him after what seemed like a long day to a sixteen-year-old.

He turned on the television, hearing its buzz and waiting for the screen to warm up. He turned on the Playstation and the familiar noise was drowned out by the sound of him singing along to "Spice Up Your Life." The foreign voice in his right ear, the thundering voice of masculinity, was always telling him how he was failing at being a man.

> STRAIGHTEN YOUR SHOULDERS!
> HOLD YOUR HEAD UP!
> YOU THREW THAT FOOTBALL LIKE A GIRL!

His own voice in his left ear was often silent, drowned out by the thundering voice of masculinity. The booming voice always thought that he was wrong.

It's okay to prefer acting over sports.
It's okay that you like to sing!
You are great how you are!

He had accepted that he would never want to be like his brothers. His friend's mother was a feminist. She had sat him down and talked to him about hegemonic masculinity; how boys are shamed for not acting like men, to perpetuate the patriarchy; how we are filled with messages from media and the people around us to conform or face the consequences (Myers, 2012). She was proud that he didn't act like all the other boys; that he was making his own path.

The voices decided to chime in about his music tastes.

> YOU KNOW, IT'S PRETTY GAY THAT YOU
> LIKE TO LISTEN TO THE SPICE GIRLS.

It's a whole lot gayer
that you like men.

He felt his pupils dilate and his jaw drop. He wanted to grab his controller and start to lead Cloud and Tifa against Sephiroth,[4] but his arms wouldn't move. Both sets of voices were as silent as a tomb, waiting for him to respond. But all he could do was blink in stunned silence. He felt the blood rush and pound in his veins. He could feel every nerve in his body, his heart racing. His eyelid twitched and a hair tickled his ear. By the time he could form a coherent thought the sky was pitch black, a cold desolate landscape spread out twenty miles before him. His mother was yelling up the stairs calling him to dinner.

Just go eat.

> YEAH, THE FAGGOT NEEDS TO EAT.

71

AT MY DESK: PART THREE

The realization that I was gay was shocking. I knew how gays were treated, and I knew how they were less of a man. I was always told that I wasn't enough of a man already. I started to wonder if I was becoming gay because I wasn't enough of a man, or if I was failing as a man because I was gay.

But it was also a relief. I always loved acting, and I knew that gay men were welcomed in the theatre. I also knew that gay men could act like women, as I had always been accused of doing, and it was expected of them. It was validating to think that I could be with gay men, and be myself, and they wouldn't police my actions. I thought that if I told people I was gay maybe they would realize that they didn't need to police my actions and make me more of a man.

TAKING THE PODIUM: PART THREE

I fell asleep
The next thing I knew I was being flipped
Onto my stomach
Like I was a ragdoll
Face slammed against a wall
"You're lucky faggot"
B whispered in my ear
"You're gonna get fucked by a real man tonight."

As I spoke of my past self's experience I felt strength building up in my chest. Support beams that had long since rotted away were being reinforced by the liberation of my words. I quickly sniffed the air, and all I could smell was dusty chalk and a faint whiff of a sweet cologne. I hadn't spoke of him in twenty years. My past self was long dead, a corpse rotting behind a closed door. A jagged knife driven into his chest by a close friend. His throat slit by people he considered friends, people who were supposed to support and protect him.

But the line between him and me started to blur. Our voice was back, and we started to fight the thundering masculinity again. My past self had been a victim of rape. But now *we* were becoming a survivor of rape.

LEARNING MANHOOD: PART THREE

Sweat flowed from his palms, which he kept wiping on the sheets. He had been planning to tell B all night. Slowly and deliberately preparing the words and polishing them like a prize jewel. He had shared his most intimate secret before, but he wasn't sure how B would take the confession. The words stuck in his throat every time he tried to say them, but he repeated them twenty times in his head.

He's one of your good friends.
Go on and tell him!

YOU HAVE ALREADY TOLD TOO MANY PEOPLE.
HE'S JUST GOING TO HURT YOU.

The room smelled like B's manly deodorant, with slight notes of vanilla and spice. B's sweat, an intoxicating manly musk that B always had after the long weekends working together. B's clothes, a salty ocean tide that always carried him away. The unmistakable sound of Pink Floyd flowed through the room, carrying them away on the breeze. They always slept in the same bed after working the weekend at the Ren Faire. Finally, he built up the courage to tell his long hidden secret. The words erupting from his mouth, releasing pressure like a steam valve opening. "B, I'm gay."

"Oh, okay," was B's curt response. B rolled his athletic form over and settled in to go to sleep. He closed his eyes and smiled, lifting up like he was on cloud nine. B didn't hate him. With the weight of a thousand secrets off of his chest, he drifted into sleep, expecting pleasant dreams of running free.

See, it went well!

HE'S GOING TO HURT YOU.

He was awakened by being roughly flipped onto his stomach. B whispered into his ear, "You're lucky faggot. You're gonna get fucked by a *real* man tonight." He felt fingers scratching and digging into his back as his pants were jerked down and he felt B enter him. He fell limp and tried to ignore the ripping pain, feeling like he was tearing apart like a battered sheet of paper. "All in all you're just another brick in the wall" played in the background. The words burned themselves into his brain, a cruel, harsh message from the world. Carving themselves into every wall in his consciousness. His best friend opened the door, a blinding beam of light shining on the deadly abomination happening in the dark, cold room. She peeked in quickly, smiled, and then the door slammed shut loud enough to shatter the brittle foundation of the cocoon he had hidden himself in. Tears formed in his dead eyes, his only hope of a savior ripped out of his soul. *She thought this is what he wanted.* B finished with a grunt and then rolled over to go back to sleep. He got up and stumbled to the bathroom, blood running down his legs in a river of shame, fear, and regret.

YOU SHOULD HAVE LISTENED TO ME.

[silence]

AT MY DESK: PART FOUR

Over the next few years, I tried to get help numerous times. Many programs for victims of rape were only available for women. I tried to go to six different support groups, and the best reaction that I got was someone telling me that there were no programs that I would be allowed in. One group told me that I would not be allowed in because men don't get raped. Another group said they had a number I could call. When I called the number, it was a number for men who were abusers, and how they could get help to stop abusing women. I went to a group that explicitly stated, "All survivors of sexual assault are welcome to speak." I was turned away by a woman who stated that she was not a victim of sexual assault. But she told me that I wouldn't understand what it was like to be a victim, as I was not a woman. At that point, I decided that it was useless to try and get help as a victim of rape.

Around 2005, I started to look for online resources. Everything that I found was women-focused as well, except for a few groups of men who had got together to support each other. But the groups of men were very large, and the stories were all the same. "Man up," "Men don't get raped," "Yeah, like a woman could hold you down and have sex with you if you didn't want to do it." Since I had started acting "like a man" I had become used to people listening to me. So I looked for ways I could help raise awareness of men who were victims of sexual assault.

TAKING THE PODIUM: PART FOUR

I didn't talk to anyone
Everyone thought I was sick
But I couldn't tell
I just sat
And bled
Wishing I bled out
For seven days
When I tried to talk to the police
They said they couldn't help me
Because men don't get raped
When I finally talked to my best friend
She congratulated me
I told her I was raped
She said I wasn't fighting him
She saw it
She didn't hear me struggle
I told her I couldn't
And she told me
"Men can't be raped."

As I started to speak louder, I became comfortable using "I" to describe what happened to him. A switch flipped in my head, shining a warm healing light on the battered bleeding body of who I once was. I had always felt like I died that night, alone and wallowing in my misery. Killing my past self was a way to dissociate from what happened to me. Dissociation "involves a variety of psychological processes (such as amnesia, depersonalization, derealisation and identity confusion) that serve the function of reducing awareness of intolerable information

74

(both internally and externally derived)" (Kennedy et al., 2004). I inhaled deeply through my nose and savored the crisp, clean smell in the air.

LEARNING MANHOOD: PART FOUR

> I couldn't tell my parents
> I didn't want them to know
> They didn't know I was gay
> I tried to tell a teacher
> One whom I really trusted
> But she just said
> "Men can't be raped"
> That's when I knew
> No one would believe me
> So I started to lie
> I said I was fine
> I smiled
> I quit theatre
> Because every moment of my life was acting
> I lied and said that
> Every night I didn't wake up screaming
> Dreaming my sheets were soaking up blood.

Not a single soul believed him. He desperately tried to tell his best friend, his teacher, and the police. He bled for a week, shocked at the rivers of blood escaping his body. He felt the cold grasp of imminent death, and he didn't care. "Men don't get raped. Men can't get raped," was repeated to him twenty times. Each repetition pushed him a little closer to welcoming the peace of death. His final fleeting thoughts were that he was a useless blight on humanity. The already bleak world would be better if he was dead. Ahrens (2006) speaks about the effects on rape survivors when they receive negative reactions to disclosing rape:

> … for most survivors, no matter what they did or how they behave, they are likely to be blamed for the assault. For some survivors, this blame may be so traumatizing that they are effectively silenced by the negative reactions they receive. (p. 270)

The silencing led to his death.

> SEE IF YOU LISTENED TO ME AND
> ACTED LIKE A MAN THIS WOULDN'T
> HAVE HAPPENED TO YOU.

[silence]

With the spark of a stolen red lighter, I lit my first cigarette and decided I would be a man.[5] Because men don't get raped.

My entire identity had changed. I always smelled like smoke now, a cowboy with his hat tipped to the front, a cigarette hanging from my lip. I hated him, a vile ugly hatred that filled me with sadness and rage. It was his fault that I was hurt. He deserved to die like the useless weak piece of trash that he was. I would live like a man and make sure that I was never raped again.

The world became my stage.

MEN DON'T GET RAPED.

I grew a beard.

MEN DON'T GET RAPED.

I worked out every day.

MEN DON'T GET RAPED.

I stopped being an actor and started playing football.

MEN DON'T GET RAPED.

AT MY DESK: PART FIVE

The issue of sexual assault is so focused on gender, women as victims and men as aggressors, that every time I tried to speak up, I was immediately shot down as a rape apologist, a misogynist, or a troll. I was told that men didn't need to speak about sexual assault because it was a thing that happened to women. I was told that if I tried to raise the awareness of sexual assault on men that I would be doing a huge disservice to women, who were the real victims of abuse. Because they couldn't protect themselves when men could.

Even in 2017 it's difficult to find any scholarly articles on men who are victims of sexual assault. Almost everything I have cited uses "women" and "rape victim" interchangeably, while using "men" and "rapist" or "perpetrator" interchangeably. When this is brought up, instead of being seen as an issue, it is made to look like an attack on women. Men aren't allowed to speak on sexual assault even if they are victims, or else they risk being branded as a man in power trying to somehow infiltrate and dismantle women's rights.

TAKING THE PODIUM: PART FIVE

I need to be a man
"Men don't get raped"
I need to grow a beard

> I need to cut my hair
> I need to be a man
> I can't cry
> I can't feel
> I need to be a man
> Men don't get raped

As I saw the startled faces of my classmates, the realization of the toll my silence had had on others started to settle in. Ahrens (2006) describe the societal effects of rape survivors being silenced.

> Sadly, when rape survivors are silenced by negative reactions, their experiences and perspectives are concealed and our ability to identify the causes and consequences of rape are obscured. Such silences thereby obstruct our ability to engage in social change. (p. 270)

I saw tears streaming down their horrified faces. Streams of empathy I had never seen for him … for me. For the first time I realized that I missed him. I needed to clean out the festering wound where he had once been and make room for him again. I wondered how different he would have been. How different I could be.

Standing in front of a group of strangers and talking about something I had hidden for twenty years brought him back to life, back to me.

AT MY DESK: PART SIX

At the end of the semester, three young men and a young woman from my class cornered me. The three men each thanked me for letting them know they weren't alone. The woman told me that her brother had been raped and no one, including her, believed him. After my presentation she called him crying and apologizing. She said her brother sobbed and said to thank me for letting him know he wasn't alone. Hot burning tears filled my eyes, caused by the sting of wounds healing. A poet who had come to our class to watch the presentations hugged me, both of us sobbing. She said I inspired her to write again. Her writing about my story influenced another man to speak about his experience with rape for the first time. He spoke in front of a large audience who applauded him and cried with him. One telling of my story had changed at least seven lives. That effect spread and changed others' lives, and will hopefully keep spreading.

But stories like mine are silenced. My story has been silenced so much that I still have trouble accepting that people believe it. I often feel like people are just placating me, telling me that they believe me just to get me to stop talking about it.

> 20 years after it happened
> And I write about it
> Hesitantly
> For the first time
> I express myself

Honestly
For the first time
In front of a group of strangers
But it doesn't matter
No one will believe me
Even though I still wake up
On the 24th of each month
Screams stuck in my throat
Just like that night
Dreaming of blood
No one will believe me
Because men don't get raped.

NOTES

[1] I am in no way trying to demean the experiences of survivor-victims who identify as women or non-binary. In my experience there are more resources and avenues of support for those who identify as non-binary, and especially, as women, than there are for cisgender men.

[2] Text in italics aligned to the left represents my own non-hegemonic masculinity. Text in all caps on the right represents the voice of hegemonic masculinity. When I hear this voice, it echoes in my right ear. Every "tip" that I received to "man up" when I was younger came from men in my life standing to my right and putting their arm around me.

[3] I refer to myself in the third person when speaking about my past self to emphasize a difference in identities between the past "I" and the current "I." The separation and merger of identities is critical in the story.

[4] Cloud, Tifa, and Sephiroth are characters from the video game *Final Fantasy 7*. Video games were an acceptable masculine hobby and became an important way for me to bond with other males.

[5] Smoking has been a traditional way of signaling masculinity in U.S. American culture. See Starr (1984) for a more detailed look at smoking and masculinity.

REFERENCES

Ahrens, C. E. (2006). Being silenced: The impact of negative social reactions on the disclosure of rape. *American Journal of Community Psychology, 38*(3/4), 263–274. doi:10.1007/s10464-006-9069-9

Bhana, D., & Mayeza, E. (2016). We don't play with gays, they're not real boys ... they can't fight: Hegemonic masculinity and (homophobic) violence in the primary years of schooling. *International Journal of Educational Development, 51,* 36–42. doi:10.1016/j.ijedudev.2016.08.002

Cheng, C. (1999). Marginalized masculinities and hegemonic masculinity: An introduction. *Journal of Men's Studies, 7,* 295–315. doi: 10.3149/jms.0703.295

Dyer, R., & Pidduck, J. (2003). *Now you see it: Studies in lesbian and gay film.* London, England: Psychology Press.

Farrell, W. (1993). *The myth of male power: Why men are the disposable sex.* New York, NY: Simon & Schuster.

Fausto-Sterling, A. (2000). *Sexing the body.* New York, NY: Basic Books.

Kantor, K. [Button Poetry]. (2015, April 5). *"People You May Know" (CUPSI 2015 Finals)* [Video file]. Retrieved from https://www.youtube.com/watch?v=LoyfunmYIpU

Kennedy, F., Clarke, S., Stopa, L., Bell, L., Rouse, H., Ainsworth, C., Fearon, P., & Waller, G. (2004). Towards a cognitive model and measure of dissociation. *Journal of Behavior Therapy and Experimental Psychiatry, 35,* 25–48. doi:10.1016/j.jbtep.2004.01.002

Kimmel, M. S. (2004). *The gendered society*. New York, NY: Oxford University Press.

Kleiman, S., Spanierman, L. B., & Smith, N. G. (2015). Translating oppression: Understanding how sexual minority status is associated with White men's racial attitudes. *Psychology of Men & Masculinity, 16*, 404–415. doi:10.1037/a0038797

Locke, A. (2011). The social psychologising of emotion and gender: A critical perspective. *Critical Studies, 34*, 185–205.

Myers, K. (2012). "Cowboy up!": Non-hegemonic representations of masculinity in children's television programming. *Journal of Men's Studies, 20*(2), 125–143. doi:10.3149/jms.2002.125

Scott, D. A., & Robinson, T. L. (2001). White male identity development: The key model. *Journal of Counseling & Development, 79*(4), 415–421.

Starr, M. E. (1984). The Marlboro man: Cigarette smoking and masculinity in America. *Journal of Popular Culture, 17*(4), 45–57.

West, R., & Turner, L.H. (2014). *Introducing communication theory: Analysis and application*. New York, NY: McGraw Hill.

O. J. Duncan
Department of Communication Studies
Southern Illinois University Carbondale

CHRIS GODSEY

9. MAKING A BIG DEAL OUT OF NOTHING

Patriarchy, White Supremacy, and Teacher Preeminence

Although most individuals have little difficulty identifying their own victimization within some major system of oppression—whether it be by race, social class, religion, physical ability, sexual orientation, ethnicity, age or gender—they typically fail to see how their thoughts and actions uphold someone else's subordination.
– Patricia Hill Collins (2000, p. 287)

When whiteness is so seeped into your being, might giving it up necessitate a threat to one's safety and existence?
– Kevin Rigby Jr. and Hari Ziyad (2016, para. 18)

Any attempt to impose your will on another is an act of violence.
– Mahatma Gandhi (quoted in Pence & Paymar, 1983, p. 96)

Because if I am not what I've been told I am, then it means that *you're* not what you thought *you* were *either*!
– James Baldwin (1998b, p. 682)

"But this is all in your *head*," an audience member chided with smiling contempt during comments after my presentation at the March 2015 Summit on Equity, Race, and Multiculturalism on the university campus where I teach. "There could be something to some of it, but overall you're making a big deal out of *nothing*." Another White woman at the same table, arms crossed and face tight with grinning Midwestern spite, emphatically shook her head yes, yes, yes.

I was a few months away from finishing coursework for my Ed.D. in teaching and learning. The presentation, *Meeting Students Where They Are (Not Where* We *Are) (Not Where We Think They* Ought *to Be)*, was a chance to workshop the confrontational claim I will address in my dissertation: teachers who feel entitled to compliance from students share fundamental beliefs with men who feel entitled to compliance from women, and with White people who feel entitled to compliance from people of color and indigenous people. The claim came from insight I had learned through almost 20 years of teaching writing and first-year-seminar courses, five years of co-facilitating critical-dialogue groups among men arrested for using violence against women, and two years of Ed.D. inquiry into intersections among patriarchy, white supremacy, and authoritarianism among teachers.

S. L. Pensoneau-Conway et al. (Eds.), Doing Autoethnography, 81–93.
© 2017 Sense Publishers. All rights reserved.

Since before starting the doctoral program I'd been obsessively pondering normative dominance and reflecting on where I sit in various cultural and institutional hierarchies. During the program I added scholarly inquiry to that constant ponder-and-reflect process. I also found and created as many opportunities as possible to defy dominant (and dominance-based) academic norms from within a system designed to perpetuate them.

I told the Summit audience of about 100 local educators that my teaching and dissertation intentions are based in theories that problematize dominant social and academic norms: feminist theory that says men's violence against women is a symptom of patriarchal entitlement to enforce dominance over and submission from women; Paulo Freire's *Pedagogy of the Oppressed* (1970/2010) philosophies about education as a collaborative process of inquiry instead of a dominant-to-compliant information bequest; work by James Baldwin (1998a), bell hooks (1989, 1992, 1994, 1997) and other authors of color and indigenous authors who name the United States as definitively white-supremacist and patriarchal; indigenous epistemologies that expose limitations in dominant (patriarchal, white-supremacist, and colonialist) academic notions about what defines knowledge, truth, credibility, intelligence, and "evidence."

During the presentation I worked hard to embody changes toward compassion and accountability I wish to see among men, White people, and teachers. I always try to do that and I feel as though I seldom succeed. I tried to describe why I feel like a fraud if I claim to oppose patriarchal and White-supremacist dominance over women and people of color but fail to interrogate my sense of entitlement to enforce students' compliance. Many folks in the audience nodded affirmatively, kept consistent eye contact, and smiled throughout the presentation. Some gave insightful feedback and asked interesting questions, but I assume the women who dismissed my presentation weren't alone. I still feel grateful for their candor. I'd have felt skeptical and a bit let down if politeness were the only reaction. Pushback let me know I was onto something.

* * *

In summer 2010 I began co-facilitating critical-dialogue groups in a program designed to help men arrested for battering women develop insight about why they use violence and how to stop. The work has given me insight about how entitlement to compliance works among men, White people, teachers, and anyone else for whom dominant authority is considered "normal."

Radical-feminist women who created the program believed, after spending hundreds of hours in dialogue with women trying to survive men's violence, that battering is a gendered social problem solvable only by eliminating the patriarchy and violence it enables. They designed men's groups not as anger management, counseling, therapy, or treatment—responses to legitimate problems that may exacerbate patriarchal violence but don't *cause* it—but as compassionate, problem-posing dialogue facilitated according to Freire's (1970/2010) admonition that "at the point of encounter there are neither utter ignoramuses nor perfect sages, there are only people, together, trying to learn more than they now know" (p. 90).

When we co-facilitate dialogue—always in (cisgender) man-woman pairs—we're not trying to convert men to feminism or our other beliefs. We are trying to problematize dominant-culture notions that "some people have the legitimate right to master others" (Pence & Paymar, 2011, p. 17) and patriarchal norms that entitle men to dominate and enforce compliance from women. We try to help the men see how our (men's) beliefs about women and relationships affect what we expect, do, and say as boyfriends and husbands. As co-facilitators we name examples of how women must constantly, at their own expense, adjust to men's unexamined entitlements. We co-facilitate from the belief that "when relationships of dominance become the norm in a culture, then all individuals within it are socialized to internalize those values or exist on the fringe of society" (Pence & Paymar, 2011, p. 19), and we ask a lot of questions about what happens to men and women who resist patriarchy's mandate that men dominate and women comply.

During my initial three-day co-facilitation training in late May 2010 I felt self-impressed and noble; certain violent guys would benefit from my insight about how to live the right kind of life. My only worry was that I would struggle, as a man who had never used violence against any woman, to earn credibility and form connections. Barely 30 minutes into the first group I observed as preparation for co-facilitating, I started realizing how abusively I had always treated girls and women in relationships since high school—how entitled I had felt to *punish* girlfriends and the woman I'm married to for displeasing me—and how my main tactic for keeping that truth from myself had been believing and saying, "I may be a jerk sometimes, but I'm not like *those* guys."

I spent the next year-and-a-half co-facilitating one 90-minute group per week and observing then becoming a full participant in two others. Since mid-2012 I've co-facilitated at least once weekly. Here's some of what all that dialogue time has helped me come to believe: even though I've never tried to physically hurt a woman, I have intimidated many women I dated and the woman I am married to without being conscious of what it means for them that I am 6'2" and 215 pounds—much larger than all of them—and stronger than I realize; I have often felt contempt toward women for displeasing me in intimate relationships, and I have brutally conveyed it by using my eyes, facial expressions, body language, and tone of voice with cruel intentions I would never have toward anyone in a casual relationship; I have habitually *tried* to hurt girlfriends and the woman I'm married to in gendered ways I believe are uniquely available to men who want to inflict pain upon women who don't comply; I have often used my facility with written and spoken words to coerce, shame, instruct, patronize, dismiss, gaslight, and punish every woman I've been with; I have justified treating friends, acquaintances, and strangers with much more kindness and patience than I have shown to women I claim to love; I have tried to enforce compliance from women I considered *mine* without realizing that's what I was doing or feeling; even though I have always sincerely liked women and taken them seriously in general, for a long time my thinking and behavior toward women in dating relationships and marriage included abusive intents, impacts, meanings, and patterns. I know many "non-violent" men for whom different versions of all those same things are true.

Before I saw any of that on my own, a few girlfriends and the woman I'm married to accurately described how relentless I could be about "proving" them wrong or myself right. They said part of what made those times feel especially painful and confusing was that I also often treated them kindly, and the constantly conflicting messages eroded their confidence and trust. I aggressively disagreed with it all. Mansplained why they were wrong about what they believed they were experiencing. Suggested they take a look in the mirror. Told them about guys I knew who were *actually* mean to their girlfriends and wives. I sometimes gently and sometimes caustically told them they had no idea what they were talking about and I believed what I was saying and I had "facts" to convince myself it was true: I listen to Ani DiFranco and I *feel* what she sings; I am still moved by everything I learned in Introduction to Women's Studies my first year of college; I understand how the men in Glaspell's *Trifles* (1996) are too clueless to grasp what Mrs. Wright's life with her husband must have been like, and I grieve for the woman in Gilman's *The Yellow Wallpaper* (1996) and Edna in Chopin's *The Awakening* (1996); I advocate for radical feminism, sometimes more strongly than women around me; I always dated assertive, physically strong, non-deferential women, then I married one; I have always felt more comfortable around women than around men; I truly, platonically *like* women, and women have told me it's obvious—they've told me I feel safe to be around, and that they can talk to me about things other men have no interest in or patience for.

"If you actually think I'm mean," I'd tell them, "that's on you."

"If this chick actually thinks I'm mean," I'd tell myself, "that's on her."

Which is exactly what a lot of men who use violence against women say. Some of those men get arrested. Most don't. As a 45-year-old cis-hetero white man raised in the U.S. I have more than 40 years of internalized lessons about who does and doesn't deserve to be taken seriously, who's entitled to dominate and obliged to comply, and who punishes and gets punished when those rules are broken. I have decades of experience among men who talk and behave according to those lessons, and who constantly police each other's compliance with them.

Many men ordered to attend groups see themselves and each other as good, struggling guys who did nothing violent or maybe did do some stuff they shouldn't have done, but either way don't deserve to get labeled as abusers or be forced to sit through a bunch of man-hating feminist bullshit. I've never believed feminism is bullshit, but if my formative group experience had including feeling like I was sent there to punish me for being a man, I probably—based on what I know about my thinking until I was in my late 30s—would have shared a version of the perspective a lot of guys enter group with: we're not the problem, the problem is these women. Not all women. Just the difficult ones. The ball-busters. The shrews. The emasculators and the spoiled brats who think they deserve everything they want. The feminists.

As a boy and younger man my most obvious enactment of patriarchal entitlement wasn't in failing to see that boys and men get some privileges at girls' and women's expense. I saw the basic inequity clearly even if I had a *lot* to learn about its subtleties. My entitlement showed itself most powerfully in how strongly I believed my own thinking and behavior transcended that inequity. I thought I was enlightened enough to be above the problem. That's a dangerous thing for someone who uses violence to believe.

I'm not saying patriarchy imbues every young man with my version of mean and dense. I'm not saying normative gender and culture hierarchies are the only forces that have wreaked havoc in my brain since I was a boy. I *am* saying I believe normative patriarchy, which teaches all women and men to take everything about men more seriously than we take anything about women, had a lot to do with why and how consistently I treated girls and women as if their greatest value in relationships was doing what I wanted.

For a long time I inhabited an "intersection between overconfidence and cluelessness" (Solnit, 2012, para. 3) I've come to believe is common in unique but related ways among men, White people, and teachers. Many men—I actually believe most of us—are ignorant to our ignorance about how constantly women must adjust to and account for our patriarchal privilege, and we're sometimes most clueless when we think we're being most understanding and aware. White people and teachers are often similarly clueless about how our entitlements to dominance damage the people of color and students whose compliance we expect.

I'm certain that had I been court-ordered to participate in the men's group I co-facilitate I would have understood why it exists, why it's based in radical feminism instead of gender-neutrality, and why the other guys were there. I probably would have agreed with patriarchy-based explanations for men's violence against women. And I would have had trouble seeing how any of it applied to me. "Look, I understand the reason for this group," I can hear myself saying on my first night. "I know I shouldn't have done what I did. I get all that. But I'm not like the rest of these guys. I don't have a problem with women. I believe in equality, and I treat everyone with equal respect."

A lot of people believe men who haven't been arrested for abusing women are better human beings than guys who have. In the past I may have agreed. I now believe that even men who haven't directly used physical or emotional violence against women are almost always colluding with it. We're enabling it by not actively trying to stop men who use it. We are *complicit*. Constantly. Please don't misunderstand: I have no time for dangerous false equivalencies that minimize men's intentional physical or emotional violence against women. I am, though, unreservedly saying that most men who consider ourselves non-violent don't care to acknowledge or cede the same entitlement that enables all forms of patriarchal violence against women. I agree with Jimmy Carter (2015): "The average man might say, 'I'm against the abuse of women and girls' while quietly accepting the privileged position that we occupy." I am also saying, with equal intensity, most White people and teachers quietly accept—and sometimes vocally defend—entitled positions that protect us at the expense of people of color and students.

I expect many of you to disagree. I dismissed those same ideas about patriarchy and White supremacy for a long time after first hearing them. But now I have to admit that even though I know a lot of men who have never used overt physical violence against women, I know very few men—in fact I don't believe I know *any*—who avoid benefiting from our patriarchal entitlement and *obligation* to dominate women or from women's patriarchal duty to please men. The same is true, experience and inquiry tell me, about how White people and teachers accept our entitlements to dominate people of color and students. Expectations driven by normalized patriarchy, White supremacy, and *teacher preeminence*—my term for the normative hierarchy that entitles teachers to dominate and enforce deference from students—imbue everything. Watch what happens to folks who challenge those norms. Defy the norms on your own and see how people—even ostensibly liberal, progressive, *woke* people—treat you. Or pay attention to how folks invested in feeling morally and intellectually superior respond when called out for their entitled, unexamined complicity with any normative hierarchy.

* * *

As often as possible, I used Ed.D. coursework to explore the idea I workshopped in the Summit presentation: teachers who enforce compliance from students share fundamental beliefs about authority-based entitlement to dominance with men who enforce compliance from women. Nothing I found makes the same connection so directly, but hooks (1992) and Yancy (2014) both write about teacher preeminence without using the term, and hooks' (1989, 1992, 1994, 1997) description of the United States as a "white supremacist capitalist patriarchy," which Yancy (2012, 2014) draws on frequently, is part of what led me to use White supremacy and patriarchy as dissertation tools for interrogating teacher preeminence. In future works, I hope to expand my scope of inquiry to include exploring how teacher preeminence intersects with hierarchies based in income and gender expression and identity. I am especially drawn to interrogating hierarchies that subordinate Turtle Island (North American) indigenous epistemologies. For now, hooks (1989, 1992, 1994, 1997), Yancy (2012, 2014), Baldwin (1998a), Cook-Lynn (1996), Deloria (1999), and many more writers who are women, indigenous people, and people of color, along with Freire (1970/2010) and Rogers (1969), inspire me to interrogate teacher preeminence by comparing it to patriarchy and White supremacy. Ignoring our ugly entitlements as teachers puts us in company with people whose violence we claim to deplore.

* * *

In the United States, says hooks (1989), "Black people and white people can socialize in a friendly manner, be racially integrated, while deeply ingrained notions of white supremacy remain intact" (p. 115). By "white supremacy" she and like-minded writers mean something much more banal than neo-Nazis, Stormfront.org, the Ku Klux Klan, or the "alt-right." They mean whiteness.

Sarah Ahmed writes, "It has become commonplace for whiteness to be represented as invisible, as the unseen or the unmarked, as non-colour, the absent presence or hidden referent, against which all other colours are measured as forms of deviance." According to George Lipsitz, "Whiteness is everywhere in U.S. culture, but it is very hard to see." He goes on to say, "As the unmarked category against which difference is constructed, whiteness never has to speak its name, never has to acknowledge its rule as an organizing principle in social and cultural relations." Richard Dyer writes, "In fact, for most of the time white people speak about nothing but white people, it's just that we couch it in terms of 'people' in general." Finally, as Terrance MacMullan sees it, "White people remain ignorant of white privilege because of the fact that all aspects of our lives—our institutions, practices, ideals, and laws—were defined and tailored to fit the needs, wants, and concerns of white folk." (Yancy, 2014, pp. 6–7)

Echoing other black and indigenous authors, hooks (1997) says most White people simply "do not imagine that the way whiteness makes its presence felt in black life, most often as terrorizing imposition, a power that wounds, hurts, tortures, is a reality that disrupts the fantasy of whiteness as representing goodness" (p. 341). She doesn't mean just overtly "racist" White people, and neither do Ziyad and Rigby (2016), who say, "Whiteness is upheld by all white people. White people cannot escape upholding it" (para. 2), then continue, "White people should move comfortably in neither Black spaces nor white spaces. Even those who are well-meaning should drive themselves into the ground trying to figure out how to occupy a positive whiteness—because it is impossible" (para 8).

Yancy (2014) says, "Being neither a 'good' white person nor a liberal white person will get you off the proverbial hook" for normative white supremacy, which Ahmed (2004), Baldwin (1998a), Cook-Lynn (1995), Deloria (1998), hooks (1989, 1992, 1997), and Yancy (2012, 2014) equate with the basic belief that, "whiteness represents goodness and all that is benign and non-threatening" (hooks, 1997, p. 169). Even many sincerely anti-racist white people have no idea how deeply we assume everyone else wants and needs our physical, intellectual, cultural, and moral characteristics (Baldwin, 1998c; Cook-Lynn, 1995; Deloria, 1998; Wilder, 2013). That's one way white supremacy resembles patriarchy and teacher preeminence: the assumption that Others would be a lot happier and easier to deal with if they were just more like us.

hooks says:

It is the very small but highly visible liberal movement away from the perpetuation of overtly racist discrimination, exploitation, and oppression of black people which often masks how all-pervasive white supremacy is in [U.S.] society, both as ideology and as behavior. When liberal whites fail to understand how they can and/or do embody white-supremacist values and beliefs even though they may not embrace racism as prejudice or domination (especially domination that involves coercive control), they cannot recognize the ways their actions support and affirm the very structure of racist

87

domination and oppression that they profess to wish to see eradicated. (1989, p. 113)

Cook Lynn (1996, 1997) and Deloria (1998) illustrate "all-pervasive white supremacy" (hooks, 1989, p. 113) in higher education (Wilder, 2013) by using examples from literature, science, Native American studies, and other disciplines to show how White scholars often dismiss or mis-appropriate indigenous knowledge. Absolon (2010), Barnhardt and Kawagley (2005), Hester and Chaney (2001), Hoffman (2013), Kovach (2010), Lavallée (2009), Rahman (2013), Tuhiwai Smith (2005), Weber-Pillwax (2004), and Wilson (2000) say white-supremacist epistemological entitlement is based in a fundamental assumption that white truth and knowledge are universal. Wilder (2013) bluntly shows how White men designed U.S. colleges and universities to sustain white supremacy and patriarchy and destroy people of color and indigenous people. That all makes sense based on Baldwin's admonition to teachers that "the whole process of education occurs within a social framework and is designed to perpetuate the aims of society" (1998b, p. 43).

Experience and inquiry tell me a primary aim of U.S. society has always been to maintain systems based in the foundational belief that "some people have the legitimate right to master others" (Pence & Paymar 2011, p. 17). Dialogue and self-reflection about men's violence against women show me that another societal aim is to protect patriarchy. Learning about whiteness from people of color and indigenous people, and through self-reflection, helps me see that another aim is to maintain White supremacy. Existing forty years as a student and teacher, and paying attention to most teachers' core intentions, tell me academic society exists to perpetuate teacher preeminence.

* * *

I'm typing this in a coffee shop near two college campuses on the Monday after Fall Semester Finals Week. DJ Shadow is pumping through my noise-canceling headphones much too loudly because within distracting earshot at least three tables of teachers are talking each other through the agony of resolving point percentages with perceptions of students' performance. As often happens when teachers commiserate, they're speaking of students as adversaries and problems instead of as fellow human beings who deserve compassion: this kid only submitted two pages when the major assignment demanded five; that one did all the work impeccably but missed a bunch of days; another girl constantly asked questions the syllabus clearly answers; a few just wanted to be told exactly what to do; some seemed like they *didn't. even. care.* (which always elicits the most angry or funereal or woe-begotten responses). "I'm just tired of caring about their grades more than they do!" one of the teachers might say. "It's like they just saw the class as an obligation instead of an opportunity. I gave them *so many* opportunities!" Of course, none of that apparent laziness, apathy, or lack of appreciation can stand. Points must be deducted because that somehow suggests "rigor."

Occasionally one of the teachers gushes something like, "Oohhh I loved *this* kid, though," then tells a story replete with directions followed, grades cared about, and authority respected—a fairytale of perfect compliance. The tale often ends with, "Why can't they *all* be like this?" Not once has any of the teachers wondered aloud about whether "their" students *learned* anything. No one stops to ask, "I mean . . . what if all these rules and policies and expectations I've been enforcing are ultimately arbitrary? What if 'good' grades indicate nothing more than complying with my arbitrary rules? What if all an 'A' tells me about a kid is that they brilliantly played a game I started then judged them for playing? What if we've been believing stories about ourselves, and about teaching and learning, that simply aren't true?"

Quick quiz!
Which of these groups often uses the phrases listed below?

Group A. Men assigned to critical-dialogue groups after being arrested for using violence against women.
Group B. White people on social media discussing recent protests around the U.S. led by indigenous folks and Black Lives Matter.
Group C. College and university teachers talking about students.
Group D. All the groups above.

Phrases
Somebody has to be in control. They're constantly looking for ways to take advantage of us. Are we supposed to just let them get away with it? You go ahead and show some vulnerability and see how it works out. We'll give them respect as soon as they start giving it to us. All they care about is themselves. But we're right. But they're wrong. The system favors them. They know how vulnerable we are to them. They *want* us to control them, and I've heard some of them say so. They don't know what to do on their own, so they need us to decide for them. Ever seen what happens when we give them freedom to make their own decisions? I don't think they're smart enough for us take them seriously. Some of them just won't ever get it no matter how many times we sit them down, clearly explain it, and make them repeat it back to us. Maybe if we _____ we can get them to _____. What's *wrong* with them? Why do they have to make it so hard? It's their sense of entitlement that really pisses me off. They just want everything handed to them. We have what we have because we worked for it; why should they get to expect anything different? This is what happens when you just *give* things to people for so long that they forget how to work hard. If everyone went back to knowing their roles there wouldn't be all this conflict. Those people just don't know how to behave. It's tough to take them seriously when the things they believe are important are so stupid and misguided. If they act stupid we're going to treat them like they're stupid. They know exactly how to push our buttons, then we get criticized for protecting ourselves. It's like

saying anything honest about them has become a crime. Not to stereotype, but why do they all _____? This PC culture has just gotten to where we can't even open our mouths because we know we'll get in trouble for what we say. This whole place is set up just for them, and we're sick of it. They just want to turn the tables. Sometimes they just need to do what the people in charge tell them to do. We know more about what's good for them than they do. We shouldn't have to tell them; they should just know. It's not our fault if they don't know how to work hard. It's not our fault if they're stupid. It's not our fault if they're lazy. It's not our fault if they have no common sense. Why can't they just set the example we follow?

Answer: Fairly sure you know by now.

Teacher preeminence enables and depends on what (2010) calls "the banking concept of education," in which "knowledge is a gift bestowed by those who consider themselves knowledgeable upon those whom they consider to know nothing" (p. 72). It assumes definitive teacher superiority and student inferiority—tells us we have a legitimate right to master students (Pence & Paymar 2011, p. 17). Much like patriarchy and White supremacy, it justifies clueless and conscious patronization, condescension, and dehumanization. It leads to syllabi and assignment descriptions focused on punishments for granular infractions unrelated to actual learning. It uses dominance and compliance as evidence of "good" teaching and learning. "Projecting an absolute ignorance onto others, a characteristic of the ideology of oppression, negates education and knowledge as processes of inquiry. The teacher presents himself [sic] to his students as their necessary opposite; by considering their ignorance absolute, he justifies his own existence" (Freire, 1970/2010, p. 72). By believing seductive stories about the basis of our institutional entitlement to dominate students, we justify enforcing compliance and calling it "learning."

* * *

Or maybe those women who dismissed my presentation were right. Maybe this is all just in my head, and I'm making a big deal out of nothing. Maybe patriarchy, white supremacy, and teacher preeminence don't resemble each other. Maybe "teacher preeminence" doesn't even exist. Maybe I ought to find a better dissertation idea.

But I don't think so.

I believe everything this chapter says, and I agree with Eber Hampton (1995):

Emotionless, passionless, abstract, intellectual, academic research is a goddamn lie, it does not exist. It is a lie to ourselves and a lie to other people. Humans—feeling, living, breathing, thinking humans—do research. When we try to cut ourselves off at the neck and pretend an objectivity that does not exist in the human world, we become dangerous to ourselves first, and then to the people around us. (p. 52)

I'm not interested in bracketing or detaching or affecting objectivity or doing anything other than passionately telling the truth as I see it. I'll be able to do that best by doing autoethnography, and I'm going to problematize teacher preeminence until it no longer exists.

Those dismissive comments from a couple years ago aren't outliers. They get echoed all the time by men, White people, and teachers who can't or won't acknowledge the damage we inflict by demanding compliance from people we claim to care about. I embodied that passivity for far too long, and I'll abide it no longer. By doing autoethnography for a dissertation about unjustified dominance, I intend to create danger for me and other men, White people, and teachers in the spirit of Yancy (2014): "By 'dangerous' I mean *threatening* to a white self and a white social system predicated on a vicious lie that white is right—morally, epistemologically, and otherwise." I intend to answer "yes" to Rigby and Ziyad's (2016) question, "When whiteness [or patriarchy or teacher preeminence] is so seeped into your being, might giving it up necessitate a threat to one's safety and existence?" (para. 18) I intend to heed Rigby and Ziyad's (2016, para. 8) admonition by driving myself into the ground trying to figure out how to occupy a positive whiteness, patriarchy, and teacher preeminence.

REFERENCES

Absolon, K. (2010). Indigenous wholistic theory: A knowledge set for practice. *First Peoples Child & Family Review, 5*(2), 74–87. Retrieved from http://journals.sfu.ca/fpcfr/index.php/FPCFR/article/view/95

Ahmed, S. (2004). Declarations of whiteness: The non-performativity of anti-racism. *borderlands e-journal, 3*(2). Retrieved from http://www.borderlands.net.au/vol3no2_2004/ahmed_declarations.htm

Baldwin, J. (1998a). *Collected essays.* New York, NY: Library of America.

Baldwin, J. (1998b). A talk to teachers. In *Collected essays* (pp. 678–686). New York, NY: Library of America.

Baldwin, J. (1998c). Down at the cross. In *Collected essays* (pp. 296–347). New York, NY: Library of America.

Barnhardt, R., & Kawagley, A. O. (2005). Indigenous knowledge systems and Alaska native ways of knowing. *Anthropology and Education Quarterly, 36,* 8–23. doi: 10.1525/aeq.2005.36.1.008

Carter, J. (2015, May). *Why I believe the mistreatment of women is the number one human rights abuse.* https://www.ted.com/talks/jimmy_carter_why_i_believe_the_mistreatment_of_women_is_the_number_one_human_rights_abuse?language=en

Chopin, K. (1996). The awakening. In S. M Gilbert & S. Gubar (Eds.), *The Norton anthology of literature by women: The traditions in English* (2nd ed., pp. 1013–1101). New York, NY: Norton.

Cook-Lynn, E. (1996). Why I can't read Wallace Stegner. In *Why I can't read Wallace Stegner and other essays: A tribal voice* (pp. 29–40). Madison: University of Wisconsin Press.

Deloria, V. (1999). *Spirit and reason: The Vine Deloria, Jr. reader.* Golden, CO: Fulcrum Publishing.

Freire, P. (2010). *Pedagogy of the oppressed.* New York, NY: Continuum. (Original work published in 1970)

Glaspell, S. (1996). Trifles. In S. M Gilbert & S. Gubar (Eds.), *The Norton anthology of literature by women: The traditions in English* (2nd ed., pp. 1351–1360). New York, NY: Norton.

Gilman, C.P. (1996). The yellow wallpaper. In S. M Gilbert & S. Gubar (Eds.), *The Norton anthology of literature by women: The traditions in English* (2nd ed., pp. 1133–1144). New York, NY: Norton.

Hampton, E. (1995). Memory comes before knowledge: Research may improve if researchers remember their motives. *Canadian Journal of Native Education, 21*(19), 46–54.

Hester, L., & Cheney, J. (2001). Truth and native American epistemology. *Social Epistemology 15*(4), 319–331. doi: 10.1080/02691720110093333

Hill Collins, P. (2000). Toward a politics of empowerment. In *Black feminist thought: Knowledge, consciousness, and the politics of empowerment* (pp. 273–290). New York, NY: Routledge.

Hoffman, R. (2013). Respecting Aboriginal knowledge in the academy. *AlterNative: An International Journal of Indigenous Peoples 9*(3), 189-203. doi: 10.1177/117718011300900301

hooks, b. (1989). *Talking back: Thinking feminist, thinking black.* Boston, MA: South End Press.

hooks, b. (1992). *Black looks: Race and representation.* Boston, MA, South End Press.

hooks, b. (1994). *Teaching to transgress: Education as the practice of freedom.* New York, NY: Routledge.

hooks, b. (1997). Representing whiteness. In R. Frankenberg (Ed.), *Displacing whiteness: Essays in social and cultural criticism.* Durham, NC: Duke University Press.

Kohn, A. (1997). How not to teach values. *Phi Delta Kappan, 78*(6), 428–439.

Kohn, A. (1999). From degrading to de-grading. *High School Magazine, 6*(5), 38–43.

Kohn, A. (2002, November 8). The dangerous myth of grade inflation. *Chronicle of Higher Education.* B7.

Kohn, A. (2004). Challenging students—and how to have more of them. *Phi Delta Kappan, 86*(3), 184–193.

Kovach, M. (2010). Conversational method in indigenous research. *First Peoples Child & Family Review, 5,* 40–48. Retrieved from http://journals.sfu.ca/fpcfr/index.php/FPCFR/article/view/172

Lavallée, L.F. (2009). Practical application of an indigenous research framework and two qualitative indigenous research methods: Sharing circles and Anishinaabe symbol-based reflection. *International Journal of Qualitative Methods 8,* 21-40. Retrieved from https://journals.library.ualberta.ca/ijqm/index.php/IJQM/article/view/943

Pence, E. (1987). *In our best interest: A process for personal and social change.* Duluth, MN: Minnesota Program Development.

Pence, E., & Paymar, M. (1993). *Education groups for men who batter: The Duluth model.* New York, NY: Springer.

Pence, E., & Paymar, M. (2011). A theoretical framework for understanding battering. In *Creating a process of change for men who batter: The Duluth curriculum* (pp. 15–20). Duluth, MN: Minnesota Program Development.

Pharr, S. (1988). *Homophobia: A weapon of sexism.* Berkeley, CA: Chardon Press.

Rahman, K. (2013). Belonging and learning to belong in school: The implications of the hidden curriculum for indigenous students. *Discourse: Studies in the Cultural Politics of Education, 34,* 660–672. doi: 10.1080/01596306.2013.728362

Rigby, K., & Ziyad, H. (2016). White people have no place in black liberation. *RaceBaitR.* Retrieved from http://racebaitr.com/2016/03/31/white-people-no-place-black-liberation/

Rogers, C. (1969). *Freedom to learn.* Columbus, OH: Charles Merrill Publishing.

Solnit, R. (2012, August). Men still explain things to me. *The Nation.* Retrieved from https://www.thenation.com/article/men-still-explain-things-me/

Tuhiwai Smith, L. (2005). Building a research agenda for indigenous epistemologies and education. *Anthropology & Education Quarterly 36*(1), 93–95.

Weber-Pillwax, C. (2004.) Indigenous researchers and indigenous research methods: Cultural influences or cultural determinants of research methods. *Pimatisiwin: A Journal of Aboriginal and Indigenous Community Health 2,* 77–90. Retrieved from http://www.pimatisiwin.com/uploads/1470824524.pdf

Wilson, S. (2000). What is an indigenous research methodology? *Canadian Journal of Native Education, 25,* 175–170.

Yancy, G. (2014). *Look, a white! Philosophical essays on whiteness.* Philadelphia, PA: Temple University Press.

Chris Godsey
Department of English, Linguistics, and Writing
University of Minnesota Duluth

STEPHEN HENRY

10. HIT HIM AGAIN

An Autoethnography of Violence and Masculinity

I kick my legs back and forth futilely. I can't touch the ground. Gathering my strength, I thrash my upper body side to side. There. I feel a slight tear. Victory is short, though. I can hear him walk back into the room.

"What are you doing? Let's fix that tear." The tone of his voice is incredulous, imitating some surprise at my actions. When he walks back in front of me, the look on his face is innocent. My cool big brother.

His hands clutch together; one wrapped around the cylinder, the other grasping the end of a hanging strip. As he snaps his hands outwards, a growl is released. The sound of duct tape being pulled from its roll is filled with life, terrifying life. It's animalistic. It speaks to the power that the adhesive provides in capturing its prey. It helps make a man feel strong, another weak.

Placing the center against my chest, he smooths out a long strip, casually tears it off from the rest, and presses the edges down. Satisfied at my reassured entrapment, he moves to the other side of the room.

From behind me, I can hear him mumbling in theatrical contemplation. I wait for him to make a choice. Once ready, he announces his tool of torture playfully as he makes his way back to my front. Lightly tapping my chest with his instrument, he jokes with me about the situation in words I don't recall, but in ways I'll always remember. Ways I would learn to imitate.

My eyes are glued to the wood now pressed against my stomach. I'm too anxious waiting for the first hit to try and beg or plead. It is going to happen. He doesn't keep me waiting too long. Taking a dramatic but tiny stance, he swings and smacks the tiny baseball bat into my stomach. It is a light hit, so only a slight yelp escapes my lips as the punching bag I'm attached to sways back slightly. Once it is back in position, another swing is made. A bit harder this time. Another hit. The phrase "human punching bag" takes on new meaning. I know the duct tape won't release me anytime soon. Another hit.

I *will* the tears to flow. It hurts to hurt to the point of tears, but I know that will be my salvation. Another hit. It's not manly, but it would end things. Another hit. Once I start crying in any of these moments, he apologizes and lets me go from whatever fun sibling bonding time he has decided on. From the corner of my attention, focused outside the growing pain in my abdomen, I see him rear back slightly in his stance before swinging.

This one is faster. It hits harder. My stomach indents around the bat slightly at the swing, and the punching bag jerks violently in response rather than follow the

S. L. Pensoneau-Conway et al. (Eds.), Doing Autoethnography, 95–104.
© *2017 Sense Publishers. All rights reserved.*

energy gently pushing it back. The pain is enough. I focus on it, wrapping myself in it, until I feel my eyes watering and my already labored breath collapsing into hiccups. The cry has begun, and I'm free. It ends faster than normal, luckily. The play has achieved its goal.

Disgruntled at the quick end to his fun, he rips at the duct tape. "Quit crying you fucking baby. That didn't hurt. Such a little bitch." Once the tape is ripped away (thankfully there is not yet hair on my arms), I fall to my hands and knees and clutch my stomach. My cries are soft, not full blown sobs. The danger remains.

Barely conscious of what any of the sounds mean, I hear metallic clanking above me. He grunts with effort, and I hear sand squishing. I don't want to look up and alert him to my recovering state, so I continue ducking my head into my chest while moaning.

An explosion of pain occurs.

Absolute shock prevents any recognition of what is happening. My world narrows to pain, and I scream.

The pain centralizes to my neck, hands shoot up to grasp at it. The cries pouring forth now are at their most critical. This kind of cry was rare. These weren't everyday tears pouring out with high pitched whines. Deep, hoarse rattles far lower than anything that should be able to leave my prepubescent throat are choking me. My eyes are wide open, my eyes are squeezed shut. No tears are flowing, as if my body recognizes it would add nothing to ease the suffering. Rolling side to side, I bump into the punching bag now laying on the floor beside me.

He starts freaking out, apologizing. "It was an accident," he says. He says it again and again. He didn't think it would hurt so much, he says that I'm ok. "You're ok, you're ok, I'll give you my Snickers!" Mom brings us candy each day after work. I'll be ok, he tells me. I can have his Snickers, and I'll be ok. He tells me he loves me.

He doesn't lose his patience as the pain drags me through minutes of agony, and he is gentle with me when he pulls me up and walks me to my room where I lay down and am conscious of how it is impossible to lay without putting weight on your neck.

When Mom gets home, she can tell I was crying. I get the candy, and he gets yelled at. Over the years, my sweet tooth becomes incredible, and he...he loses interest with chocolate as he forgets the taste.

* * *

This chapter traces a youth spent learning violence. I do this to argue that violence is not simply a symptom of masculinity, but rather the vehicle and driving force of it. Masculinity is toxic to all who come in contact with it and, through violence, it is taught, learned, and reified. While masculinity manifests differently in cultures around the world and even within any particular nation (Alcalde, 2011; Landreau, 2012; Nilan, Demartoto, & Wibowo, 2011), discursively it is broadly characterized by an imperative to dominate others in order to assert one's self (McCarry, 2010). Masculinity as a performance of gender empowers men to assert their self-importance as if in direct competition with those around them. Such domination, in my definition of masculinity, is only accomplished through an intimate connection with violent behavior and thought.

Violence may eventually manifest differently as an individual's masculinity twists to accommodate particular life paths. However, there is always a background of physical violence, experienced or performed, for the initiated cisgender man. Masculinity is the discovery, expression, and reaffirmation of self-worth through violent domination. This theoretical formulation which I put forth is purposefully single-minded. There are broader nuances, and cultural specificities to what guides an understanding and formation of masculinity, but in this chapter I identify violence as the vehicle in which to teach and perform masculinity in US American society. We are taught violence in our families, in our schools, by authority figures, and even on our playgrounds with other boys we have never met before.

* * *

Writing autoethnographically, I examine my gradual introduction to violence through various narratives, discuss the reasons I had in perpetrating it further, and finally question the place for change. This work is not a plea for pity, nor a justification of the damages I have done to others. I write to "show the view from the country club," as it were (Sherwood, 2009). Standpoint theory offers the (often controversial) understanding that those who have been oppressed and marginalized can provide special, unique commentary on social practices that those insulated in power cannot (Kramarae, 1981; Matsuda, 1995). We know, and have known for a while, the stories of those under the boot of masculinity (Hamner, 1992; Koivula, 1995). Critique of violence for the sake of the harmed is woven into broad cultural discourse in the USA. While some legislation and institutional measures have occurred as a result, we still generally accept that "boys will be boys."

To confront violent masculinity, I call for a different, concerted front in the battle against masculinity. This is the autoethnography of one who has known power and domination, and found fulfilment through both. I hope to reflexively work with the inescapable opacity of attempting to understand my own privileged gender performance and offer valuable commentary from a white, lower class standpoint privileged in violent masculinity. The viewpoint of a bully can offer an understanding of masculinity that the stories of the bullied never will. I believe that dissecting masculinity from a history of power is necessary for dismantling violent masculinity, and more research on masculinity is moving towards this goal (Mullaney, 2007; Johnston & Kilty, 2015).

I started this essay with my brother by necessity. Violence is a learned habit. We are not, as (cisgender) men, violent by nature or instinct. My brother was my teacher. He was the most present manifestation of strength in my life, and the most … interactive.

* * *

You'd love my brother. Really. He is the kind of guy who would answer his phone at two am and drive two hours to help pull your car out of a ditch. He has an electric and attractive personality. He could sell your own car back to you, and you'd leave thinking he was giving you a deal. If you met him, he'd probably make you laugh. He'd buy you a drink (if you didn't like alcohol, cool, no pressure), make you comfortable in whatever group, and sing badly off tune with you to your favorite song.

He taught me how to make tuna properly and use a sewing machine to make a kitchen apron. He taught me how to drive, and he taught me how to shave. When I confessed my feelings to a girl for the first time in high school and was turned down, he was the one I called and he was the one who helped me get through the disappointment. He encouraged me to keep going in school, because he dropped out of high school himself. When he was unable to attend my undergraduate commencement ceremony, my mom told me about the way he cried. He was my biggest fan two years later when I walked for my Master's.

He is so careful with and caring to his nieces with disabilities. When someone is cruel to them, he is the first to soothe their tears with whatever gentle means necessary. He has been that manager at a store after an armed robbery who immediately looks after his workers and ensures them the company would take care of any counseling services or time off they may need. He hates the thought of those he feels responsible for being scared and scarred by violence.

My brother grew up as the abused, neglected, and mentally ill middle child of a single mother of four. His grandmother took her senile rage out on him and his older brother. His father blamed outbursts of anger on him and abandoned him when anger led to crime and crime led to police warrants. His mother was always working, so she couldn't protect him from the inner city gangs that wanted to harry younger kids who walked through their neighborhood on the way home from school. If my brother wrote autoethnography, you would feel the pain in his experiences.

* * *

Autoethnography, a method of cultural analysis, acts to unveil systemic horror in the general by analysis of the specific. As a method of inquiry, autoethnography seeks to connect individual memories and experiences to cultural phenomenon and, through examination and explanation, critique social structures "responsible" for the events (Berry, 2013). Moments of great harm find voice and credibility through the structure of autoethnography (Douglas & Carless, 2013). Discussions of taboo topics are brought to the forefront, and writers are viewed as epistemic sources of new knowledge on under-examined concepts. Through autoethnography, scholars have examined rigorously the raw, remembered instances of sexual assault (Moeller, 2014; Ronai, 1995), bulimia (Tillman-Healy, 1996), homophobia (Adams, 2011), and the demands of masculinity (Drummond, 2010) in ways different than how we can understand such topics through other research methods. When I say that if my brother wrote autoethnography you would feel his pain, I recognize the harms he has experienced, the systems of power which pushed down on him, and how they have shaped him into the man that he is.

* * *

My brother, however, is also a monster. He acts and speaks in ways that can be read as racist, sexist, transphobic, and truly, horrifyingly violent. In response to someone shooting a firework at his car, my brother shattered the man's jaw with a punch so hard it broke his hand. I broke windows through playful accidents; he broke walls in blind rage. I've seen him try to sit down while balancing plates of food, drop one, and fly into a rage, throwing the other plate and knocking over things around him while cursing at everyone. If a server at a restaurant got his "simple" order wrong, he could leave them crying.

My brother's identity is complex. It is one constantly at battle with masculinity. Violence has shaped it, but violence also unshapes it. He has learned to be strong through hurting others, but also always carries the scars and disgust for doing so. He's declared many times that if he has kids, he would never be like his father. Much as I want to believe him, masculinity isn't so simple. Butler (1990) tells us gender performance is performative and, thus, cumulative. Unlike Riviere (2008) who positions gender as a mask that one learns to put on and take off as a situation calls for it, Butler suggests that the continued relationship to an identity cements it on one's expression of self.

There isn't a simple binary of a violent, masculine identity and an underlying, real, caring identity. We live in a play of various discourses, each hierarchically positioned and contradictory in their demands of our loyalty in performance (Weedon, 1987). An individual's identity is influenced by each, altered and nuanced by the intersections of cultural relations. Still, masculinity is *sticky* (Berggren, 2014), leaving residuals through any contact and infesting other discourses. Whatever identity markers that a person may forefront in their performance of self, masculinity plays a particularly insidious role in shaping it. So when my brother tells me about the patience he would have with his children through the pains he has suffered, I remember the number of times I was slapped upside the head for not doing mental math quickly enough. Violence is taught and learned through repeated performance of seemingly mundane actions.

* * *

He hands me a foam cup. A surprise frosty from Sonic. The whip cream looks delicious, so I take a bite. Shaving cream fills my mouth, and he helps me to rinse it off by pushing my face in the toilet. What a mean little trick he played, I think. I think, "He sure got me good."

* * *

I'm promised a fun time playing on the trampoline. He congratulates my jumps and flips, and I'm happy to be praised. When he promises more fun, I don't even hesitate to follow along and do what he says. As I hang from a sleeping bag 50 feet up in the tree for the next 8 hours, waiting for my mom to get home and bandage me up, I discover suspicion for family bonding. I begin to realize that these activities aren't meant to be fun. For me, at least.

* * *

The sun beats down on me, but I am happy. I swing my arms, barely feeling the weight of my backpack. It's been a good day at school, and I get to practice my violin when I get home. The sun beats down on me, but soon I'll be in the cool air of my welcoming home. As I make my way down the alley to my house, I see a bike coming out of my driveway. Without saying a word, my brother rides towards me. I fear. He reaches me, and I have no words of protest and I have no flight instinct. The sun beats down on me, and so does my welcome home. I accept it, knowing this is how it goes.

* * *

Masculinity demands a victim to be dominated. In this, it also demands a dominator. While my brother loves me, and I do not doubt this, masculinity calls to him. The decision to ignore it is not present in our society, especially for a lower class white man confronted with what he sees as enemies on all sides (Wellman, 1997). And, besides, why not do it when it is fun?

In my experiences of pain, I have learned to fear masculinity. My story diverges from the typically heard marginalized tales and merges with the more common tales by taking this fear as something to instill in others. Masculinity, in pressing down upon me, showed itself to be an escape as well. By shifting the violence from my body onto other bodies, I could change my relationship with masculinity from one of the dominated to the dominator.

* * *

I watch in silence from the couch as the bodies flop on the floor. They punch and kick, grab and pull, and the grunts of pain are constant. Cheers from the voices around me show much more enthusiasm than I feel.

An arm twisted the wrong way, a frantic smacking at the ground, and the match ends. As my friend gets up from the ground, his exuberance is obvious. He is victorious in the battle of masculinity, and his efforts show that it was a worthy claiming of prestige.

"See, it's so fun! I wanted to get him in a chokehold when he rolled over after I punched him, did you see that? Ugh, he got lucky, and I couldn't wrap my arm around his neck. But that armbar, did you see that? Cool, right? So are you gonna go? I'll let you start on top since it is your first time. Look, I'm even already kinda tired. Come on."

I'm tentative, terrified, but this is something I cannot say "no" to. The question of our friendship isn't heavy on my mind. Neither is how he could spread stories about me at school for being a wimp. There isn't a reason to debate and weigh options, as violence is just what has to happen. I am here, I am a boy, and I am going to fight.

I fumble with uncertainty on top of him and worry that I'm doing it wrong. This isn't happening the way I'm used to at all. I wonder as we move, "Did he really hit me? They looked like they were hitting hard before, so why didn't that kick hurt?

Is he being really nice and going easy on me?" The confusion continues as I push him down again and again. It continues as I punch him and choke him and my hands leave pain in their wake. At the end of it, I stand in confusion as he lays in tears. I realize that I am not completely weak. I'm not a fucking baby, a wimp, or any other names I have been called by my brother during beatings. My brother is eight years older than me, so I can't fight back. Compared to him I'm nothing. Compared to my peers, though, the weak younger brother that is abused daily and tries pointlessly to fight back is an unbeatable warrior. This taste of power is intoxicating. I know I need to say something, and I have a script ready. "I'm sorry. You're ok, I'm sorry. I didn't mean to hurt you, I really didn't. I promise to go easier on the next person, just please fight me already. I want to feel good."

* * *

Masculinity was something that could not be escaped or watched passively from the sidelines. It was a fact of reality—something I naturally had to participate in. Rather than just be the dominated, I had to make someone else my victim by dominating them. Of course, we each were simultaneously victims and dominators in a system that required each man to be both. It's a "dog-eat-dog" world. Men learn to fear that truth, but also relish in the eating. The convolutedness is lost when we choose or are forced to participate. It is fun because we think it is natural, but we make it fun because we are scared of the natural way of things that we cannot change.

Violence is a reaffirmation of self. Masculinity requires such tributes in endless ways. When it's threatened, of course it needs to be defended and shown to be right. When it is in doubt, the need is just as strong. When it is docile too long, reaffirmed. When it is working well … well, it can't hurt to hurt. Just to be sure. Many moments of hurting others serve no actual purpose. There is no scheming little thought in the action itself, but a lot of positive payoff. Growing up, I heard more times than I could count, "What were you thinking when you did that?" There was no answer. I didn't understand why it was fun, and those moments of having to admit as much never went far enough to stop it the next time.

* * *

A sneer curls my lips. I lean forward and smack his skull. He jumps from where he was sitting on the bench, eyes full of rage, silently quivering.

"WHAT? Huh? Yea, sit your bitch ass down."

I laugh with my friends as his eyes lower and he turns around. Do I see a tremble in his lip before he is facing away from me again? Oh. Whatever. We mimic his reaction, making a tale out of the moment. No backstory, no believable character arcs, but a bestseller nonetheless. It doesn't matter exactly where, when, or why it happened. I don't even need to remember his name. It happened. It will happen again. For now, I'll carry this pleasure the rest of the day. And then, when I feel a loss of happiness or control for some reason in the future, I'll remember how to get it back.

* * *

I run. I retreat into myself. I hide in books, unable to be hurt and unable to hurt others. Landreau (2011) shares the experiences of those who discover feminist critiques of masculinity because of their attempts to flee it. A Gender and Communication course re-opens my mind, and I see a way to be happy without hurting others. I see where masculinity has betrayed me, even as it filled me with joy and arrogance. The chance to live without the expressed performance of masculinity allows the freedom to breathe freely. Constant tension that filled my every moment, analyzing eyes looking for weakness around me, these relax as my gender performance does. But what do I do with these hands stained red, quite literally, with the blood of others? Even as I do not purposefully perform masculinity, I still benefit from the privileges that my presentation of maleness and masculinity grants me. Do I hide my hands in shame and hope I cannot be mistaken for powerful by anyone, or do I repurpose them?

* * *

I can never fully escape the desire to hurt others or the ingrained drive to do it. Coward (2000) has taught me that violence is not an instinctual part of the male psyche. Men aren't internally geared towards domination by biology, just as women aren't submissive by nature. I remember these things, but I also remember the many years learning violent practices. While I may not be thinking about how rigid my walk looks and mean my face looks anymore, the remembered performance still surfaces carelessly.

I know the discourse of masculinity. I have learned how men acquire gender performance through policing and violence all through youth (Hamner, 1992). I know how not to be manly, I know what kinds of manly I actually want to express, and I know which ones disgust me. But I also know that my consciously knowing and wanting isn't always the clear and direct motivator of my actions. Kristeva (1986) says learned discourse has sway on our subconscious and the resulting formation of consciousness. I think back to times of domination, and recall the joy I experienced in asserting my power. I can never tell if my joy is my own, or the joy of masculinity. Can I rewrite my attempts at masculinity to critique it?

Weedon (1987) warns about the risks in agentically appropriating a discourse. I can try to co-opt masculinity to work towards undoing its dominating potential, but there's no guarantee I'll succeed. I may even advance the powerful centrality of masculinity in discourse. Heasley (2005) tells me to use my position of privilege to challenge the system and change it from within, but Lorde (1984) always reminds me that "the master's tools will never dismantle the master's house."

I struggle with where this leaves me as a man. I want to fight the patriarchy, and I want to fight masculinity. I want to end the violence, but I know just how little those calls to "stop fighting, please!" meant to me when I belonged to the cult of violence. I feel compassion for the tales of those who are bullied, and who masculinity has done wrong by. I had compassion for them even as I was making new stories just like them for those around me. As a scholar, an activist, and a concerned man who still displays signs of violent masculinity that can influence the eyes staring up to me for instruction, I don't feel that those narratives will change things.

We need to know the stories of those who hurt others. Only in shining the light on the bully rather than the bullied will we disgust those who think to emulate. Masculinity thrives on repetition of learned violence. Performance of power that is typically seen as positive and good to imitate must be exposed as ugly. We men who want to destroy the system that did us so much harm have to acknowledge where we contributed to reaffirming it (Flood, 2011). Harding (1991) calls for men to epistemically produce feminist knowledge that benefits the struggle against patriarchal domination. Where men should learn from and primarily listen to feminism, they can also play a role in contributing to the fight for equality. By drawing on feminist voices, men can learn and push back against the systems they benefit from and have had a hand in building and upholding. This is our chance. This is my chance. I must make violent masculinity disgusting to those who love it.

REFERENCES

Adams, T. E. (2011). *Narrating the closet: An autoethnography of same-sex attraction.* Walnut Creek, CA: Left Coast Press.

Alcalde, M. C. (2011). Masculinities in motion: Latino men and violence in Kentucky. *Men and Masculinities, 14*(4), 450–469. doi: 10.1177/1097184X10376743

Berggren, K. (2014). Sticky masculinity: Post-structuralism, phenomenology and subjectivity in critical studies on men. *Men and Masculinities, 17*(3), 231–252. doi: 10.1177/1097184X14539510

Berry, K. (2013). Spinning autoethnographic reflexivity: Cultural critique, and negotiating selves. In S. Holman Jones, T. E. Adams, & C. Ellis (Eds.), *Handbook of autoethnography* (pp. 209–227). Walnut Creek, CA: Left Coast Press.

Butler, J. (1990). *Gender trouble: Feminism and the subversion of identity.* New York, NY: Routledge.

Coward, R. (2000). The instinct. In N. Badmington (Ed.) *Readers in cultural criticism: Posthumanism* (pp. 14–22). New York, NY: Palgrave.

Douglas, K., & Carless, D. (2013). A history of autoethnographic inquiry. In S. Holman Jones, T. E. Adams, & C. Ellis (Eds.), *Handbook of autoethnography* (pp. 84–106). Walnut Creek, CA: Left Coast Press.

Drummond, M. (2010). The natural: An autoethnography of a masculinized body in sport. *Men and Masculinities, 12*(2), 374–389. doi: 10.1177/1097184X09352181

Flood, M. (2011). Men as students and teachers of feminist scholarship. *Men and Masculinities, 14*(2), 135–154. doi: 10.1177/1097184X11407042

Hamner, K. M. (1992). Gay-bashing: A social identity analysis of violence against lesbians and gay men. In G. M. Herek & K. T. Berrill (Eds.), *Hate crimes: Confronting violence against lesbians and gay men* (pp. 179–190). Newbury Park, CA: Sage.

Harding, S. (1991). *Whose knowledge? Whose science? Thinking from women's lives.* Ithica, NY: Cornel University Press.

Heasley, R. (2005). Queer masculinities of straight men: A typology. *Men and Masculinities, 7*(3), 310–320, doi: 10.1177/1097184X04272118

Johnston, M. S., & Kilty, J. M. (2015). You gotta kick ass a little harder than that: The subordination of feminine, masculine, and queer identities by private security in a hospital setting. *Men and Masculinities, 18*(1), 55–78. doi: 10.1177/1097184X14549998

Koivula, N. (1995). Ratings of gender appropriateness of sports participation: Effects of gender-based schematic processing. *Sex Roles, 33*(7/8), 543–557. doi: 10.1007/BF01544679

Kramarae, C. (1981). *Women and men speaking*. Rowley, MA: Newbury House.

Kristeva, J. (1986). *The Kristeva reader*. (T. Moi, Ed.). Oxford, England: Blackwell.

Landreau, J. C. (2011). Queer intersubjectivity: Doing and undoing masculinity in women's studies. *Men and Masculinities, 14*(2), 155–172. doi: 10.1177/1097184X11407044

Landreau, J. C. (2012). Refusing masculinity: The politics of gender in José María Arguedas. *Men and Masculinities, 15*(4), 388-405. doi: 10.1177/1097184X12455784

Lorde, A. (1984). *Sister outsider: Essays and speeches*. Berkeley, CA: Crossing Press.

Matsuda, M. (1995). Looking to the bottom: Critical legal studies and reparations. In K. Crenshaw, N. Gotanda, G. Pellar, & K. Thomas (Eds.), *Critical race theory* (pp. 63–79). New York, NY: The New Press.

McCarry, M. (2010). Becoming a "proper man": Young people's attitudes about interpersonal violence and perceptions of gender. *Gender and Education, 22*(1), 17–30. doi: 10.1080/09540250902749083

Moeller, L. (2014). *Remembering through relational experience: Family construction of memory in sexual assault*. Unpublished Master's thesis. Angelo State University, San Angelo, TX.

Mullaney, J. L. (2007). Telling it like a man: Masculinities and battering men's accounts of their violence. *Men and Masculinities, 10*(2), 222–247. doi: 10.1177/1097184X06287758

Nilan, P., Demartoto, A., & Wibowo, A. (2011). Young men and peer fighting in Solo, Indonesia. *Men and Masculinities, 14*(4), 470–490. doi: 10.1177/1097184X11409359

Rambo Ronai, C. (1995). Multiple reflections of child sex abuse: An argument for a layered account. *Journal of Contemporary Ethnography, 23*(4), 395–426. doi: 10.1177/089124195023004001

Riviere, J. (2008). Womanliness as a mascarade. In N. Badmington & J. Thomas (Eds.), *The Routledge critical and cultural theory reader* (pp. 25–33). New York, NY: Palgrave.

Sherwood, J. H. (2009). The view from the country club. In M. T. Berger & K. Guidroz (Eds.), *The intersectional approach: Transforming the academy through race, class, & gender* (pp. 136–153). Chapel Hill: The University of North Carolina Press.

Tillmann-Healy, L. M. (1996). A secret life in the culture of thinness: Reflections on body, food, and bulimia. In C. Ellis & A. P. Bochner (Eds.), *Composing ethnography: Alternative forms of qualitative writing* (pp. 76–108). Walnut Creek, CA: AltaMira Press.

Weedon, C. (1987). *Feminist practice & poststructuralist theory*. Oxford, England: Blackwell.

Wellman, D. (1997). Minstrel shows, affirmative action talk, and angry white men: Marking racial otherness in the 1990s, In R. Frankenburg (Ed.), *Displacing whiteness: Essays in social and cultural criticism* (pp. 311–331). Durham, NC: Duke University Press.

Stephen Henry
Department of Communication Studies
Southern Illinois University Carbondale

CHRISTINA L. IVEY

11. GOING HOME

Alienating Emotional Relational Talk with Brecht-olage

My dad is the type of person who expects me to call once a week, preferably on Sunday after church. During these calls, I can expect a myriad of topics that center around two things: his concern that I live so far away, and politics. Specifically, he seems to receive all of his political news from the darkest depths of the alt-right cesspool. The Obama administration in particular angered him, making him the type of person that would sarcastically say, "Thanks, Obama." He has also referred to Michelle Obama as a monkey, mocking her beautiful features and strong will as traits unbecoming a genteel woman. Lately, conversations turn to "crooked" Hillary Clinton, and how much she will "ruin" our great country.

"It is time," he says, "for a great businessman to take over."

Despite countless attempts to inform him of Donald Trump's unimpressive business record, my dad still thinks Trump is exactly what this country needs. Normally, I awkwardly giggle at these statements, say something to the extent of, "Yeah, Dad. But I don't really think that would work." He responds with one final thought, thinking the last word means he has won, and that will be the end of the conversation until next Sunday.

My dad is the type of person who built a man cave. He lives on a small piece of land in the country, surrounded by three cows, two donkeys, and a couple of dogs. He used to have a chicken pen, until he came across a snake as he was trying to fetch eggs for his breakfast. No more chicken pen. His garage-turned-man-cave is roughly half the square footage of his house—with a work bench, wood burning stove, beer fridge, meat freezer, a couple of four-wheelers, and gator utility vehicle. It is a close model to the shed his father had behind the house he grew up in, which included a rebel flag proudly hanging from the rafters. The difference between my grandfather's flag and my dad's flag is that my dad's flag features a picture of Hank Williams Jr., framed by the words, "If the South had won, we'd have it made." Like Plato's Cave, my dad's man cave serves as an homage to the illusionary spectacle of what lies beyond it, where losers of (the Civil) War continue to live out the remainder of their days in the dark. A space which poses a threat to anyone returning with knowledge of what lies outside of the spectacle.

Despite this, my dad has a heart of gold. I have seen him do more for a neighbor than most people do for their own family members. He is easily one of my biggest influences in regards to placing the well-being of others before myself, which carries over into the teaching and research I do.

S. L. Pensoneau-Conway et al. (Eds.), Doing Autoethnography, 105–113.
© 2017 Sense Publishers. All rights reserved.

My dad is the type of person who resembles many dads in the South: a conservative, religious, foulmouthed, beer drinking, hard working, servant leadership type of man. As such, in this chapter, my dad is my dad; yet, he is not my dad.[1] He is born from stories told by students who visit during office hours to ask my advice about how to talk to their folks. He is born from friends sharing their experiences with the "hard-headed," "over-bearing" male figures in their lives. He is born from Facebook statuses, Fox News interviews, and right-winged radio rants. He is born from my "memory and imagination" as a child growing up in the South, who has a difficult time returning home (Giorgio, 2013, p. 407).

Going home is difficult because communicating with my father is difficult. Although I, like my dad, grew up in a small Texas town situated in the Bible Belt, I am a first generation college student. As such, the expectation was that I come home and put my education to good use in our small hometown. I was supposed to be married and teaching at the local high school, presumably with children of my own who would attend the same school. I was not supposed to find love while away (especially not queer love!), nor was I meant to spend an extra six years in school completing graduate work. Now that I have veered so far off course and have experienced enough of the world to disagree with former expectations, how do I talk with/to my father? Talk plays an integral role in connecting change and communication—neither exists without the other (Pelias, 2011). Where do I gather the "equipment for living" with my dad when our respective lives seem to fight on opposite sides of a war (Burke, 1937, p. 304)? This question, in essence, presents itself every semester through students in similar situations with their own families.

My tumultuous relationship with my dad makes the communicative process even more difficult. Though I stand against my father on many issues, I love him. I want him to be a part of my life, and to be involved in his. This fact, however, convolutes conversations by allowing a space for heightened emotional responses to his seemingly disregard for my beliefs and personal attacks toward me. Put simply: my dad's ignorance pisses me off. It makes me cry and question the wonderful memories I have growing up in the South. It prevents me from engaging with him through talk to initiate change. Spry (2011) argues that "autoethnography is not just the articulation of a personal story; the autoethnographer is articulating critical cultural knowledge that is intended to be epistemologically generative for an *audience*," but can the same also be said of the author (p. 147)? Can I learn to combat the underlying emotional turmoil I feel toward my father, and reconcile my love/hate relationship with him during our war with each other?

BERTOLT BRECHT + BRICOLAGE

War is a common theme found throughout the work of German playwright Bertolt Brecht. Though his last work was written more than sixty years ago, Brecht's work is still perceived as a general instrument to promote political messages and heal those affected by war. Because he did not "conceive [his] plays as a form of propaganda to be performed by an audience, but rather 'exercises' for the Communist participants in which the goal was to promote critical thinking," his approach often called for alienating techniques (such as masks, use of slides, and ending a scene before the climactic moment) that would disrupt the audience and force them back into reality (Pan, 2009, p. 224). As drama therapist Renee Emunah (1994) explained, "emotional distance was required to help people think objectively instead of responding subjectively, and objective thinking was necessary to activate social and political change" (p. 9). Because his tactics were geared toward downplaying the emotion and enhancing critical reflection in a particular context, drama therapists often utilize his work to do the same:

> Rather than allowing an emotionally charged and potentially volatile action to continue, I will shout *freeze!* in the middle of the action, at which point I will incorporate a distancing device, such as 1) directing the client/actors to reverse roles (thereby lessening their identification with their character, and facilitating deeper understanding of the other character); 2) asking the client/actors, or the clients watching the scene, to think about what has taken place and to decide what should follow (thereby fostering reflectivity and the capacity to perceive choices and options); 3) asking the client/actors to speak about their characters, in the style of a television interview show (promoting objective analysis of the characters). (Emunah, 1994, p. 9)

With these techniques, drama therapists teach their clients how to contain emotions and develop observational skills that aid in better communication. Put differently, drama therapists utilize this strategy to demonstrate to clients how to better control their emotions when affect hinders communication.

Brecht's method of thinking about evocative performances critically and reflexively have inspired autoethnographic approaches, but a full exploration of Brecht's alienation has yet to be investigated (Denzin, 2013). In this chapter, I demonstrate how Brecht's alienation effect can be used in autoethnography when discussing relational talk saturated in emotional, affective reactions. To do so, I turn to Emunah's (1994) advice (objective analysis of characters; reversing roles; asking what should follow) and combine it with "bricolage," a familiar autoethnographic method. The bricoleur accumulates elements and meanings of the "dominant culture" to "challenge and disrupt that culture" (Edgar & Sedgwick, 1999, p. 32). The fragmented elements are then woven together to create a new way of viewing the culture. Here, I weave stories about my father with Emunah's guidance, creating a Brecht-inspired bricolage—a Brecht-olage, if you will.

"FACEBOOK POSTS"—OBJECTIVE ANALYSIS OF CHARACTERS

My dad and I often engage in battle on Facebook by sharing various memes, articles, videos, and quotations as a form of argumentation. For example, he posted a picture of the new XM556 Microgun (hand-held Gatling gun) within minutes of also posting, "You do realize if democrats stop shooting people, gun violence would drop by 90%." I responded with the PBS recording of President Obama explaining the Democratic party has no intention of "taking them away." When he posted a meme with the phrase "HOW TO BREAK UP A BLACK LIVES

MATTER PROTEST" above a photograph depicting a crowd of black men running away from a small child asking, "Are you my dad?" I entered a Judith Butler (2010) quotation, "We judge a world we refuse to know, and our judgment becomes one means of refusing to know that world," next to a picture of the poem *Allowables* by Nikki Giovanni (2013, p. 156).[2] And, of course, when he forwarded a picture of 2 Timothy 3: 1–5 highlighted in his Bible, I simply distributed an illustration of Jesus saying "Blessed are the poor" being interrupted by a disciple correcting Him with "Blessed are ALL lives, Jesus."[3]

Typically, these posts seem to be in good fun: I make a game out of trying to match his silly, misinformed posts with something that has crossed my feed. One day, however, he posted something I could not forget: a meme which read, "REMEMBER: Just because you went to college doesn't make you smarter than anyone else…Common Sence [sic] doesn't come with a Degree." This post seemed more hurtful than the others. As I stated before, I am a first generation college graduate—no one else in my family has ever even *attended* college. Though he could have been directing it to whoever read it, it felt like a direct attack on me. I have been called a "sell-out," and a "fake" for going to school and never coming home. Was my father reiterating this narrative?

Freeze!

Speaking objectively about my dad proves to be easiest after this story: I just need to flesh out the statistics that have led to his responses. Butler referred to instances like the one described above as "modes of address," and can simply be a "way of speaking to or about someone," or "describe[s] a general way of approaching another such that one presumes who the other is" (Yancy & Butler, 2015). Through these modes, assumptions are easily made about the other, so a quick search online can alleviate some of my anger and shock at his post.

According to a Columbia University study, out of 2.8 million shares traced on Facebook, 75 billion potential views, and 9.6 million actual clicks, 59% of links are never opened on the social media site (Gabielkov et al., 2016). In other words, most people share information without ever reading it. To emphasize my point, I posted the interview with Butler (cited in the previous paragraph), and my dad liked it. I am assuming that is because it is entitled "What is Wrong with All Lives Matter?" *not* because he had actually read the interview.

A lack of research or knowledge gained by *engaging* with the material can motivate a lack of understanding in dealing with the issue. Butler argues that this happens with the #alllivesmatter counter to the #blacklivesmatter movement:

> It is true that all lives matter, but it is equally true that not all lives are understood to matter which is precisely why it is most important to name the lives that have not mattered, and are struggling to matter in the way they deserve. (Yancy & Butler, 2015)

Many poor White Americans struggle with the concept of privilege because they cannot see the ways the system works for them. Whiteness has "its own internal hierarchies," but mistaking those hierarchies for systemic discrimination further positions Black individuals as something to be feared (Yancy & Butler, 2015). This logic is exacerbated by decisions of police review boards and grand juries who refuse to go to trial.

My father and I are separated by this knowledge. My attempts to "educate" him are silenced by the thunderous roar of his social position.

"GUNS"—ROLE REVERSAL

For Christmas, dad had gotten himself a new hunting rifle. *Another* one. Instead of a traditional gun, or one that served a practical function for hunting, this gun looked different. If someone were to say, "picture an 'assault rifle,'" you would have a pretty clear depiction of this gun.[4] He brought it out to show us, much like a child does when they receive a new favorite toy.

"What do you think about this?" he asked, smiling. I looked at my partner, whose eyes had grown wide and fearful.

"It's...uh, well...it's nice, Dad," I said, trying to slowly position myself between my partner and the gun. I didn't make it in time.

"Do you want to hold it?" he asked, while pushing the gun into my partner's chest. She almost dropped it from surprise. I stepped in to catch the rifle and prevent her from exploding.

"Nah, Dad. You should probably hold on to it. Wouldn't want it to break. Actually, maybe we should put it up? There are a lot of children around."

"You sound like Obama—coming for my guns," he grumbled.

Brushing off the misinformed political comment, I smiled and continued, "C'mon, Dad. Why do you need such a big gun like that? What could you possibly be shooting? Deer? A squirrel? Surely nothing that poses that much of a threat."

"How would you know anything about hunting? You've never been!"

This was a lie. He had taken me hunting quite a few times as a kid. He didn't remember. Now, the situation had gone beyond a mere back and forth of (mis)information: he was denying a memory I had from childhood. More importantly, he insisted that one of the few *good* memories I had of the two of us together was not worth remembering. I sank back. My partner could tell the comment had upset me, so she ushered me outside before I could respond.

Freeze!

I chose role reversal for the gun story because the moment that triggered an emotional response came down to indifference. "Indifference," Pelias (2011) wrote, "is a failure to stop, to look, sometimes driven by efficiency or practicality and sometimes indicative of status or ego" (p. 48). It can be "used as a statement against history," a weapon programmed to erase the past (p. 48). Not only did I feel as though my father felt indifferent about erasing some of our good history together, but also that I have grown indifferent to leaving him. I am glad that I no longer live in that small town surrounded by the same people I knew growing up.

109

When I was younger, though, I was Daddy's little girl. I followed my father everywhere: we fished, we hunted, we played catch after dinner. He would admit that I was his favorite whenever we were on those special trips. I witnessed his heart break the first time I no longer felt the need to kiss him goodnight. Watched as his eyes tear up when I came home and wanted to talk to mom about school instead of him. The only time I remember seeing him cry was when I walked across the stage at my high school graduation. When he and my mother divorced, I was the only one to visit him. When I met my partner and came out to him, I did not go home for four years.

Even though this exercise is supposed to be a role reversal, I cannot imagine loving someone so much only to watch them leave and *stay gone*. I cannot imagine feeling as though what little family I had left despised me. My father's response makes sense, as painful as it is, because he did not initiate the indifference.

#BLACKLIVESMATTER—ASKING WHAT SHOULD FOLLOW

This past summer, I thought my father and I were doing well together. We had a couple of beers and were, for once, talking about the details of my teaching.

"Do you like working for a college?"

"Yes. My students are so imaginative—they push how I think about things."

"I'm super proud of you. Do you know that?" he asked. I blushed and giggled. This time, though, was a real reaction. I knew he was proud of me, but hearing him say it is always a treat.

"Do you have any of them *niggers* talking about black lives matter?"

Silence. I was stunned. Even though I sensed this conversation might happen, I did not expect it to happen during such a sweet moment. The mix of timing and the use of *that* word violated the usual script. It snapped me out of our odd couple game of Conservative-Daddy-and-Liberal-Daughter-Make-Conversation.

He crossed a line, and I could not take it anymore.

"Dad, you shouldn't talk about things you don't understand. If you don't get why they *need* to spend time telling people like you why their lives don't matter to the greater society, then just shut up."

Normally, this is where I sweetly chuckled and respectfully moved the conversation away from controversial topics. My change in tone and deliberate disrespect had crossed his threshold of patience.

"See, all that damn schooling has brainwashed you. You would never talk to me like that when you were little!"

"No, Dad. 'All that damn schooling' taught me that individuals matter. It taught me that society allows certain type of persons to succeed. We need people talking about Black lives matter so that they *can* matter for once."

"What about 'all lives matter?' Everything didn't just fall into my lap. I had to work for everything that I got. All that hard work put a roof over your head, didn't it? I didn't teach you to go against your own people."

"But, you did teach me to love everyone and respect them."

"I just can't understand why you'd want to respect anybody who acted like savages. *Savages*, Christina. They use all of this as an excuse to loot the poor shop owners and places that are around them. Now, you tell me, why would anyone trying to save their community steal from it? It's 'cause they're like animals."

"Dad, I'm going to need you to turn off Fox News occasionally. Yes, that happens, but nowhere near as often as ..."

"What about those who block hard working people who are just trying to go to their jobs by standing in the road? What about the animals that shot up all those cops in Dallas? Who are they going to call if their crack house gets robbed? The same police officers they say are targeting them."

"Crack house? Really, Dad? The movement doesn't condone what happened in Dallas. Again, stop watching Fox News ..."

"Don't talk to me like I'm one of your students. I'm your father, damn it. They're a terrorist group. Plain and simple. And you're over here trying to defend them. How are you going to learn anything if you think you know it all already?"

I had heard this statement several times throughout my life. He said it during moments he thought were "teachable moments." It always sounded like an insult, like he anxiously awaited those moments when he could intellectually get the best of me. I felt the emotions bubble up again. Tears swelled, stomach tightened, breath quickened. I held them in, while he continued to rant. I don't remember exactly what he said, I was just acutely aware of the dangerous space I was in.

Freeze!

Asking what should follow after such a dangerous battle can be one of the only ways to make it through. Shots fired from both sides. I purposely used larger words to make him feel inferior. Butler (2010) claimed that wars brought about to protect a community are justified when that community is "a) threatened with elimination, or b) subject to coercive transformation of its way of life" (p. 152). He is from a culture that is taught to fear those who claim to be "educated"; they will manipulate the "weaker minded." I made myself his enemy.

He, however, purposely used a nasty term to instigate the fight. It is too easy to say I should win because I take the more "moral side." That is not why I wrote this chapter. I did not write to congratulate myself on making it through the war with my pride still intact. I wrote this to move forward because "it never feels satisfying to win" the war (Pelias, 2011, p. 33).

To take back control of my emotions, I must learn to control the communication that initiates them. For situations in which I feel targeted, I must use silence as my "weapon" (Pelias, 2011, p. 33). "Silence can be a plan/rigorously executed," and I should "not confuse it/with any kind of absence" (Rich, 1978, p. 17).

As such, my response to my father *should* be: "You're right, Dad. But, the same could be said to you. I'm ending this until we can have an informed, adult conversation. You know, like the kind I teach my students to have."

I can take back my emotions. I can take back my relationship.

DEBRIEFING AND CONCLUDING

An important element of the drama therapy experience occurs at the end of the session when the client processes what has occurred. Specifically, Emunah (1994) warns that after unpacking emotional baggage, "extreme stress revolves not only around the prospective dissolution of the new self-image, but more complexly, the feared annihilation of the previous negative self-image" (p. 296). Autoethnography is equally transformative. Given the realizations revolving around redefining my dad, accepting my role in our relational neglect, and taking back my emotions through silence, the vulnerability encouraged by adopting Brecht-olage through autoethnographic praxis motivates me to offer some concluding thoughts.

Autoethnographers "embrace vulnerability with a purpose," exposing themselves in order to challenge beliefs and offer insight into social phenomena (Adams et. al, 2015, p. 40). Though purposeful, this vulnerability, like the work of drama therapy, can leave the autoethnographer at risk of emotional stress. Considering this emotional baggage, the "Freezing" technique adopted in drama therapy lends itself well to the autoethnographer, providing a space to inhabit the vulnerability of an autoethnographic bricoleur. Drama therapy practices, such as the Brechtian approach, offer insight in how autoethnographers can simultaneously remain vulnerable with their audience as well as protect themselves during that process. Through autoethnography, like drama therapy, "the story is witnessed, honored, and validated by the audience, providing positive feedback and acceptance ... [and] allows the self to be seen openly in public—a powerful experience *for those who are ready for it*" (Bailey, 2009, p. 377, my emphasis). Essentially, combining a powerful autoethnographic technique (bricolage) with a drama therapy strategy (the Brechtian approach) allowed me to explore a hostile moment of vulnerability in a relatively safe way. Future autoethnographic studies could explore this Freezing technique by expanding upon various ways to Freeze, as well as strategies for merging autoethnography with drama therapy.

NOTES

[1] Essentially, "my father" is a composite character, compiled from all of the sources listed. Much of these stories are fictionalized, yet based on true accounts, news interviews, and everyday interactions. As Ronald Pelias (2011) warns, writing intimately about family members (even composites of their character) poses the risk of leading readers to negatively perceive those individuals. I harbor no ill feelings toward my father, nor anyone who may have contributed to this composite. If you should feel negatively toward the character, "Blame the writing, condemn the writer, but not those about whom I have written. They would have their own way of telling, and I would love to listen, to lean in" (Pelias, 2011, p. 186). For more on composite characters and autoethnographic ethics, see Ellis (2007), Tullis (2013), and Hernandez and Ngungiri (2013).

[2] The poem mentioned here can be found in her book *Chasing Utopia: A Hybrid.*

[3] "But mark this: There will be terrible times in the last days.[2] People will be lovers of themselves, lovers of money, boastful, proud, abusive, disobedient to their parents, ungrateful, unholy,[3] without love, unforgiving, slanderous, without self-control, brutal, not lovers of the good,[4] treacherous, rash, conceited, lovers of pleasure rather than lovers of God—[5] having a form of godliness but denying its power. Have nothing to do with such people" (2 Timothy 3:1–5, New International Version).

[4] After many conversations with my dad, I realize that there is no such thing as an "assault rifle." My rationale for using this description is to summon that aesthetic, not the functionality of the weapon.

REFERENCES

Adams, T. E., Holman Jones, S., & Ellis, C. (2015). *Autoethnography: Understanding qualitative research*. New York, NY: Oxford.

Bailey, S. (2009). Performance in drama therapy. In D. R. Johnson, R. Emunah (Eds.), *Current approaches in drama therapy* (pp. 374–391). Springfield, IL: Charles C. Thomas.

Burke, K. (1937). *Attitudes toward history*. Berkeley: University of California Press.

Butler, J. (2010). *Frames of war: When is life grievable?* London, England: Verso.

Denzin, N. K. (2013). Interpretive autoethnography. In S. Holman Jones, T. E. Adams, & C. Ellis (Eds.), *Handbook of autoethnography* (pp. 123–142). New York, NY: Routledge.

Edgar, A., & Sedgwick, P. (1999). *Key concepts in cultural theory*. New York, NY: Routledge.

Ellis, C. (2007). Telling secrets, revealing lives: Relational ethics in research with intimate others. *Qualitative Inquiry. 13*, 3–29. doi: 10.1177/1077800406294947

Emunah, R. (1994). *Acting for real: Drama therapy process, technique, and performance*. New York, NY: Brunner/Mazel Publishers.

Gabielkov, M., Ramachandran, A., Chaintreau, A., & Legout, A. (2016). *Social clicks: What and who gets read on Twitter?* Paper presented at ACM SIGMETRICS/IFIP Performance 2016. Antibes Juan-les-Pins, France.

Giorgio, G. A. (2013). Reflections on writing through memory in autoethnography. In S. Holman Jones, T. E. Adams, & C. Ellis (Eds.), *Handbook of autoethnography* (pp. 406–424). New York, NY: Routledge.

Hernandez, K. C. & Ngunjiri, F. W. (2013). Relationships and communities in autoethnography. In S. Holman Jones, T. E. Adams, & C. Ellis (Eds.), *Handbook of autoethnography* (pp. 262–280). New York, NY: Routledge.

Pan, D. (2009). Sacrifice as political representation in Bertolt Brecht Lehrstucke. *The Germanic Review. 84*, 327–352. doi:10.1080/00168890903291468

Pelias, R. (2011). *Leaning: A poetics of personal relations*. New York, NY: Routledge.

Rich, A. (1978). *The dream of a common language*. New York, NY: Norton.

Spry, T. (2011). *Body, paper, stage: Writing and performing autoethnography*. New York, NY: Routledge.

Tullis, J. A. (2013). Self and others: Ethics in autoethnographic research. In S. Holman Jones, T. E. Adams, & C. Ellis (Eds.), *Handbook of autoethnography* (pp. 244–261). New York, NY: Routledge.

Yancy, G., & Butler, J. (2015, January 12). What's wrong with all lives matter? *New York Times*. Retrieved from http://opinionator.blogs.nytimes.com/2015/01/12/whats-wrong-with-all-lives-matter/

Christina L. Ivey
Department of Communication
Boise State University

DIANAH MCGREEHAN

12. LOST IN HOPE

(De)constructing Hope in "Missing Person" Discourses

I'm watching the opening sequence of *The Lost Boys* on Netflix. This 1980s classic about vampires terrorizing a seaside town starts with a popular song by The Doors.

> People are strange when you're a stranger
> Faces look ugly when you're alone
> Women seem wicked when you're unwanted
> Streets are uneven when you're down. (Morrison & Kreiger, 1967)

The music plays over images of missing persons posters. Posters layered over more posters of forgotten faces. Pictures of young girls, boys, and assumed run-aways flash across the screen. Worn and torn posters peeled from wooden poles, as weathered as the rusty nails which once secured them in place.

Posters put there by loving parents, sisters, and brothers. Posters walked by without a single pause or glance. Re-watching the film, I think about these faces. I am curious which ones were taken by the monsters.

* * *

Since 2002, I have found myself existing in a liminal space between hope and reality. This is the year my younger sister, Roxanne McGreehan, vanished at the age of twenty. It is her story/my story/our stories that inspired my interest in better understanding the narratives surrounding missing person discourses.

In this chapter, I explore the architectural narratives and discourses that enclose family members of missing persons in a labyrinth of hope to express the difficulty of seeking an ultimate truth through the shadow of ambiguity and trauma. Meandering through the messy maze of hope and grief, I follow the crumbs of the academic scholars before me to develop a pathway toward understanding ambiguous loss (Boss, 1999). I begin to (de)construct the protective walls of hope to reshape and reconstruct fragments of meaning. By sharing my personal stories, I shed light on the trepid space between hope and traumatic loss. I emphasize how the relational construction of identity and reality binds and links our personal experiences and narratives. Twisting and turning through doing *my* autoethnography, I aim to connect myself with readers so we can form a communal space of support and begin our path of resilience.

S. L. Pensoneau-Conway et al. (Eds.), Doing Autoethnography, 115–126.
© *2017 Sense Publishers. All rights reserved.*

Our collective hope and grief hardens our demand for protection from the dangerous monsters hidden in the cracks of society. For the survivors coping with ambiguous and traumatic loss, social constructionism and relationalism (e.g., Gergen, 1973, Gergen & Gergen, 2000, Gergen & Walter, 1998) allow multiple meanings of truth. In the co-active process of dialogue, I (re)make my reality to transform new meanings from the confusion of complicated grief.

The therapeutic nature of narrative as an intervention for sharing and reconstructing identity (Boss, 2006) allows the autoethnographic approach to serve as a communication process with relational others co-creating experiences of surviving the fatal blows of death (Bochner & Ellis, 2006). Sharing my stories of ambiguous and traumatic loss, I work to provide a space for myself and readers to communicate the complexities of the cultural phenomenon of missing person discourses. I reinforce how the doing of autoethnography requires an active participatory speaking, listening, and processing of lived moments of struggle.

The messiness of morass moments are fragmented on these pages and scattered through temporal shifts in time. Layered accounts invoke an "emergent experience" for both writers and readers (Rambo Ronai, 1992, 1995). Through "layers of reflection" (Rambo Ronai, 1992), I share interpersonal encounters throughout the life, death, and disappearance of my sister. I share my vulnerable self through my narrative text to help reflexively gaze back and forth between social and personal experiences of uncertainty (Ellis & Bochner, 2000). Sharing these lived stories of loss functions to reveal the intersubjective connection of shared identities and meanings between survivors of trauma. I (re)claim my voice and intertwine it with the utterances of others to write through pain (Adams, 2012) and dialogically shift (Baxter, 2011) the construction of meaning as a communal space for sense-making.

HOPE: THE LIMINALITIES OF LIFE AND LOSS

I pull up to the three-way intersection. Rolling slowly to a stop, I tug at my turn signal. It blinks—left, left, left. My complete stop has signaled the driver on the left to enter straight into the intersection. His car passes in front of me. My eyes follow—left to right. Dilating pupils fixate on the woman waiting diagonally on my right side. As his car drifts in front of hers, I am suddenly awakened from my daydream—the mundane mechanics of this moment.

It's Roxanne! She is right in front of me. Dark brown roots of hair transition into store bought streaks of faded blonde, which makes a strange orange shade in the sun. Blotchy tanned skin flashes as she lifts her arm up and runs her fingers through her over processed hair. Her blinker pulsates—left, left, left. I can only see the profile of her face. Her face is now half hidden under this dye job. Maybe it's the disguise she has chosen to help her remain hidden in plain sight.

I stare intensely as she enters the intersection. My eyes blink like the shutter lens of an old Canon camera. Frames of reality—blink, blink, blink. She crosses in front of me and now toward me. The shutter speed of my lashes adjust—blink, blink,

blink—to slow down reality as I hold that frame; an image of my sister is in front of me. In that same flash, I internalize and ponder so many thoughts.

She looks happy—blink.
Maybe she does want to be missing—blink.
Should I tell people I've seen her? Or, should I let her keep her secret—blink.
How can she do this? Why is she hiding from us? Maybe I should follow her—blink.
She's alive after all this time. And she's been here—right in front of me. Right?
Blink.

I adjust the f-stop. The light hits my eyes, as I follow her passing car—left to right. This new exposure is so revealing. I am staring at this stranger so intensely. I can see her face clearly now. Her full lips lightly sing along to an unheard song. Painted nails hang over the steering wheel. Although she is not my sister, I stare at the curves of her face just to make sure. She never looks at me. She doesn't know I am looking at her.

My head turns as I continue to stare. I look over my shoulder as her car starts to drive away from mine. I enter the intersection. Moving forward through the years, I see my sister in random places and in random faces.

* * *

The hot water of a morning shower rushes over me. I take in a deep breath. Yawning, I struggle to keep my eyes open. I take in a deep breath. The hot water running over my face awakens me to the day ahead. The drain is covered. Water slowly rises above my ankles. I wish I could rest, lie down and let my body slowly submerge into the water. I wish I could sink down and escape into its comforting warmth. I turn off the water and unplug the drain. I breathe in, watching the water recede. I step out of the tub and into the reality of the day. I am running late. I grab a towel. It wraps around me like a mother's inviting embrace. I step into my room and turn on the morning news.

I breathe out, a deep gasp. The news anchor's words hit me like a tidal wave. Words ripple through the room and smack me: "After five weeks of searching, police officers have finally found the body of 25-year-old, Ophelia Walton." Ophelia was a high school friend. She was last seen alive on August 11, 2007. The day she went missing, she was enjoying the water of a warm summer's day. She was with friends floating on tubes down a nearby river. River water – drinks – laughs – drinks – sun – drinks – fun – drinks – river water. Then night came. According to the news, Ophelia was highly intoxicated. Her friends didn't want her to drive. But she got into her car to make her way home. That was the last time anyone saw her alive.

For five weeks, images of her beautiful, porcelain, creamy white face and wavy red hair were broadcasted over the airwaves of local and national news networks. Her mother was pleading with the viewers for information. She was offering money for knowledge of her daughter's whereabouts, bargaining against death. She longed to wrap her arms around her daughter again. Her mother, family, and friends fought to keep Ophelia floating on the surface of this liminal space she was now plunging into. For the family and friends of missing people, we hold our breath. We hold our breath in shock. We fight to breathe. We gasp. We hyperventilate. But then ...

We breathe in
    Hope fills the air
We breathe in
    Hope fills our lungs
We breathe in
    Hope fills this liminal space
We breathe out
    Our denial deepens

Five weeks of subjunctive voices in the media created an "as if," a space of possibility. Today, the water of that nearby river finally receded. Hope receded. Reality emerged. Ophelia's body was found trapped in her vehicle just eight feet beneath the water's surface. Her cause of death, drowning.

* * *

The funeral service is over. Ophelia's grieving family and friends slowly seep out the doors. I step out of the doors and into the warmth of the sun. I breathe in the September air. I see Ophelia's best friend in the crowd. Her face is drenched in tears. I make my way toward her to let her know I have great empathy for the pain she has suffered over the past five weeks. She takes a deep sobbing breath in, and then painfully utters back to me,

"I wish they never found her."

I could see in her eyes hope was lost and she was suddenly drowning in the depths of this reality. She was still fighting for a different interpretation, hoping for some greater reason behind it all. She tells me about the bruises seen on Ophelia's arms during her autopsy. She felt the bruises were from fighting off some unknown enemy—death. But according to the police, the only thing Ophelia was fighting for was air—life.

We breathe in hope.
    We breathe out denial.

* * *

Since 2002, my mom makes a birthday cake on March 28th. I am not there for the ritual. Instead, my three younger half-sisters, my stepfather, and mom partake in the celebration. I picture them there gathered in the dark, year after year. I can see my mom turning the corner with candles lit; flickers of light dance and swirl with shadows of smoke against the walls. A heavenly glow is cast upon their faces as they sing, "Happy birthday to You." I picture my mom tightly closing her eyes with concentration. As if saying a prayer, she bows her head to softly mumble words. She makes *the wish*. It's the wish we have all held on to. This wish has escaped my lips time and time again.

I see her slowly opening her eyes. The tension of the in-between is in the air. She wants to make the wish. As she celebrates this ritual of birth, she is not quite ready to blow out the flames.

* * *

I've been waiting for my refurbished cell phone to arrive in the mail for over a week. It was originally sent to the wrong address or not sent at all. It's frustrating not having a phone. I am excited when it finally arrives in the mail. As I let the phone charge for a bit, I am anticipating the number of missed calls I may have.

Once I see the little battery symbol on the top right corner is half alive, I start to review my missed calls. My first message is from an unfamiliar number. I am assuming it's someone trying to sell me something or some random promotional message. But if a company leaves a message, I will listen to it. I press the play button on the message first. At this point, the message is nearly a week old.

A deep male voice reverberates in my ear. The recorded voice says, "Hello, this is detective Harry Smith. I am the lead detective investigating the murder of who I assume is your sister, Roxanne McGreehan. If you can please give me a call at the station or on my cell phone as soon as possible, that would be great. I would like to ask you a few questions."

Although I let the message play all the way through, my mind went into a little a bit of shock when I heard him say he was investigating the murder of my sister. For the past 11 years, my sister has been a missing person. What does he mean, investigating my sister's murder? My jaw and heart drop. I grab a pen and piece of paper. I play the message again. I urgently write down his name and phone numbers he has provided me.

I pace back and forth. My heart races as I pick up the phone and begin to dial his cell number. With the ring, anxiety and nervousness shake my body. On the second ring, I sit down on the sofa and start rocking slightly back and forth. Luckily enough, I am home alone. Only the dogs and cats watch the anxiousness take over my body while I wait for him to answer.

I am finally greeted by his firm voice, "Hello, this is detective Harry Smith. How can I help you?"

I respond, "Ah, yes, this is Dianah McGreehan. I received a call from you about a week ago regarding my sister, Roxanne McGreehan. I am sorry I didn't call back right away. I lost my phone a couple of weeks ago, so I just got your message." I felt I had to apologize.

Relieved to hear my voice after a week of waiting, "Yes, I wanted to ask you a few questions."

I quickly interrupt, "In your message, you mentioned you were investigating my sister's murder … is that right?" I find myself suddenly holding my breath.

"Yes, I am the lead detective on your sister's case," he confirms.

I let out a gasp, and my voice starts to shake. I blink and thick tears run down my face. Years of hoping that she was alive—years of hoping for information—years of hoping to know the truth collided with his calm confirmation. My body starts to shake as I try to gather myself. I suddenly feel a little numb. I apologize for my emotional outburst. I breathe in and then let out a deep exhale.

Wiping my tears, my voice cracks, "I am so sorry … this is just shocking news."

He comforts me, "It's okay. I know that this must be really hard to hear. Are you okay to talk right now or do you need to call me back later this afternoon?" His firm voice softens.

I reassure him, "No … no, I can talk. I want to talk. And please, I know that this is hard to hear, but I would like as much information as possible."

"Well, first I wanted to ask you about your brother Ronald McGreehan. Did you know Ronald hired a private investigator a couple of month ago?" he questions.

I am a bit thrown off from his first question, "No."

He continues, "So you don't know why your brother, after 11 years of your sister being a missing person, hires a private investigator now?"

In a slight defensive tone, "My brother has looked into my sister's disappearance in the past. But he has never hired a professional, private investigator. This is the first I am hearing about it. I think my brother has just always wanted to do something to help Roxanne or just wanted to try to get some information. Why are you asking this?"

He expounds, "I am only asking because … well, I guess your sister was never filed as a missing person when she first disappeared in 2002. Looking at our system, your sister was filed as a missing person for the first time two months ago by this private investigator. Well a month after she was listed, a man who was being interrogated in prison … just randomly, out of the blue, confesses to your sister's murder in detail."

I am not sure what he is insinuating, so I quickly assert, "Well, have you spoken to Ronald about this. My brother is a really great guy. He is an officer in the Air Force … umm he was the captain of his football team. He is a really good guy, and I am sure he was just trying to be a good brother. He was just trying to find out what happened to Roxanne."

He corrects his approach to the conversation, "Actually you are the first and only person from your family who I have spoken to about this. No… no… no, I don't think your brother was involved in anyway. I am so sorry if I gave off that impression. I am just amazed by the miracle of it all. If your brother didn't hire that private investigator, your sister would not have been listed as a missing person. If it wasn't for that, we would not have been able to trace back the murder. Your brother is actually quite the hero in this situation. I don't know, it just seems like a miracle. I really was just curious why he suddenly, after all this time, was moved to hiring this investigator."

I have a short sensation of relief. The detective and I talk for what feels like an hour. He tells me details about the man who confessed. He lived next door to where Roxanne was staying during her visit to San Antonio. It seems Roxanne had asked him for a short ride to the corner store, but that would not be her final destination.

The detective says they believe he murdered my sister. The detective believes this because of how detailed his confession was. The prisoner described what she was wearing that night. Her murderer gives details about the way he looked at her. He retells their conversation. Roxanne was so happy to be starting her life. Roxanne told him about how she was going to be joining the military. She described her daughter, Beth, and how she was finally going to be able to get her back. She was so excited to start her life. She talked about traveling to see Beth in California next. Roxanne talked about Beth so much that this man, Roxanne's assumed murderer, could still remember Beth's name.

* * *

I had a friend ask me the other day how my writing was going. I just said, "Oh, you know, I write for an hour and then I cry for two." She laughed so hard when I said that. Except, I wasn't joking. I said it as though it was a joke, but it really has been my pattern the last few days. As I emotionally recall and transform past experiences into thick descriptions on the page, it triggers something in me.

I keep going back to my conversation with the detective who is investigating my sister's murder. I guess I keep thinking about that moment. Because for me, that moment was when my sister died. Although she was murdered in 2002, for me, it was that day my sister died—that call.

The synchronicity of life is so strange. It had been over a decade since I had last seen my niece, Beth. But two weeks before the detective's phone call, I finally reconnected with her in person. She looked so much like my sister—like her mother. She is so sweet. I asked her what kind of things I could get her for future holidays and birthdays. And you know what she said? Do you know what she wanted? She just asked that I send her photos of her mother. That was all she wanted … just to see pictures of her mom.

* * *

So I have been having these daydreams about that moment. Not the moment when he kills my sister. I have been having dreams about the moment my sister knew that something was wrong. That something was out of place. That she was out of place. The moment her happy conversation turned to fear. The moment she knew she would never see her daughter again.

* * *

After I finished the call with the detective, I was in a stage of shock. Some scholars suggest there are seven stages of grief while others argue there are five. The first stage of grief is always denial. My denial came during my sister's disappearance. My family and I denied death and replaced it with hope—hope that somehow my sister was alive. But hearing the details, the reality, of my sister's death, gave me a sense of shock. I can't tell you how long I was in a stage of shock. But I can tell you after that initial shock, all of the other stages—of anger, bargaining, and depression—have been an entangled blur, which come in ebbs and flows.

It was the middle of the second summer semester when I received the call from the detective. I wasn't taking a class at the time, so I was able to process that shock before I moved out to West Texas to attend classes in the communication graduate program at Angelo State University. I think I used my "stage of anger" toward my research and work my first academic year. My pain and loss felt so disenfranchised. As I discussed the disappearance and death of my sister with my colleagues during the fall semester, they weren't able to grasp the internalized anger, pain, and guilt I was experiencing.

* * *

I killed my sister today. This time sh...sh...she's screaming and she's begging him to stop. She doesn't play possum this time. No, this time she's scared—as he leans over to the passenger side of the car to smell her flesh. She fights back—as he grabs her and drags her from the car toward the wooded area by the creek. Hitting the ground, she claws at the dirt—gripping for some hope of escape. As his hands squeeze and tighten around her throat, he presses her into the ground. Her eyes are open and she is looking right at him. Tears are seeping from the small corners of her eyes. She's gasping for air, fighting for life. I can hear her soul scream as it escapes from her body—from the cracks in her skull that met the rock. Her soul is yearning for her daughter, her family, somewhere safe, somewhere to call home. She's lost—her soul is lost.

* * *

After I finish sharing my dream with my therapist, he confirms that I am suffering from PTSD and prescribes me Prozac. Later that evening, I take a pill and wait. I wait for the pill to take away the depression and anxiety. I wait for justice. I wait to find meaning. I wait to grieve. I pretend "as if" life can somehow be normal again.

SEARCHING FOR MEANING

As I share my struggles with making sense of the insensible nature of ambiguous loss and homicide, I am haunted by stories and images of children who have disappeared throughout history (e.g., Etan Patz, Adam Walsh). I recall hope lingering on the lips of newscasters, as well as in the hearts of volunteers combing empty fields—hands placed over hands. I hoped for them. I hoped for the ones missing, but more importantly for the ones searching. "I hope they find her," I would mumble from my mouth as I changed the station.

By sharing my own personal stories of ambiguous loss, I show the communal and intersubjective nature of hope for the missing. Collective hope and loss transforms our relational connections and shared realities. During the disappearance of my sister, hope became an inescapable narrative which shaped the societal expectations and actions I placed on myself and on others (Betz & Thorngren, 2006). Hope became a paradoxical action against ambiguity, which trapped me and my family in a liminal space between absence and presence.

Boss (2006) offers, "How we see the world will determine how and what we hope for" (p. 179). In seeking to understand the impact of collective hope and collective loss on survivors of ambiguous loss, I came to learn how the phenomenology of meaning is formed collectively through shared stories and interactions with others. If a family hopes for a story with a happy outcome, their collective hope suspends the life of their loved ones in a positive state of possibility. Hope covers the deep cutting reality of death.

When death is certain, collective rituals also govern the process of grieving. Social ghosts (Gergen, 1987) haunt families coping with the ambiguity surrounding cold case homicides. As I sought to understand collective loss, I found the normalcy of death to be a myth. Death ruptures our sense of identity and leaves us emotionally wounded in its wake. Healing begins as we redefine meaning and redefine ourselves through shared experiences and stories of loss. By reframing and reforming symbolic rituals, stories, and performances surrounding death, families and communities experiencing complicated grief can share in a new collective memory and mourning of the missing.

I (re)tell my personal narrative to (re)learn my identity as a survivor and to begin relationally (re)constructing meaning (Attig, 1996). Walls in the labyrinth of hope begin to collapse as I forgive myself for past events—assumed failings as a sister. Interior liberation (Levi, 1958/1987) occurs in/through the sharing of my survivor story. For so many years, I was reluctant to share my story of loss with friends and acquaintances. My story disrupted the mythos of a "good death." Autoethnography liberates my story from the shackles of societal scripts and strengthens my own voice as a source to legitimize my own experiences of loss. I write to overcome and understand trauma (Pennebaker, 1990). I have to let go of the hindering hope for definitive and complete answers. Cooper (2000) explains how the "ability to create, resurrect, challenge, modify, and even renounce our hopes is as good as any other definition of health" (p. 73). My autoethnographic inquiry offers me the space to understand the power of renaming and redirecting hope. In discovering a new form of hope, families can learn to live with ambiguity and gain resiliency to the absurdities of life (Boss, 2006).

Autoethnographic narrative engages and forms a connection between self and others. Everyone, at some point in life, will be a survivor of loss. For those suffering from loss due to a disappearance or cold case homicide, autoethnography provides an outlet to relationally recognize the complications of grief formed from uncertainty. By telling my story, I share self and/with/through the identities of others to reinforce a shared interconnection and commonality in our lived experiences of loss.

The accessibility of narrative allows readers to reflect on their moments of vulnerability, supporting a communal experience of transformation and healing (Custer, 2014). Together, we amplify our voices and break free from suffering in silence. I/we bear witness and testify to the cultural phenomena of ambiguous loss (Denzin, 2004; Ellis & Bochner, 2006). Therapeutic healing occurs as we legitimatize and destigmatize our stories of loss. By exposing trauma I experienced during the disappearance and death of my sister, I emancipate the voices of an underrepresented sub-culture of victims/survivors in an academic context. I tell my/our stories with/through others to gain resilience to ambiguous loss.

As I share my story, I recognize it is through my personal lenses and filters. I am guided by Boylorn's (2013) approach to writing a storied self as I share my experiences of loss and trauma:

> I realize that my story is never my story alone. I am not always able to fully protect the anonymity of the people in my life, nor do I want to. Auto/ethnography acknowledges that truths, memories and perspectives are subjective. (p. 9)

Pelias (2011) warns readers to blame the writer for any negative perceptions they believed may have been conveyed in autoethnographic writing. The stories I share are mere glimpses of a lifetime of stories which have collectively shaped my self-identity. Just as I reflexively understand these stories to form meaning, I ask readers to also participate in moments of sense-making.

HONORING THE MEMORY OF ROXANNE MCGREEHAN

This autoethnography constitutes symbolic space for homage to my sister as I memorialize/d her in these pages (Bochner, 2007). The ritual of writing was like visiting and tending to her grave. Repeating, typing, and reading her name within these pages is like etching the epitaph of her memory onto her gravestone. If autoethnography is always a co-constructed story of self with other (Allen-Collinson, 2013), I needed moments of self with her. Much like the obituaries in the back of a daily newspaper, I could only share a portion of her life experiences in the limited space.

Through sharing my story with readers, I offer an invitation to visit her plot, her story. Her memory becomes something readers and I now share (Ellis, 2013). As I reflexively form meaning from my narrative, readers also participate in making sense out of life's complex tales of loss. Readers experience the tensions of absence and presence as they subjectively form their own understandings of meaning surrounding her/our story (Boylorn, 2013).

As I type and repeat the name Roxanne McGreehan within these pages, I solidify the importance of her story. Even though her story never made headline news, her story matters. Her story is a representation of the "missing-missing" individuals (Quinet, 2007) who go unreported and untold. I share stories of our lived experiences as a symbolic cenotaph for all missing individuals and for the families searching for meaning. Through the communal sharing of my/her story, I hope to begin the communal process of healing.

REFERENCES

Adams, T. E. (2012). The joys of autoethnography. *Qualitative Communication Research, 1*, 181–194. doi: 10.1080/13645579.2014.854015

Allen-Collinson, J. (2013). Autoethnography as the engagement of self/other, self/culture, self/politics, and selves/future. In S. Holman Jones, T. E. Adams, & C. Ellis (Eds.), *Handbook of autoethnography* (pp. 281–299). Walnut Creek, CA: Left Coast Press.

Attig, T. (1996). *How we grieve: Relearning the world*. New York, NY: Oxford University Press.

Baxter, L. A. (2011). *Voicing relationships: A dialogic perspective*. Thousand Oaks, CA: Sage.

Betz, G., & Thorngren, J. M. (2006). Ambiguous loss and the family grieving process. *The Family Journal: Counseling and Therapy for Couples and Families, 14*, 359–365. doi: 10.1177/1066480706290052

Bochner, A. P. (2007). Notes toward an ethics of memory in autoethnography. In N. Denzin & M. Giardina (Eds.), *Ethical futures of memory in qualitative research: Decolonizing the politics of knowledge* (pp. 197–208). Walnut Creek, CA: Left Coast Press.

Bochner, A. P., & Ellis C. S. (2006) Communication as autoethnography. In G. Sheperd, J. St. John, & T. Striphas (Eds.), *Communication as ... : Perspective on theory* (pp. 110–122). Thousand Oaks, CA: Sage.

Boss, P. (1999). *Ambiguous loss: Learning to live with unresolved grief*. Cambridge, MA: Harvard University Press.

Boss, P. (2006). *Loss, trauma, and resilience: Therapeutic work with ambiguous loss*. New York, NY: Norton.

Boylorn, R. (2013). *Sweetwater: Black women and narratives of resilience*. New York, NY: Peter Lang.

Cooper, S. H. (2000). *Objects of hope: Exploring possibility and limit in pscyhoanalysis*. Hillsdale, NJ: Analytic.

Custer, D. (2014). Autoethnography as a transformative research method. *The Qualitative Report, 19*, 1–13. Retrieved from http://nsuworks.nova.edu/tqr/vol19/iss37/3

Denzin, N. K. (2004). The war on culture, the war on truth. *Cultural Studies ⇔ Critical Methodologies, 4*, 137--142. doi: 10.1177/1532708603256627

Ellis, C. (2013). Crossing the rabbit hole: Autoethnographic life review. *Qualitative Inquiry, 19*(1), 35–45. doi: 10.1177/1077800412462981

Ellis, C., & Bochner, A. P. (2000). Autoethnography, personal narrative, reflexivity: Researchers as subject. In N. K. Denzin & Y. S. Lincoln (Eds.), *Handbook of qualitative research* (2nd ed., pp. 733–768). Thousand Oaks, CA: Sage.

Ellis, C., & Bochner, A. P. (2006). Analyzing analytic autoethnography: An autopsy. *Journal of Contemporary Ethnography, 35*, 429–449. doi: 10.1177/0891241606286979

Gergen, K. J. (1973). Social psychology as history. *Journal of Personality and Social Psychology, 26*(2), 309–320. doi: 10.1037/h0034436

Gergen, K. J., & Walter, R. (1998). Real/izing the relational. *Journal of Social and Personal Relationships, 15*(1), 110–126. doi: 10.1177/0265407598151007

Gergen, M. M. (1987, August). *Social ghosts: Opening inquiry on imaginal relationships*. Paper presented at the 95th Annual Convention of the American Psychological Association, New York, NY.

Gergen, M. M., & Gergen, K. (2000). Qualitative inquiry: Tensions and transformations. In N. K. Denzin & Y. S. Lincoln (Eds.), *Handbook of qualitative research* (2nd ed., pp. 1025–1046). Thousand Oaks, CA: Sage.

Levi, P. (1987). *If this is a man/The truth* (S. J. Woolf, Trans.). London, England: Abacus. (Original work published in 1958)

Morrison, J., & R. Krieger (1967). People are strange [Recorded by The Doors]. On *Strange Days* [LP]. Hollywood, CA. Elektra.

Pelias, R. (2011). *Leaning: A poetics of personal relations.* Walnut Creek, CA: Left Coast Press.

Pennebaker, J. (1990). *Opening up: The healing power of expressing emotions.* New York, NY: Guilford Press.

Quinet, K. (2007). The missing missing: Toward a quantification of serial murder victimization in the United States. *Homicide Studies, 11,* 319–339. doi: 10.1177/1088767907307467

Rambo Ronai, C. (1992). The reflexive self through narrative: A night in the life of an erotic dancer/researcher. In C. Ellis & M. Flaherty (Eds.), *Investigating subjectivity: Research on lived experience* (pp. 102–124). Newbury Park, CA: Sage.

Rambo Ronai, C. (1995). Multiple reflections of child sex abuse: An argument for a layered account. *Journal of Contemporary Ethnography, 23,* 395–426. doi: 10.1177/089124195023004001

Dianah McGreehan
Department of Communication Studies
Southern Illinois University Carbondale

SONDRA S. BRIGGS

13. TEACHING WHILE LESBIAN

Identity and a Case for Consciousness in the Classroom and Beyond

> When I refuse to listen to how you are different from me, I am refusing to
> know who you are.
> – Linda Martín Alcoff (2006, p. 6)

The implicit resistance among educators and in institutions of learning towards discussions around LGBT (lesbian, gay, bisexual, transgender) issues perpetuates the marginalization of these identities and the real students and teachers who live these identities every day. In K-12 schools and college classrooms the prevailing silence sends disturbing messages about the treatment of adults and children when their sexual orientation fails to fit neatly into prescribed binary classifications. As one who has been silent as well as silenced, I understand this dichotomy from a unique perspective. Moreover, my lived membership within diverse cultural and racial groups that have been routinely marginalized through institutionalized practices in educational and social contexts provides a complex lens through which to examine and complicate notions of heteronormativity, identity, and otherness.

As proposed by Ellis (2009), using an autoethnographic approach as the qualitative method for this chapter positions me "at the intersection of the personal and the cultural, thinking and observing as an ethnographer and writing and describing as a storyteller" (p. 13). This intersection appeals to my sense of responsibility and kinship to the politics of pedagogy while it also addresses my need as a writer to express my observations, reflections, and desires in a narrative form that is accessible to readers. But autoethnography goes beyond being merely accessible. Bochner (2012) insists that it is "not intended to be received, but rather to be encountered, conversed with, and appreciated" (p. 161). So, as I stand at the juncture described here, there is space for constant interchange between researchers and readers. This methodology opens avenues for readers to interact with narratives authentically, reimagining and reconstructing more inclusive worlds along with researchers and participants who are inextricably linked.

This chapter was born in large part from my dissertation, *Teaching While Lesbian and Other Identities: Sexual Diversity, Race, and Institutionalized Practices through an Autoethnographic Lens* (Briggs, 2015). That study was initially intended to be an inquiry into the silence that exists in our educational institutions around a single discourse—homophobia. But like my faceted and multidimensional approach to the world (*Should anything ever be viewed in isolation?*), my work soon encompassed the intersectionality of race, colorism, class, and sexual diversity. It is through my ways of identifying that I tell my story.

S. L. Pensoneau-Conway et al. (Eds.), Doing Autoethnography, 127–137.
© 2017 Sense Publishers. All rights reserved.

These pieces are interwoven with threads tinged by the complexity of family, culture, advantage and disadvantage, within the racial and social contexts that I have lived. The five sections that follow in this chapter are arranged in reverse chronological order; the narratives that illustrate the theme of each section span roughly 75 years. The first section describes how the initial premise for my dissertation work came to be. Section two depicts an experience at the first school where I taught in Cobb County, Georgia; its significance helped cement my view of teaching as a political act. In sections three and four, I introduce the reader to my mother as I address colorism, religion, forms of capital, and marginalization; these narratives journey back through my childhood. To close, I invite the reader on an historical excursion with Mama, a vital influence in my life.

SCHOOLS AS HETERONORMATIVE SPACES

In California in the late 1990s, the dialectical dynamic of being an out lesbian in my personal life and teaching in an elementary school—closeted only by the limitations of my presumed heterosexuality—found relief in small pockets of everyday experience. The Long Beach chapter of GLSEN (Gay, Lesbian & Straight Education Network) periodically held their meetings at my school, and I attended regularly. I held hands with my girlfriend in public and even brought her to my school's holiday event months before returning to the South. However, in ultra-conservative Cobb County—the suburb of Georgia where I teach—the term *significant other* had an entirely different meaning when it appeared on the staff invitation to the year-end party: it presumed heteronormativity. Teaching first at the middle school level (where my students regularly inquired about my marital status) and later in a K-5 setting, I experienced an increasing furtiveness around my lesbian identity—a singular facet of how I identified—and it weighed on me, perhaps more than I was willing to acknowledge. Johnson (2014) aptly notes, "As much as we conform to meet our labels, we are merely hiding bits and pieces of our identities that, eventually, will leak out" (p. 93). I had remained hidden in plain view for nearly seven years before my closet of silence became too deafening. The revelation was inevitable and, in the immediate aftermath, inconsequential.

Under the assumption of heteronormativity, heterosexuality is not only the sexual norm, but the social and cultural norm as well; other expressions of sexuality, thus, are pathologized (Biegel, 2010; Sue & Sue, 2008; Thornton, 2003). Such views have been deeply entrenched in our society and the silences are so loud, even in the academy. Clark (2010) recounts her textual practices in the late 1990s and being startled by how inexplicit she was in naming categories (both in her syllabi and in discussions) outside of what was standard practice. Reflectively, she wrote, "even as I asked my students to consider silencing around issues of race, I failed to interrogate my own silence around gender and sexuality" (p. 45). Even in an environment that many might consider safe—a graduate course in cultural literacy, where some students might identify as LGBT—language pertaining to sexual diversity remains starkly absent. It was in just such a university setting in 2011 that the seed for what grew into my dissertation began to take root. The students were fellow educators from multiple school districts and employed in every facet of teaching and administration. When the discussion was tainted by a homophobic comment, the unfortunate giggles were followed by a long moment of uncomfortable silence. The most palpable was my own.

The semantic uses of *diversity* and *inclusion*, both of which are employed in discussions on culturally relevant pedagogy, rarely include or even allude to LGBT-relevant terms. In fact, Alvarez and Schneider (2008) point out the conflict that exists between these two terms, which are often used interchangeably: "Universities will proudly announce their commitments to a diverse community of learners but will offer very limited possibilities for meaningful inclusion" (p. 73). At the same time, LGBT and related terms (most often, *gay* and *lesbian*) to denote sexual orientation are frequently referred to in isolation, as if there exists mutual exclusivity between diverse ways of identifying and sexual orientation. Yet, in the context of education and pedagogical practices the undeniable intersectionality that does exist should not be overlooked. Kumashiro (2002) argues that "to speak of identities always and only in their separate(d) incarnations...not only denies ways in which identities are already intersected, but more importantly, masks ways in which certain identities are already privileged" (p. 56).

IDENTITY AND THE PRIVILEGE OF NAMING

I came to realize that, along with teaching English learners, completing what seemed like massive amounts of paperwork on each pupil was part of the territory of being an English to Speakers of Other Languages (ESOL) teacher. Although permanent records were accessible, I noticed that the veterans in the department sometimes relied on one another and their—often presumed—knowledge of their students when it came to filling in demographic information required for test forms. As the newest teacher in the department I may have been hyper-aware of the ramifications of challenging a colleague's judgment. But in one instance that concerned presumption around a student's racial identity, I felt I had no choice. The student was from Brazil and, based on discussions around culture that I'd conducted with my 8th graders, the student had verbalized her self-identification as both White *and* Black. The teacher in this case insisted on marking solely the White box, purely on the basis of the student's skin color. Since it was so "obvious," she questioned how I could dispute her claim. I, in turn, questioned her willingness (or need) to impose a racial identity on a student who might view herself differently—based on criteria that was not so readily apparent.

We are a society that is used to naming and labeling in stereotypical and dichotomous ways. Should people be categorized in so expedient a manner, giving little to no regard to the subject of the naming? And what is the purpose of such naming—the preservation of our own comfort level? Or something more insidious, such as who has power over whom? I was the only ESOL educator of color in the department, and the only one present who questioned what was transpiring. Coincidence, or an occurrence that felt all too familiar? Alcoff (2006) points to the "arbitrary nature of social identity designations" (p. ix) learned early on by those of us who have lived in and between multiple racial contexts. She argues that while the objective nature of identity is inescapable, the experiential components and those centered in subjectivity can be ascribed more significance.

"HALF-BREED" AND A BOATLOAD OF CAPITAL

"What are you?" was the most common way they'd phrase the question. Sometimes the question just sounded curious. Often, though, the edges were tinged with something else. At times I'd shrink inside knowing they'd detected something different. "How come you talk so good?" "Where'd you get that good hair?" Those angry attacks were clues to the differences, none of which I could change. "Your sister's real smart, huh?" I shook my head in futile denial though I guessed the neighborhood already knew she was headed to The Bronx High School of Science in the fall. "You think you're better than anybody else 'cause you're wearin' that dress?" Vicky[1] was surrounded by her usual group of friends that day in the schoolyard; it was the day I wore my new sailor dress.

It was sleeveless and navy blue down to below the hips where the pleats began. They were crisp white and razor sharp. The sailor collar, too, was white and hung down perfectly squared in the back. The edge of the collar had thin red cording sewn all the way around, and a wide bright red sash was tied in a loose knot below the V-neck in front; another crimson sash around my hips separated the navy bodice from the pleated skirt. I slowly retreated, my *"No"* barely a whisper, knowing the doors to the school were locked until the bell rang. Vicky then asked me for a nickel to buy an Italian ice from the bakery across the street. My other nickel was in the purse that was slung across my shoulder. "I don't have any money." She hit my shoulder hard and then told me to hit her back. I said nothing. She shoved me again, even harder, and I felt frozen in place. A crowd started to gather as she pushed me violently, yelling ugly remarks like "half-breed." It was the most hurtful. Somewhere in the commotion my lemon ice in one of those pleated paper cups fell to the ground. Vicky then punched me in the stomach with such force that I vomited my lunch. I wondered if I'd soiled my dress. After my mother went to school the following day I never had to worry about Vicky again.

Mama had a way of brandishing her unique form of cultural capital. In the projects of Spanish Harlem her sense of pride, disarming dignity, and European accent stood out like a sore thumb. And she knew when to make the most of it. Her biggest weapons, though, were her razor-sharp intelligence, uncanny grasp of the law, and a fervent inclination to always speak truth to power. So when Mama marched out of the house the next morning to meet with the principal, I knew instinctively that I'd be okay from then on.

At JHS 45 students were leveled according to reading ability. Every grade (7th to 9th) had classes that were labeled from single to double digits, 7-1 to 7-19; the higher the number, the lower the reading level. Following a suspension, Vicky was removed from her respectably average single-digit classroom and placed in an embarrassingly high double-digit room; this ensured that our lunch and gym schedules did not coincide. She was also threatened with expulsion if she ever again laid a hand on me. Even then I was aware of the unfairness of that system: Vicky wasn't stupid, just mean. Yet before her first year of junior high had ended, Vicky's sense of self, her place in the world, and her academic future had been impacted by a powerful and equally negative blow.

I often think of that sailor dress—the one Mama had bought for me at the Salvation Army. It cost no more than three dollars. It was part of the outer and inner trappings that helped shape my identity and influenced how that identity was perceived by others. There was never enough money for clothes in our family and barely enough for food, but outsiders would not have known that; my mother's innately good taste always picked up where the money from the semi-monthly public assistance checks left off. It was the particular kind of "wealth" with which Mama had inculcated us and which we in turn projected into the world that likely was so threatening to the "Vickys" in our neighborhood. The girl who pushed me would never know I was wearing a used garment that day or, as the youngest of three girls, many of the clothes I wore to school routinely had been worn by at least one of my older sisters. There was, of course, much more at play that day: all the stuff that sits just below the surface primed for just the right spark to set it aflame.

Mine is a story about otherness. However, the veracity of that statement would lie in someone else's perspective—not my own. Otherness can only find truth in opposition to that upon which has been placed greater value or significance. It is true that I have occupied spaces within multiple cultural contexts. It is also true that I have been an unwitting participant in my own labeling and identification by those in dominant as well as dominated cultures. Yet through it all, I have developed what feels like an inherently complex understanding around my identity.

PRACTICING JUDAISM

In Manhattan, the geographic demarcation line that separates classes is 96th Street. That divide is most recognizable on Lexington Avenue, where the landmark is four blocks south: the 92nd Street Y, host to such luminaries as Leonard Cohen and Adrienne Rich. Two more stops and you arrive in Yorkville, the Upper East Side hub of the German-Jewish elite. Congregation Kehilath Jeshurun is located just one and a half blocks west. The summer before junior high school, my mother decided against sending my sisters and me to sleep-away camp. Instead, she bought each of us a black composition notebook and a ballpoint pen and, in her fiercely determined style, subjected us to countless hours of transcribing her dictated readings in preparation for Hebrew school at the site of that synagogue. That was also the summer I learned about the Holocaust and a whole other reality about my extended maternal family, those I would never get to meet.

My mother loved the traditions associated with Judaism, even though the only one she remained devoted to throughout my childhood was Passover. We never had the proper extra set of plates and silverware, but would wash the everyday dishes more carefully whenever we prepared for that first Seder. Chanukah, for us, turned out to be mostly about the dreidel and chocolate gelt, although I loved the lighting of the candles; whenever we did observe, I'd make a personal contest out of watching the wax melt until the final flicker. For Purim, Mama would surprise us (when money allowed) with the most delicious buttery hamentashen from the bakery near Hebrew school; her and my favorite were the ones with poppy seed filling. Some years we'd all take the bus downtown to hear the blowing of the shofar on Rosh Hashanah. And Mama usually put the traditional fasting for Yom Kippur (the highest holy day) up for a vote. We would typically agree to it; not eating for an entire day was more fun when we made a contest out of it.

Because of Mama's fondness for the cantor's chanting of the Kol Nidrei, Yom Kippur's special prayer, we all headed to the synagogue. Even before leaving the house, I had decided that I'd be the one to touch the Torah during the procession of the scrolls as they were paraded along the aisles. So when we were seated and I saw that only two people separated me from my goal that evening, I felt pretty confident. When the time came, the entire congregation rose to their feet and as the elaborate, heavily encased Torah scrolls inched closer, I prepared myself: in my gentlest and most refined voice, I said, "Excuse me" to the well-dressed graying lady standing beside me. And I stretched out my left arm. The sudden shock of my hand being slapped away was supplanted only a moment later by the woman's vindictive glare as our eyes met. What followed was the hiss of a single two-syllable word, the force of which felt as if it were being spat in my face. It was a word that I had not heard before in a language that I could only presume was German. Suddenly, as if she herself had been struck, my mother's entire being seemed to overtake the narrow pew where we stood and emitting from her mouth in the most threatening torrential wave were more German words than I had ever heard her speak before or since.

Mama made it a point to guide my hand to one of the passing scrolls before she proudly marched her brood of biracial children out the doors of the synagogue and into the chilly fall evening. She explained that the word, yelled in Yiddish, was *schvartze* and that its literal meaning was "black." The way it was used, however (and she seemed to struggle for an appropriate translation), meant "dirty." She was sorry I had to hear that, and assured me that I had every right to touch the Torah. There was a short treatise on what kind of ignorant and bigoted person would have the audacity to say something so insulting. Later that week, she kept her promise to make a full report to the head rabbi.

"You know what your heritage is," Mama had told us from an early age. "You are Austrian and White European on your mother's side and Black American on your father's side." And she would always add, "But the world will only see you as Black." During the years I and my sisters and brother attended Hebrew school, I lived in and between two distinct worlds: one White, affluent, and religious; the other, my neighborhood of Spanish Harlem—culturally and linguistically diverse and lower middle class to poor. Neither of these worlds made any sense for my identity that struggled to attach itself to some sense of belonging. Neither world accepted me fully, nor I them. I began to recognize viscerally a world brimming with preconceived notions of color, culture, and class. I was somewhere outside of the lines of what was considered the norm. For quite some time, that place of liminality felt like home. And I learned how to use it.

* * *

For much of my life I have experienced a particular and distinct level of cognitive dissonance in relationship to my Jewishness. In somewhat the same way that Collins (2000) describes the notion of being an *outsider within*, what I perceived as a lack of access has been the most troubling for me because it seemed to threaten the profound connection that I have with my mother, and all of the exotic pieces of history tragic and joyous that I had yet to piece together.

On my mother's side, I am a first generation U.S. American. In New York City's Spanish Harlem, where my siblings and I were raised, we were one of two biracial families. At our Hebrew school there were no other children of color. My lack of capital in some respects and abundance in others led me to understand early on what it means to live in the margins. My lived experiences as a biracial Jewish lesbian have posed countless challenges in terms of how to navigate spaces—many of which allowed, but did not invite, access. It is illuminating but not altogether surprising to consider where I have placed my focus as an educator—teaching English learners. Like me, many of my students grow up straddling two or more worlds, where notions of color, culture, class, and capital impact their daily lives. Like my mother, they must navigate between and within two distinct sociolinguistic worlds. Gay (2010) asserts that language "identifies and humanizes, and gives cultures, ideas, and thoughts the capacity to speak" (p. 76). But with the desire for assimilation (often for the purpose of gaining access to certain privileges), language learners must contend with balancing that desire against the sometimes ambivalent choice to honor the culture and language that sustains them. My mother all but lost her first language in the face of such challenges.

ROOTS OF A REBEL

In his "queer of color critique," Ferguson (2004) examines the social, economic, and political forces that were in play in the mid-twentieth century with the influx of immigrants to the U.S., including how "Theodore Roosevelt endorsed the naturalization of European immigrants" and extended "white racial difference" to them (p. 33). Assimilation of these new populations was the ideal on the basis that intermarriage would occur only between and among Whites, thereby promoting the integrity of the race through heterosexual reproduction. Of course, that did not always happen. With the increasingly porous regulatory boundaries, geographical as well as sexual, came the new crisis of trying to "keep desire within the racialized confines of the heteropatriarchal household and the segregated neighborhood" (p. 36). Policing those neighborhoods was one means of carrying this out.

My mother Mimi Rosenfeld arrived on U.S. shores as an Austrian immigrant in 1940. After a brief stay in Connecticut, she moved to New York City where she would spend the rest of her life. Nonnine, my mother's first of seven biracial children, was born in 1944. Clearly, Mimi did not fit the profile of the naturalized European immigrant Roosevelt had in mind. And while her choices were certainly atypical for the time, her timely fortitude—even audacity—in the face of authority was something that deserved my constant admiration as I observed how she navigated her world. Long before DWB (i.e., driving while Black) ever came into existence, my mother had a sense of what it meant to be profiled by the police.

Mimi was on a New York City subway with Nonnine's father when a White uniformed policeman approached her. "Why are you with him?" he asked, indicating the Black man seated beside her. "You can do better than that." My mother rose from her seat and stood eye to eye with the officer. "How dare you!" and proceeded to write down his badge number. "You will hear about this!" she warned. And she wasn't kidding: she penned a letter to Mayor Fiorello La Guardia (in office for three terms, 1934–1945). My mother was most proud of the fact that she received a reply from the mayor, who apologized for the officer's impropriety with an assurance that the policeman had, indeed, been reprimanded. In this scenario, the familiar intersection of policing and the Black body is clear. Even while the officer's direct interaction took place only with my White mother, the message was that she should disassociate herself from the inferior Black man. In addressing my mother, the police officer was apparently aligning himself with her on the basis of what appeared to be a "Whiteness" with which he was familiar. But one can only wonder what went through his mind when my mother first uttered her rebuke: her Viennese accent that remained with her throughout her life was distinct and pronounced. The concept of *Whiteness* in the United States, embodying all of its structural underpinnings, exists only in direct opposition to that which is considered other: Blackness (Ferguson, 2004; Muhammad, 2010; Sue & Sue, 2008). This same concept could not have existed in mid-twentieth century Austria. In fact, her first sighting of a person of color (in this case, a turbaned man from India) occurred after my mother arrived in England at the age of 19. So, the rich conundrum of intersectionality that took place on that 1940s New York City subway may have been Mimi Rosenfeld's early glimpse into a U.S. American legacy with a long and convoluted shadow.

* * *

I come to this chapter with the knowledge that my experience with otherness in and outside of sites of learning has helped to create the pedagogical framework upon which I rely to create access to spaces for meaningful expression. Describing my ways of identifying is born out of a commitment to reflexivity—a term not to be confused with reflection. Reflexivity is essential to understanding our experiences as socially constructed, a view that supports our engagement with our social world and the kinds of practices that can lead to critical change. Importantly, reflexivity is also a teachable skill; practitioners can acquire the tools that lead to uncovering assumptive reflexes, and learn how intentional *self*-consciousness and outside dialogue can lead to meaningful social action (Cunliffe, 2004; Johnson, 2009).

An ACLU Special Report that utilizes extensive nationwide sources exemplifies accounts of racial profiling commonly known as DWB, a reference to the widely documented and pervasive problem of racially motivated, pretextual traffic stops to which predominantly Black and Latino/Latina citizens are subjected (Harris, 1999). Driving while Black, of course, parodies DWI, or driving while intoxicated—the *actual* crime. DWB is a painful reality for those being profiled, and a powerful commentary on the structural racism experienced by those who are often deemed as other. Similarly situated acronyms have become popular shorthand for expressing instances of intolerance or injustice experienced predominately by those who are culturally and linguistically diverse. Such acronyms—including those spelled out below—push back upon and interrogate our society's widely accepted cultural stereotypes. There are startling statistics for three highly profiled groups "caught in the act" of Driving While Black, Flying While Arab, and Walking While Latino (in Arizona, after the passage of that state's controversial SB 1070 immigration law in April 2010). In a related Gallup poll, a majority of White respondents denied that excessive profiling targeting certain groups was taking place; the same respondents felt that "race, ethnicity and overall appearance" were factors that should be considered for airport passenger searches (Dawkins, 2010).

I have chosen to use Teaching While Lesbian as the opening phrase for the title of this chapter because of my stance on the unspoken imposition on LGBT teachers to be closeted; it is an implicit form of discrimination imposed by educational systems and state-sanctioned legislation. Naming a practice of discrimination where it lives exposes it for what it is—in this case, a strategy for social stratification that is used as a tool to perpetuate LGBT marginalization.

The riskiness of placing the words *teaching* and *lesbian* within the same phrase is a reality that does not escape me. I am aware that it goes well beyond the realm of comfort for many; among them, very likely, the majority of my colleagues. Pellicer (2008) contends that pursuing anything worthwhile will involve significant risk, not unlike trapeze-jumping. The use of these words in my title feels like a decision fraught with risk—like stepping out on a far-flung tree limb.

In the policies on student conduct for the school district where I teach, the language pertaining to student harassment has evolved over the past few years. Those covering elementary, middle, and high schools currently use appropriate protective language to define *harassment*—terms include *sexual orientation* and *gender identity*. Although the meaning of diversity in education may have expanded in certain respects in recent years to become more inclusive of LGBT student populations, there has been little impact on the extension of protections or the most basic collegial acceptance for educators who choose to practice outside of the boundaries of the closet. Since sexual orientation is not a protected class for educators (or any school employees) in the state of Georgia, the District Administrative Rule for Equal Opportunity Employment in the district where I teach states explicitly: "The District will not tolerate harassment, discrimination or retaliation against any employee based upon legally-protected status."

That limb on which I often find myself has been in some ways a regular theme in my life, and one with which I feel significant familiarity. In most instances, it feels less precarious than straddling fences for the mere sake of safety. When she describes the important work of telling our stories, memoirist Judith Barrington (1997) asserts, "For members of marginalized groups, speaking personally and truthfully about our lives plays a small part in erasing years of invisibility and

135

interpretation by others" (p. 14). My commitment to using an autoethnographic approach to tell my story is about doing this process in the full light of authenticity.

I tell this story from the margins; within those margins are the multi-layered intersections along which I have lived and taught and loved. I know that to be fully engaged with my research and to allow others into the credible space of my writing means allowing my identities to surface, and opening myself to uncommon degrees of vulnerability. I also know that within this process lies an expansion of understanding about how to speak to and deconstruct the myths and institutionalized practices we as educators and as a society rely upon so heavily to maintain a status quo.

The ongoing challenge is how to speak to one another. There is a gaping hole where dialogue should be, and it continues to fuel intolerance and injustice—often in the form of tiny annihilations that occur daily and are virtually invisible (but to those who are the intended or unintended victims)—in every part of our society. While no amount of legislation can dictate beliefs or behavior, we surely know that *any* kind of exclusion results in a loss for someone, or everyone. Messages that announce (even implicitly) "you are not welcome here" carry a heavy burden for adults and children alike. Such messages happen far too often in places where they shouldn't—our schools. We must ask ourselves: What are we teaching? What are we learning? What haven't we learned? Why do we continue to choose the path of exclusion? Can we begin to learn how to use the language and understandings that *do* exist to articulate the contradictions and imbalances that are present and unaccounted for in the institutions we rely on most? Surely we can find the dignity that exists on the other side of every intolerant action.

My own story is the one I know best. Although it is uniquely subjective, it is also fundamentally connected to a vast catalog of like narratives for the mere fact that we are each linked by our humanity. For this reason, I hope that readers will be able to glimpse facets of truth that resonate with their own immediate experience. For in that mere recognition may exist the very seeds of commonality that help erase essentialist concepts like otherness; and maybe in their place an acknowledgment and deep embrace of our inevitable differences. After all, is it not the critical consciousness that can only derive from within a pluralistic society that has been humanity's enduring strength?

NOTE

[1] For the purpose of confidentiality, I use pseudonyms in this narrative for all persons not directly related to me. "Vicky" is a pseudonym.

REFERENCES

Alcoff, L. M. (2006). *Visible identities: Race, gender, and the self.* New York, NY: Oxford University Press.

Alvarez, S. D., & Schneider, J. (2008). One college campus's need for a safe zone: A case study. *Journal of Gender Studies, 17*(1), 71–74. doi:10.1080/09589230701838461.

Barrington, J. (1997). *Writing the memoir: From truth to art.* New York, NY: Eighth Mountain Press.

Biegel, S. (2010). *The right to be out: Sexual orientation and gender identity in America's public schools.* Minneapolis: University of Minnesota Press.

Bochner, A. P. (2012). On first-person narrative scholarship. Autoethnography as acts of meaning. *Narrative Inquiry, 22,* 155–164. doi: 10.1075/ni.22.1.10boc.

Briggs, S. S. (2015). *Teaching while lesbian and other identities: Sexual diversity, race, and institutionalized practices through an autoethnographic lens.* Unpublished doctoral dissertation. Kennesaw State University, Kennesaw, GA.

Clark, C. T. (2010). Inquiring into ally work in teacher education: The possibilities and limitations of textual practice. In M. V. Blackburn, C. T. Clark, L. Kenney, & J. M. Smith (Eds.), *Acting out: Combating homophobia through teacher activism* (pp. 37–55). New York, NY: Teachers College Press.

Collins, P. H. (2000). *Black feminist thought: Knowledge, consciousness, and the politics of empowerment.* (2nd ed.). New York, NY: Routledge.

Cunliffe, A. L. (2004). On becoming a critically reflexive practitioner. *Journal of Management Education, 28*(4), 407–426. doi: 10.1177/1052562904264440.

Dawkins, M. A. (2010, June 9). *Driving while Black, flying while Arab, walking while Latino.* Retrieved from http://www.alternet.org/speakeasy/2010/06/09/deterred-and-discouraged

Ellis, C. (2009). *Revision: Autoethnographic reflections on life and work.* Walnut Creek, CA: Left Coast Press.

Ferguson, R. A. (2004). *Aberrations in black: Toward a queer of color critique.* Minneapolis: University of Minnesota Press.

Gay, G. (2010). *Culturally responsive teaching: Theory, research, and practice.* New York, NY: Teachers College Press.

Harris, D. A. (1999). Driving while black: Racial profiling on our nation's highways. *An American Civil Liberties Union Special Report.* https://www.aclu.org/report/driving-while-black-racial-profiling-our-nations-highways

Johnson, A. L. (2014). Negotiating more, (mis) labeling the body: A tale of intersectionality. In R. M. Boylorn & M. P. Orbe (Eds.), *Critical autoethnography: Intersecting cultural identities in everyday life* (pp. 81–95). Walnut Creek, CA: Left Coast Press.

Johnson, C. W. (2009). Writing ourselves at risk: Using self-narrative in working for social justice. *Leisure Sciences, 31,* 483–489. doi: 10.1080/01490400903199815

Kumashiro, K. (2002). *Troubling education: Queer activism and antioppressive pedagogy.* New York, NY: RoutledgeFalmer.

Muhammad, K. G. (2010). *The condemnation of blackness.* Cambridge, MA: Harvard University Press.

Pellicer, L. O. (2008). *Caring enough to lead: How reflective practice leads to moral leadership.* Thousand Oaks, CA: Corwin Press.

Sue, D. W., & Sue, D. (2008). *Counseling the culturally diverse: Theory and practice* (5th ed.). Hoboken, NJ: John Wiley & Sons.

Thornton, S. J. (2003). Silence on gays and lesbians in social studies curriculum. *Social Education, 67*(4), 226–230.

Sondra S. Briggs
Independent Scholar

SARAH HELPS

14. REMEMBER WHO YOU BELONG TO

A Story of Multiple and Temporary Belongings

Words do not on their own *do* anything: they do not stand for things, nor represent ideas. They have a meaning only in those situations in which living human beings make some *use* of them in relating themselves to other living human beings.
—John Shotter and Arlene M. Katz (1999, pp. 81–82)

The professional self cannot be separated from the personal self ... in practice a person's life experiences and ideas may inform their action in different ways at different times.
—Fran Hedges and Susan Lang (cited in Hedges, 2010)

You look like you belong here.
—Mrs. Pomeroy, teacher, to Gretchen Ross, student (*Donnie Darko*)

BEGINNINGS

This chapter offers some autoethnographically-inspired reflections on belonging, and my relationship to this theme as a systemic psychotherapist, supervisor and researcher. I offer the chapter to my patients, my research participants and my colleagues as a way of furthering a dialogue about the things that influence our therapeutic positionings. One particular position relates to how my own beliefs about the world influence the ways in which I do, and think about, my practice. In giving concrete examples of my experiences, I intend to connect with others who reflect on and are self-reflexive about their practice.

THERAPEUTIC CONVERSATIONS AS THE CREATION OF TEMPORARY BELONGING RELATIONSHIPS

The therapeutic relationship exists because patients need something from a therapist. There is a wealth of literature that highlights how the therapeutic relationship, rather than the specific tools of particular therapies, makes a significant difference to the outcome of the work (e.g., Karam, Blow, Sprenkle, & Davis, 2015). In modern family therapy practice, my specific area of psychotherapeutic work, therapists are not seen in the old-fashioned blank-canvas psychoanalytic way, but as live, embodied characters who, through their own

S. L. Pensoneau-Conway et al. (Eds.), Doing Autoethnography, 139–147.
© 2017 Sense Publishers. All rights reserved.

thoughts, feelings, and experiences, bring something unique and important to the therapeutic relationship (Bertrando, 2015; Flaskas & Perlesz, 1996; Rober, 1999).

An important part of "doing psychotherapy" involves reflection on our practice (Schön, 1987) in order to continue the cycle of professional learning and development. In reflecting on my conversations with my patients, I often start from the question, "What influenced me to say or do that then?" My replies involve all sorts of answers, loosely arranged along a spectrum from "I was moved to do it" to "I was guided by a paper that I recently read that relates to this particular issue." My potential answers therefore involve both my professional training and my own experiences as a creative, living human being (Shotter & Katz, 1999; Wilson, 2015). These experiences "call" me to respond to situations in unique ways. I situate these calls in connection to what John Shotter (2008) describes as a relationally responsive way of being in relation to an other. This way of being involves the spontaneous, living responsiveness of our bodies to those around us, which are shaped by our past and present situations. Awareness of these calls enables me to ensure that I always work in the service of my patient.

The way in which I respond to the "calls" that I notice, involves my gender, race, religion, age, ability, culture, class, education, ethnicity, sexuality, and spirituality (Burnham, 1992, 2011). These, together with other visible and invisible social differences, intersect with each other and with the "others" in the conversation (Shotter, 2009).

Because of the absolute importance of patient confidentiality, therapists don't write about their patients unless they have negotiated explicit permission to do so. Some have described, using anonymised or composite accounts, what it is like to be on the professional side of the couch (Bryon, 2014; Orbach, 2016; Yalom, 1989). Others have written of their intersecting identities of therapist–teacher—researcher (Etherington, 2004; Speedy & Wyatt, 2014). Autoethnographic research methodologies sit comfortably with the practice of systemic, dialogical, reflexive family therapists (Bertrando, 2007; Rober, 1999; Simon, 2013) who tune in to their inner and outer dialogue and embodied feelings. Indeed, in explaining the process of using her inner and outer dialogue, Gail Simon (2013) writes that

> Writing autoethnographically has offered me ways of "laying them bare" for all to see, to invite others into a privileged and otherwise unexposed view of the inner and outer workings in the life of a practitioner. Without detailed descriptions of inner and outer dialogue, there is no way of showing reflexivity in action. (para. 7)

Following Simon, I write from within the relationship with my patients. I do this not to look at "them," but to attempt to autoethnographically look at myself from both within and without. But therein lies a problem. Even if the focus is myself, I am always in relation. I exist in relation. I act in relation to real, current, imagined, and historical voices and feelings generated in relation with others.

Like many autoethnographers, I worry about what I write. Even though I have permission to share these stories, it still feels risky to share my thoughts and feelings about the ways in which my inner dialogue about them-out-there weaves its way through my personal stories. I know about relational ethics, and I try to write with an ethics of responsibility and care (Doloriert & Sambrook, 2009; Ellis, 2007; Etherington, 2007). But still, in wanting and needing to privilege the position of my current patients and any future patients, how can I do this safely?

Next I offer a collection of writings generated through my current study. I have ethical approval to conduct this research, which includes an autoethnographic layer of writing generated around the data. Patients have given their permission for transcripts (and video recordings) of their sessions to be analysed for the purposes of research. The project explores how I position myself in my first conversations with patients, when I seek to build a therapeutic relationship.

A PARTIAL STORY OF MY BELONGING

I grew up in a small town in a reasonably well off and very white part of the southeast of England UK. At least that's how it was in the 1970s.

Growing up was not without complications, and I became adept at pushing the boundaries, particularly as a teenager, as I started to move away from the family to being more influenced by my peers. Whenever I left the house, at times with unsuitable boys, at times with skirts that were too short, at times conforming to some kind of white Essex girl stereotype with my peach colored stilettos and hair all fake-curled and frothy, my mother and grandmother would tell me, "Remember who you belong to."

This phrase—remember who you belong to—would be said at every opportunity, to every family member, whatever they did, wherever they went.

For years, it was just one of those things, one of those slightly annoying, irritating things that defined our family. As I grew older and traveled further afield, whether getting on the train to go to university a few hundred miles away or going on a plane to another continent, the phrase would emerge—remember who you belong to. It's not a phrase I say to my children. The words don't seem to work in the same way, but the sentiment, the belonging, is fundamental.

I can't tell you where the phrase came from, and I can't tell you the meaning it held for my mother or grandmother. Those aren't my stories to tell. In writing this phrase now, I can tell you about the desire to create a belonging that pervades the personal and professional—emerging in my therapeutic practice, and my attempts to create spaces for my temporary belonging with and to the families I work with.

SOME THEORY

This belonging phrase forms part of my narrative inheritance (Goodall, 2005). It's a motto, an invitation, a script, an instruction, an order, a way of being in relation that was frequently said but never unpacked. Or perhaps, more specifically, never unpacked by me in relation to those who uttered the words. Even now the suitcase remains closed but the legacy of this baggage is immense.

Writing about race and gender, Robin Boylorn (2016) tells of how "there is no pause in [her] identity" and how she resists singular disconnected representations

141

of her identity (p. 49). I like the idea that we do not/cannot divide ourselves and that we need to resist others' efforts to divide our selves into separated parts. So, my relationship with belonging is with me at every moment, including when working as a family therapist. As a therapist I need to ensure that my preferred stories and beliefs do not lead or dominate the interaction or, indeed, show themselves in ways that might be unhelpful to the family. I need to hold on to my own thoughts about belonging while listening out for family stories that might be contrary to or not sit comfortably with my story.

But in doing so, I'm listening for points of connection, points of resonance, points of dialogical engagement. So I listen for how my ideas about belonging, connection, and meaning-making influence my questions and responses.

Barbara Tedlock (2013) reminds us that "the knower and the known are intricately linked" (p. 358) and that a focus on the narrative of the knower helps us bear witness and offer support for vulnerable selves within cultural and social worlds. In my therapeutic conversations with families, all participants are knowers as the "knowing" gets created as we speak together. But I wonder how much of the therapist knower needs to be known by the patient knower, how much is given away by visible markers, and how much is assumed. How much it is helpful to share in an overt way (Lee, 2014; Roberts, 2005) and how these currents of perceived knowledge get into and out of the work.

STORIES FROM PRACTICE

It's been a crazy morning, and I'm running late. The multiple hats that I wear at work (manager, supervisor, researcher, clinician) have all got jammed on at angles that don't feel at all jaunty, and the bit that suffers is time-keeping. So I'm running late. I go to meet Lauren[1] and Suzanne, her mother, and take them to the clinic room. I chat along the corridor and hear that they've had a tricky journey because the tube was really busy. Lauren is quiet, but Suzanne fills the air. Before I've had a chance to explain confidentiality and its limits or ask them both for consent to video the session (standard practice) and take part in my research, Suzanne starts to tell me how she struggles to manage Lauren. "Be quiet," I think. "I want this material on tape!" We settle in. Permission forms are read and signed. Suzanne starts to list all the things that are "wrong" with Lauren. I glance to Lauren, who sits slightly outside of the middle-aged-mother dyad that Suzanne and I form (that's my connection, but of course Suzanne knows nothing about me apart from the visible signs that she may have noticed as we talk). Lauren doesn't seem perturbed by this list of supposed failings. I jump in, interrupt Suzanne, and ask Lauren a question about the recent holiday that her mother has just described in disastrous terms.

I hear how mother and daughter have seen so many professionals, all of whom have said that they couldn't help. From Suzanne, I hear a story of frustration, despair and anger. I hear less from Lauren. I wonder how in our future conversations I will be able to help mother and daughter find ways to listen to each other, to connect with each other in ways that feel "better."

We come to the end of the hour. "Well," I say, "I'm so pleased to meet you. I'm sorry that we started late. I think you've come to the right place, and I'm sure we can help in figuring out not so much what's 'wrong with Lauren' but how she, and you, process the world and what would help to make this easier for you both."

* * *

Watching the video after the session, the messages I offer glow like beacons: "You've come to the right place." "It looks like you belong here." "Let's create something together, let's give of ourselves and belong to each other for a bit."

And I like these people, I feel warmly towards these people. But can I say that? I turn to Jane Speedy (2013), and I am reminded of her description of the young men she works with:

> I realize how in love I still am with these young men. I remember that I am always a little in love with each of my clients. Maybe not at first—it is not necessarily love at first sight—but for this work to work, there is always an element of falling in love. (p. 32)

Speedy also writes of how talking about these feelings might be seen as something close to the "critical edge and slippery slope" away from professional practice (p. 32). Is my privileging of belonging near the slippery slope? I don't think so, but what if others do?

MORE PRACTICE

I'm sitting on a semi-circular sofa in a television studio, not quite on prime time but nevertheless on national television. I'm talking about my area of expertise—autism—on a mid-morning talk show. Gone are the Essex girl visible markers (well—I still think I talk the same as I did back then). Now most noticeable to me is the gentle spread into middle-age, with greying hair, emerging wrinkles, and more comfortable shoes. Unexpectedly, someone has just, with a great deal of cheer and chatter, done my make-up.

The interview goes fine. I sound articulate. I think I make my point, and I leave feeling that I gave a good account of myself and effectively represented the needs of families where there is autism.

Two things happen in the coming days. My mother emails me and says that she had flicked the television on, was astounded that her daughter was on the screen, that she loves me and is proud of me. An ex-patient emails me and tells me that she felt proud to have shared so many therapeutic conversations with me, with someone who had just been on the television. Belonging strikes me again as taking such different forms: forever forms, temporary forms, each so valuable.

IN SHARING A STORY OF MY BELONGING IN PRINT, WHAT DOES THIS DO TO MY RELATIONSHIP WITH MY PATIENTS?

Everything that gets written and put out into the world for consumption and critique by others is indelible. I don't have tattoos on my body, but my writing is akin to the tattoo I dream of having. In choosing to share of myself in such a public way, I have to think of the consequences, to be accountable for my words.

Stacy Holman Jones, Tony Adams, and Carolyn Ellis (2013) note that we not only need to give an account of ourselves but also be accountable to one another.

Sharing a personal story with my patients and my students—this phrase, remember who you belong to—what will they make of it? Will it resonate? Will they look back on the conversations we have had together and make different sense of them? Will they say, "So that's what she was trying to do when she said, 'I'm sure you've come to the right place/I'm so glad we got to meet and to start talking.'" Will they say, "Well, that doesn't fit with my experience"? What if I pinned a copy of this paper up on the door of my office for all to read? What if they don't like it or complain?

SUPERVISION CONVERSATIONS

My door is open and my colleague, someone I supervise, pops his head in. "I need to talk to you," he says, "about something I've done. I told the X family that I am gay." "Oh," I say, "tell me more." We have a discussion about the family, about the work, and about the use of self-disclosure in family therapy. My colleague goes away seeming to have a greater understanding of and comfort with his decision-making processes. We talk the following week after he has seen the family again. I hear that the family found his comments helpful. I think of all the times I have shared personal stories about my identity, my growing up, my children and my ideas about family therapy, with families, and how different it seems to write down and fix personal stories than to spontaneously give of oneself in the therapy room in the moment-to-moment context of conversation. But perhaps these conversations are also indelible in that they sit in people's minds and bodies long after the words have been spoken.

EXTRACT FROM MY RESEARCH FIELD NOTES

I'm starting my data-analysis. Reading and re-reading the transcripts of interviews with my patients, I search for the language of belonging. Words and sentences blur, taking me back to the rooms in which the conversations happened. Despite multiple readings, I just can't find the neat paragraphs that I can cut and paste to show this thing I call belonging. But I feel it. I imagine the changing climate of the conversation. The family and I begin talking. We start, we halt, we review, and alter our language, our tone of voice, our rate of speech, seemingly to try and fit, to connect, to make a relationship, and—I think—to belong so as to get the job done. I want evidence to demonstrate how belonging creeps in to everything but can't find it on the printed page.

So, I turn, again, to John Shotter. I am reminded that language is only meaningful in relationship and that it is the embodied, spontaneous mutually adjustive connectedness that is the thing, *the thing*, that creates meaningful connection. I am reminded that:

As we give voice to our words into the world, it is not just the static form or the picturable patterns of our words that is important, but our unfolding bodily movement in their production. The others around us cannot not respond to our voicings, to our utterances. Thus others, in our presence as individual, active "I's," do not move independently of us; their movements are not wholly their own, they are "colored" by our, individual movements— but our individual movements are also colored by theirs. (Shotter & Katz, 1999, p. 84)

So there won't be a sentence or a small conversational exchange that shows belonging. It is created in the so-much-more-than-words, relationally responsive goings-on of conversations. It is created in the story I live and tell about the overarching arc and feeling of conversations, and perhaps the story that my conversational partners tell themselves and each other.

WORDS TO DRAW THIS TO A CLOSE

Some might hear the phrase "remember who you belong to" as having all kinds of connotations that I haven't thought of. From the dictionary, I am reminded that belonging has two meanings, either belonging to a group or belonging to someone as a possession. I don't want to possess my patients, my colleagues, or my research participants, and they certainly don't belong to me. But I do want to make a connection and to take care in our conversations as if the words and the experiences are something, a kind of possession that I care-fully look after.

An autoethnography can only offer a partial, punctuated, temporary glimpse of a person's life. The reader only has access to the bits of my story that I choose to write, but what if the bits I initially leave out and later on tell people, leave them feeling that they have been tricked in some way, that they thought something about me that then isn't "true"? I'm reminded of something I read that Yoko Ono said, of how once her words had been spoken, they took on a life of their own that she couldn't be held accountable for.

In the days before I finalize this chapter and send it to the editors, I read an article in the newspaper about a general practitioner (GP) who killed herself, seemingly after a patient had complained after reading a blog the GP had written on living with mental illness (Parveen, 2016). Of course I know only details reported in the article.

But this article makes me feel incredibly sad and anxious about this whole transparency/self-disclosure/autoethnography endeavour. It serves as a stark reminder of the ongoing stigma of mental distress and, or indeed, any perceived "other." It reminds me again that my writings might have unintended and unexpected consequences and that I need to try to imagine, predict, and account for those consequences (Etherington, 2007). But, I think, not to be too constrained by these; I can't control the responses of others. As a result of thinking about the GP's death, I go back to the story of belonging that I started with and I edit—removing some things, dulling some of the richness and the detail, rewriting some sentences. I feel an urge to add a sentence that the things I deleted have nothing to do with mental illness. But then I get tangled up in how such protests continue the stigmatisation of mental distress. I try to imagine what a patient or student might think about me as their therapist or supervisor. And then I think back to other autoethnographic writings that I have published and connect with the warm, unexpected, and helpful comments that have been offered, that have made me feel connected, to belong, with people I had not expected. (I remind myself that not all comments received were quite so warm and supportive, but it's those that I'll keep in mind for now.) A final read and I feel confident enough. The chapter will be pinned to my office door alongside a comments box. I await your responses.

Come in, sit down, let's talk. I think you've come to the right place.

NOTE

[1]   Pseudonyms are used to protect the individuals' identities.

REFERENCES

Bertrando, P. D. (2007). *The dialogical therapist: Dialogue in systemic practice*. London, England: Karnac Books.

Bertrando, P. D (2015). *Emotions and the therapist: A systemic-dialogical perspective*. London, England: Karnac Books.

Boylorn, R. M. (2016). On being at home with myself. *International Review of Qualitative Research, 9*, 44–58. doi: 10.1525/irqr.2016.9.1.44

Burnham, J. (1992). Approach-method-technique: Making distinctions and creating connections. *Human Systems, 3*, 3–26.

Burnham, J. (2011). Developments in Social GRRRAAACCEEESSS: Visible-invisible and voiced-unvoiced. In I. Krause (Ed.), *Culture and reflexivity in systemic psychotherapy: Mutual perspectives* (pp. 139–160). London, England: Karnac Books.

Byron, T. (2014). *The skeleton cupboard*. London, England: Pan Macmillan

Doloriert, C., & Sambrook, S. (2009). Ethical confessions of the "I" of autoethnography: The student's dilemma. *Qualitative Research in Organizations and Management: An International Journal, 4*, 27–45. doi: 10.1108/17465640910951435

Ellis, C. (2007). Telling secrets, revealing lives: Relational ethics in research with intimate others. *Qualitative inquiry, 13*(1), 3–29. doi: 10.1177/1077800406294947

Etherington, K. (2004). *Becoming a reflexive researcher: Using our selves in research*. London, England: Jessica Kingsley.

Etherington, K. (2007). Ethical research in reflexive relationships. *Qualitative Inquiry, 13*, 599–616. doi: 10.1177/1077800407301175

Flaskas, C., & Perlesz, A. (1996). *The therapeutic relationship in systemic therapy*. London, England: Karnac Books.

Goodall Jr., H. L. (2005). Narrative inheritance: A nuclear family with toxic secrets. *Qualitative Inquiry, 11*(4), 492–513.

Hedges, F. (2010). *Reflexivity in therapeutic practice*. Basingstoke, England: Palgrave Macmillan.

Holman Jones, S. H., Adams, T. E., & Ellis, C. (2013). *Handbook of autoethnography*. Walnut Creek, CA: Left Coast Press.

Karam, E. A., Blow, A. J., Sprenkle, D. H., & Davis, S. D. (2015). Strengthening the systemic ties that bind: Integrating common factors into marriage and family therapy curricula. *Journal of Marital and Family Therapy, 41*, 136–149. doi: 10.1111/jmft.12096

Lee, E. (2014). A therapist's self-disclosure and its impact on the therapy process in cross-cultural encounters: Disclosure of personal self, professional self, and/or cultural self? *Families in Society: The Journal of Contemporary Social Services, 95*, 15–23. doi:_10.1606/1044-3894.2014.95.3

Orbach, S. (2016). *In therapy: How conversations with psychotherapists really work.* London, England: Profile Books.

Parveen, N. (2016, August 26). *GP found dead after being suspended over bipolar disorder* [Blog post]. Retrieved from https://www.theguardian.com/uk-news/2016/aug/26/gp-found-dead-after-being-suspended-over-bipolar-disorder-blog

Rober, P. (1999). The therapist's inner conversation in family therapy practice: Some ideas about the self of the therapist, therapeutic impasse, and the process of reflection. *Family process, 38*, 209–228. doi: 10.1111/j.1545-5300.1999.00209.x

Roberts, J. (2005). Transparency and self-disclosure in family therapy: Dangers and possibilities. *Family Process, 44*, 45–63. doi: 10.1111/j.1545-5300.2005.00041.x

Schön, D. A. (1987). *Educating the reflective practitioner. Toward a new design for teaching and learning in the professions.* London, England: Jossey-Bass.

Shotter, J. (2008). *Conversational realities revisited: Life, language, body and world.* Chagrin Falls, OH: Taos Institute.

Shotter, J. (2009). Listening in a way that recognizes/realizes the world of "the Other." *The International Journal of Listening, 23*, 21–43. doi: 10.1080/10904010802591904

Shotter, J., & Katz, A. (1999). Living moments in dialogical exchanges. *Human Systems, 9*, 81–93.

Simon, G. (2013). Relational ethnography: Writing and reading in research relationships. *Forum Qualitative Sozialforschung/Forum: Qualitative Social Research, 14*(1). Retrieved from http://www.qualitative-research.net/index.php/fqs/article/view/1735

Speedy, J. (2013). Where the wild dreams are: Fragments from the spaces between research, writing, autoethnography, and psychotherapy. *Qualitative Inquiry, 19*, 27–34. doi: 10.1177/1077800412462980

Speedy, J., & Wyatt, J. (Eds.). (2014). *Creative practitioner inquiry in the helping professions.* Rotterdam, The Netherlands: Sense Publishers.

Tedlock, B. (2013). Braiding evocative with analytic autoethnography. In S. Holman Jones, T. E. Adams, & C. Ellis (Eds.), *Handbook of autoethnography* (pp. 358–362). Walnut Creek, CA: Left Coast Press.

Wilson, J. (2015). Family therapy as a process of humanisation: The contribution and creativity of dialogism. *Australian and New Zealand Journal of Family Therapy, 36*, 6–19. doi: 10.1002/anzf.1095

Yalom, I. (1989). *Love's executioner.* New York, NY: Basic Books.

Sarah Helps
Tavistock and Portman NHS Foundation Trust
London, UK

MINDY RALSTON

15. NOT AN ALICE

Thoughts on Body and Performance

My college theater professor once told me
that despite my talent,
I would never be cast as a romantic lead.
We do plays that involve singing animals
and children with the ability to fly,
but apparently no one
has enough willing suspension of disbelief
to go with anyone loving a fat girl.
—Rachel Wiley, "10 Honest Thoughts on Being Loved by a Skinny Boy"

* * *

I am sixteen, and I am nervous.

I file into the theater with the rest of them as my director gestures toward labeled stacks of cold reads that sit untouched on a table beside her. The boys, far too confident and far too loud, file into each other behind the wide array of scripts that are available to them. This line of prospective Hatters and Hares and Cheshires and Caterpillars seems to grow increasingly fast as more boys file into the auditorium. I take note of my options. Two stacks: One for Alice, and one for the Red Queen. The thought of being cast as the Queen of Hearts makes my own heart sink ever so slightly as I imagine playing the villain. I want so badly to earn the lead role of Alice, to be on stage for the entire show, to be gawked at and admired by every girl on opening night. But looking around, I take note that not one girl is as half as big as I am, and I suddenly feel half my size.

* * *

Like an actress being cast in a show, I learn where I belong.

I am taught, as a fat girl, that I have two choices in this society: to be "fat and lazy" or "fat and jolly" (Wilchins, 1997, p. 131). My choice to accept and perpetuate the role of the latter earns me a grim trophy of femininity when, in my final year of high school, I am crowned homecoming queen.

Here I am, waiting nervously with four other girls who seem to care about this far more than I do. Their dresses are flattering, big, and new. Mine is a rental, the

S. L. Pensoneau-Conway et al. (Eds.), Doing Autoethnography, 149–154.
© 2017 Sense Publishers. All rights reserved.

same one I used for prom last year. They clutch onto their fathers anxiously and mine whispers to me about how funny it is that I don't even like sports.

We're standing on the field, waiting nervously for the presenter to announce a king and queen. Part of me wonders if, since I so clearly don't belong, I was nominated as a joke. As I am standing next to these girls with bated breath and squeezed-tight-eyes, my brain begs me to remember that I am both inferior in beauty and a looming symbol of downward mobility (LaBesco, 2004). But, sure enough, the announcer calls my name as the capital-H, capital-Q Homecoming Queen and the crowd erupts with cheers. I quickly survey my surroundings for buckets of pig's blood, and my dad hugs me. I cry. A lot. And, as I notice minutes later when the crown is placed on my head, so do the other nominees.

This crown will sit years later on a dusty bookshelf beside my associate's degree and will serve as proof that I did high school "right." Even still, it is no secret that my name was on the ballot for queen for the same reasons my name is listed under class clown in my senior yearbook. Despite the fact that size is a "sloppy and unscientific way to judge someone's character" (Bacon, 2008, p. 157), I, at the start of high school, made the decision to take on the role of the Funny Fat Friend in order to avoid the alternative stigma of being regarded as lazy. This conscious decision earned me these rewards, but has done me no favors. My integrity, time and time again, slips from my tightly clenched fingers each time I beat others to the punch with a joke about my own body. Although I wear this identity as armor, I feel more like a jester.

The outpour of congratulations following the homecoming court decision is overwhelming and I begin to wonder, again, if I was nominated as a good deed. I feel like a punchline to a joke I never agreed to tell, and years later, I will wear the crown to costume parties and recite my story as a point of pride.

* * *

The very idea of auditioning for Alice is so absurd that, during the five-minute bathroom break, I decide to climb onto the stage with a girl a year ahead of me. She exaggeratedly takes on the role of the White Rabbit, flailing herself around the stage and making grand gestures toward a giant, pocketed, pantomimed watch. I take on her opposite as Alice and overdo it on the curtsies. I mime a skirt far too large for a stage and tip toe daintily around my funny stage partner and soak up the laughs from the sparse audience. *Are they laughing at my jokes*, I think to myself, *or are they laughing at the prospect of a fat girl playing Alice?* Regardless, the girl and I fall into each other laughing as we stumble off the stage.

* * *

Like an actress meeting her cues, I learn to respond.

Bodies like mine are written as plot devices. Bodies like mine are used as warnings to little girls. Bodies like mine are posted and projected on screens and murky corners of the Internet to be shown as secrets, jokes, fetishes. And, because fatphobia is one of the only acceptable forms of prejudice (Hartley, 2001), I am expected to laugh along. I am expected to not get upset.

I'm sitting on the living room floor of the apartment belonging to my best friend of about twelve years. She passes a blown-glass bulb filled with water to her boyfriend, who draws smoke from it, and she points to a place in my script. It's our second year of college and our director has allowed us to co-direct an entire show for the semester. Most of our nights are spent like this, laughing with each other, scribbling stage directions in our ratty scripts, swapping ideas. I write in my script by the glowing light of their muted television whereon Daniel Tosh is presenting a YouTube clip of a fat woman falling off of a table. What was it about her? I think. Why is she the butt of the joke? Anyone else and it'd end up on America's Funniest Home Videos. But add her size to the mix and it's a three-minute fat joke special on Comedy Central. I feel eyes on me and I glance toward my friend and her boyfriend. There's a long pause, and I realize that they are waiting for me to laugh. And so... I laugh. The tension is sourly lifted and they laugh, too.

The same friend who stayed up with me my first week of college as I cried over getting cast (yet again) as an aggressive ugly fat woman in the play, the same friend who watched me struggle with eating disorder after eating disorder in high school, the same friend who held me tight during my panic attacks in the junior high bathroom after being teased by the boys on the tennis team, was begging me to laugh along to a joke where I was the punchline.

There are excuses I could make for this moment. It's late, we're high, it's just Daniel Tosh. But these moments add up, and I realize that I am an actress meeting her cue. My laughter, though delayed, is part of a script from which I cannot deviate. Through day in and day out rehearsals, these delays become shorter and shorter. I grow better at my craft.

She unmutes the television and we continue to watch.

* * *

After auditions, the director pulls me aside and speaks to me in a low voice. "It was funny what you and Paula did up there," she says. "But I think you can actually do it. I think you could be Alice." I stare at her, wondering if she is continuing the joke I set up. She meets my gaze and does not break. The thought that had once seemed laughable now seems reachable and I am frozen. I think ahead to opening night, where I imagine the long, frivolous curtain call of which I am the center. I step off the stage in my Alice dress and meet a long line of little girls who beg for a hug or a picture or just one autograph, please? This idea holds me tightly.

By this time, I had been involved in the program for a while and my list of roles could be summarized in grunts and motherly sighs. I could barely imagine taking on the role of a character that matched both my age and gender. There are no such roles out there for me, for girls like me. Even *Hairspray's* Tracy Turnblad, one of the only roles on Broadway tailored specifically for a fat woman, requires a daily exercise routine.

The role of Alice, I knew, was not made for me, but I would take it graciously.

I agree to the callbacks on the condition that I take it seriously and I float home.

* * *

Like an actress stepping onto the stage, I learn to perform.

Sometimes I feel as if my dresses don't have enough flowers on them.

My wardrobe is a feminine Wonderland, with tights of all colors stacked in rows in my top dresser drawer and dresses and skirts of all kinds hanging from the metal hangers in my closet. My favorite one, a black dress that I often pair with blue tights or a scarf, hugs me in all the right places. It smooths out my rolls and the sleeves are long enough to hide my upper-arms. When I wear it, I feel like I am supposed to feel when wearing a dress; I feel like a girl.

When I come to the quiet conclusion that I am queer, my want to wear this costume fades. My body and queerness force me a handicap in which I am defaulted as masculine (LaBesco, 2004). The identity that I have taken starts to fog the way I think I should be performing. If I am queer, should I want to wear this? If I am really queer, would I?

There are days where I am thankful for this dress. I am thankful that it allows me to easily step into my role without me wondering if any part of me is "giving away" my identity that I have been taught to be ashamed of. At the same time, I wonder if my dresses are enough. Enough to cover what I am hiding. Maybe I should spend more time on my hair, or invest in some makeup. Maybe it would help if these dresses had more damn flowers on them, or if I wore a fucking bonnet. Without such a costume, it would be especially hard to perform femininity as a fat woman. I, like Susan Bordo (1989), see my body as a site of struggle. I know that a woman is defined by her weight, and that "being small and taking up as little space as possible" is part of my role as a girl (McKinley, 1999, p. 99). Knowing that I am not only unsuccessfully performing my gender, but also unsuccessfully performing my sexuality, I feel trapped. I find myself subscribing to harmful ideals that I would never actively acknowledge in the context of anyone else. I give myself rules and dress codes and strictures that guide me on how I should behave and perform. I try to unlearn them. To rewind. But the same parts of me that yearn for lead roles in plays about docile women remind me that it's easier to follow these rules. It's easier to shut up.

* * *

There's buzz around the drama room that the director has narrowed her choice for Alice. Each reaction, I overhear, is the same: An incredulous *"Her?"* There's no part of me that feels that these reactions are rude, or even unwarranted, but somehow I still feel like I'm being openly mocked. The other potential Alice, thin and fair with her blonde hair in waves down to her stomach, rocks back and forth on her heels nervously. I sense that her nerves do not come from whether or not I will do better than her, but whether or not she will lose to someone like me.

Suddenly the prospect of being a leading lady feels more like being a prop.

* * *

Like an actress learning her lines, I learn to apologize.

I rehearse often. Many of my sentences begin and end with sorries, and frequently I apologize for taking up any inordinate amount of space (which, with this body, is easy to do).

I find this rhetoric seeping into private sectors of my life. I offer sorries where sorries are not needed nor heard, and I begin demanding them from myself when I make simple mistakes. My panic attacks, aggressive and cold, far overstay their welcome as I scold myself for letting them in the door. The sorries do not stop. I am an actress glued to the stage, repeating the same line with different dynamics and blocking, unable to please my director.

It is dark, and it is bright.

He kisses me deeply and reaches for the edges of my shirt. I stop him and explain to him hesitantly and slowly. "No one's ever seen me naked," I say, wide-eyed, ruefully. He kisses me again and murmurs through deep breaths that he doesn't care. He doesn't care, he loves me, it's okay, he wants me to take my time, but he doesn't care, it's okay, he loves me, no matter what, no matter what, he loves me. I take off my clothes and all I can think of is how I might not be enough for him.

It is dark, and it is bright.

He looks at me for the first time and I am bared and cold. He holds me and offers small, sweet kisses where I allow and waits until I am ready.

"I'm sorry," I say. "I'm sorry, I'm sorry, I'm sorry."

* * *

When I lost my fiftieth pound, I had never seen my mother so happy.

Later, I would look into the mirror and see another person.

* * *

When I ask my director to reconsider my placement as Alice, I am met with disappointment. I know that she so badly wanted to make a statement, but I am not willing to *be* that statement.

The cast list is posted and I am relieved to see my name under the Red Queen's. There are so many parts of me that feel wrong about this. Despite my not wanting to be used as an object, I still feel like I'm being used as one. I'm reaffirming everything there is to say about fat bodies. That we are meant to be villains. That we are meant to be hated. I understand very quickly that there was never any winning in this situation. I was made into a statement either way.

I will come to learn in my cumulative years of theatre that I will never play an Alice. And, as I will also come to learn, I will never again *want* to be an Alice. My time is better spent not dreaming about playing boring, meek women and fighting to encourage scripts that create three-dimensional women with much more to say than hums and haws, and much more to do than provide men with motives. I will

153

learn that I find more comfort off the stage, working to cheer on scripts that demolish tropes like Alice's *and* tropes like the Red Queen's, and actively support scripts that elevate the voices, and bodies, of all women. And eventually, I will come to learn that girls like me are far more than the roles they are cast into.

* * *

Like an actress, I learn that the show must go on. I understand that I am policed and that I am monitored. I am held to stricter standards, seen under brighter spotlights. But when I am off the stage, I shine brighter.

I have learned, through stage and sound, that this body is not my own. It does not belong to me. It belongs to the stage, to the performance, to the audience, to the players, to the lights. This body is not my own, but I, alone, am not my body.

REFERENCES

Bacon, L. (2008). *Health at every size: The surprising truth about your weight*. Dallas, TX: BenBella Books.

Bordo, S. R. (1989). The body and the reproduction of femininity: A feminist appropriation of Foucalt. In A. M. Jaggar & S. R. Bordo (Eds.), *Gender/body/knowledge/feminist reconstructions of being a knowing* (pp. 16–33). New Brunswick, NJ: Rutgers University Press.

Hartley, C. (2001). Letting ourselves go: Making room for the fat body in feminist scholarship. In J. E. Braziel & K. LeBesco (Eds.), *Bodies out of bounds: Fatness and transgression* (pp. 60–73). Berkeley: University of California Press.

LeBesco, K. (2004). *Revolting bodies? The struggle to redefine fat identity*. Boston: University of Massachusetts Press.

McKinley, N. (1999). Ideal weight/ideal women: Society constructs the female. In J. Sobal & D. Maurer (Eds.), *Weighty issues: Fatness and thinness as social problems* (pp. 97–115). New York, NY: Aldine De Gruyter.

Wilchins, R. A. (1997). *Read my lips: Sexual subversion and the end of gender*. Milford, CT: Firebrand Books.

Wiley, R. (2013, August 17). *10 honest thoughts on being loved by a skinny boy*. Retrieved from https://www.youtube.com/watch?v=tRFOTqTicvY

Mindy Ralston
Department of Communication
Angelo State University

DAVID PURNELL

16. THERE IS NO HOME LIKE PLACE

LOSS OF CONNECTIONS

I am a young boy. I love going to visit my grandparents. I often find myself sitting in my grandpa's forest green leather chair with its wooden claw armrests. Sitting in this chair, I close my eyes as I envision my grandpa doing the same. I sit in the chair naked with the fan blowing on me just as my grandfather did. There is no air conditioning, and the summer heat is unbearable. The fan cools me down. This is my grandfather's chair. He picked the green leather; he tooled the wooden claw armrests. Though he made this chair, this is my chair, too. It belongs to me. I know this chair; this chair knows me. It knows my body. As a child I cannot articulate it. I simply know that when I am sitting naked in this large leather chair with the fan blowing on me, this is where I belong. I smile.

* * *

Milligan (1998) theorizes that interaction fosters attachment to place. As she states, "Place attachment is significantly based on the meaningfulness of the interaction itself (which then imbues a site with meaning), not on the inherent meaningfulness of the place in which it occurs" (p. 28). Reflecting on this statement, I realize that my first attachment to place was not my grandparents' house, but instead, the act of sitting in that forest green leather chair with its wooden claw armrests. This emotional link of place attachment affectively connects the physical environment to self-conceptualizations (Kyle, Mowen, & Tarrant, 2004). In other words, the act of sitting in the forest green leather chair with its wooden claw armrests provided a sense of connection that went beyond the security of the space of my grandparents' house. While *space* is abstract, *place* is concrete, tangible, and imbued with meaning by the interactions that take place in it (Relph, 1976). Place matters (Gieryn, 2000); place connects meanings to the storying of our lived experience.

Stories link us to our past, and they give us the opportunity to reflexively learn and grow toward a better understanding of the future. This experience brings us to appreciate place and prevent the disappearance of place from our lives. The connections to personal experiences begin meaningful conversations (see Ellis & Bochner, 2000). These conversations keep the importance of place prominent in our thinking. Placelessness creates not only a loss of affect and connection, but it also contributes to a loss of meaning associated with the experience and history (Hayden 1995; Kunstler, 1993; Relph, 1976).

S. L. Pensoneau-Conway et al. (Eds.), Doing Autoethnography, 155–162.
© *2017 Sense Publishers. All rights reserved.*

* * *

After the death of my grandfather, the family farm is sold. We move into a new townhome with new furniture and a new car. Besides the absence of Grandpa's forest green leather chair with the wooden claw armrests, I lose my connection to home. The quick change in my environment disrupts my attachment of what it means to have a home. Within the first year of trying to adjust to the move, my parents separate and eventually divorce. One day I am living in our new house, and the next night I am sleeping in the basement of the home of a close friend of my mother's. This is my first experience with placelessness. We have shelter, but no house that contains *our* belongings.

We eventually move to an apartment on the other side of town. My sense of placelessness continues in our new accommodations due to the lost relationships of both my parents. My father is a man who rarely makes an appearance in the lives of his three children after the divorce. My mother is a woman who has little work history prior to the divorce and has to work two fulltime, minimum wage jobs to provide for her children. We have shelter, but there is no connection—no sense of place. Place makes the difference between a house and a home, a neighborhood and a community. Moving into a house does not make it your home any more than moving into a neighborhood makes it your community. A sense of place is cultivated, nurtured, and matures over time (Tilley, 1994).

* * *

Places carry meaning because they are given meaning. According to Seamon and Sowers (2008), a sense of place cannot exist without an attachment made to it, which is usually strong and lifelong. The concept of place refers to the subjective experience of interaction with the physical world. Place also encompasses the memories associated with it, which enforce our connection to or disassociation from place. The experience of connecting prevents the disappearance of place from our lives and, perhaps more importantly, shows us the value of place.

What makes this work particularly unique is my orientation to the process of "place attachment," one that reflects upon my lived experiences. For this reason, I use personal narratives to paint a more evocative and intimate picture of place attachment and placelessness.

I turn to a reflection of lived experience—a journey of loss, of searching, of finding. Through this journey, I move from my inward self to an outward expression (Denzin, 1997). I want the reader to take this journey with me and see the connection to place that I had lost and then found. I want to encourage the reader to examine his or her own internal feelings of connection through the similarities of our stories—an act of reflexivity. Through this process, I show the relationship between finding place and interactions that connect us to place.

All individuals, despite differences, have a common bond. That is, we can make connections to the lived experiences of others that go beyond just hearing and listening to those stories. It is the similarities in stories that allow readers to make connections to individual accounts and help to begin a conversation regarding the complexities of losing place as well as the struggle to find and maintain connections (Ellis & Bochner, 2000). These conversations involve personal inquiry (Bochner, 1994; Rosenwald & Ochberg, 1992) and discovery (Goodall, 2000), which in turn create the relationship between the connection that is possible through the personal experience of storying (see Ellis, 1991).

This autoethnographic chapter provides a way to understand the importance of the commonalities of life, which we often take for granted. The process of "reinhabiting the old in a way that will alter it" (Russo, 1994, p. 30) allows for connections through the stories that we tell and "brings readers into the scene" (Ellis, 2004, p. 142). This "bringing in" offers readers the ability to "tap" into the "emotion, perception, and appreciation" of the narrative (Dewey, 1984, p. 350).

* * *

Before my parents' divorce, they fight often, making silence a rare and desired commodity. Eventually, fear is the only connection I have to our home. My father's constant yelling fills the house. Needing an escape, I spend most of my days outside—daydreaming into oblivion. If the weather refuses to accommodate, I hide beside the long couch in the living room. The small space between the wall and the end of the couch becomes my refuge when the vastness of being outside can't serve as my escape. Even before the divorce, I was "placeless" due to a lack of connection in our new house. We were a group of people occupying a building—not a family. My father made this even more clear to me when he kicked my older brother out for being gay (Purnell, 2013).

The next morning, my sense of placelessness deepened when I found a poem that my older brother had written the night he was kicked out of the house. I have kept the words of this poem with me all these years:

Here I am, but where is here?
Nothing is definite; nothing is clear.
All packed and ready to go.
Heading where, I do not know.
—Harold L. Purnell, Jr.

I cry over the words as I think of my brother—his life, his death,[1] his sense of placelessness. We were never what I would call close. We never hung out together. He was never the protector that older brothers can become. A connection, however, links us beyond his death. We both have shared a strong sense of placelessness— both haunted by a loss of place. Loss, like that forest green leather chair with the wooden claw armrests, knows me and fought to find a place in my life.

TRYING TO FIND CONNECTIONS

As research in studies of places such as home and childhood environments developed, researchers began to pay attention to issues involving relocation and changing family structures, making emotions more salient regarding connections to

157

place (Altman & Setha, 1992). As stated earlier, however, connections develop over time and depend on the interactions that occur.

As a teenager, school quickly becomes my sense of security. I want to be within its walls as much as possible. I escape the feeling of abandonment and replace the security of family with the protection of brick and mortar. I become withdrawn. It is the security of the building itself as an alternative space from the residence of my family that connected me to school. It is never relationships with my peers; I never develop close bonds with my classmates nor establish a network of relational support that I was seeking and wanting. For three years, my connection to the brick and mortar of school and my focus on my studies keeps me grounded. School gives me a sense of place, but graduation takes that (mis)connection away. I refer to this as a misconnection as it was never a healthy connection. I drift in and out of brief moments of pretending to make connection during high school, but the truth is that I do not recall a connection of any kind during those years.

SEARCHING

My journey of trying to find place took me to many locations, but three stand out as significant: Atlanta, Georgia; Long Beach, California via San Diego; and Tampa, Florida. In Atlanta, I begin to focus on who I am as I struggle with trying to create connection to place. I am still lost, still putting on a face "to meet the faces that you meet" (Eliot, 2015). At this point, I have moved often and never allowed myself to develop connections. Being placeless is easier in that emotions are removed. I interact with others, but I make no effort to interact with the same group consistently. I join a bowling league in Atlanta to pass time. The weekly encounters begin to cultivate a connection, though not strong enough to create an attachment to the league members. As a young man trying to find a sense of place, Atlanta was not the best choice for me. I retreated, scared to expose myself and be vulnerable. The bowling league was outgoing and "family" oriented. However, this type of inclusion was not something I had known since I was eight. It scared me that others were interacting in a way that made me think I could become a part of a strong circle of friends. I shut down and preclude the interactions from coalescing into a sense of belonging. Silent and withdrawn, I remain placeless...by choice.

I have little recollection of the words spoken during my time of chosen placelessness: the lack of dialogue throughout this account is purposeful. Relph (1976) and Hayden (1995) argue that placelessness takes away our memories associated with place, which I find to be true in my own experiences. Sure, things happen each day, but they bring no connection and no real memory of place.

While living in Atlanta, I take a road trip to San Diego. I always wanted to go to San Diego as I was born there. My family moved back to the East Coast shortly after my birth. I have no childhood memories associated with the place, but I am connected—aren't I? I love my visit to California. I love it so much I stay.

"Scott?

"Yeah."

"David here. I hate to do this to you and the other guys, but I'm moving out."

"When?"

"Now."

"Now?"

"I know it's crazy, but I'm not coming back. Sell my stuff, give it away, I don't care. Keep whatever money you can get for my things to help with the rent. I'm sorry to do this to you, but I can't come back. I need to leave Atlanta."

"Good luck to you."

"Thanks, man."

In Atlanta, I had started working in LASIK eye surgery assisting doctors with the procedure. I figure I won't have too difficult a time finding a job in San Diego. In the interim, I need some quick cash. I have just over $20 to my name, a credit card that is almost maxed out, and a car. Selling the car isn't an option. Perhaps the move was not the best idea. With no real plan, I walk into a bar and decided to get drunk and worry about tomorrow … well … tomorrow. I hear two men arguing in the back of the building. I can't make out the argument except for the last two words.

"You're fired!"

A man storms out, and I walk over to the other man.

"You in need of a bartender?"

"You know how to tend bar?"

"Absolutely!" I lied.

"Can you start today?"

"I can start right now."

"You're hired."

Jay, the owner, shows me around, gives me a set of keys, leaves the bar, and I begin my job at The Hole.[2] For two weeks, I sleep on the pool table, but that becomes too risky, as I can be fired if caught. Still short on money for required deposits and rent, I stay out all night after work then get an "early check-in" at a cheap motel. This allows me time to sleep before going to work; I then return to the hotel immediately after work and sleep some more until the noon checkout time. Every other day, I rotate between three motels until I save enough money to afford the initial deposits and rent to move into my own apartment.

San Diego isn't much different than Atlanta. It's just another placeless place for me, and I soon find myself falling into old habits of avoiding getting too close; I continue to fear being vulnerable and allowing others to know me. I need to make connections, but I find myself leaving again. I was hired for a short-lived LASIK position in too-expensive Newport Beach, California, so I move to Long Beach.

I meet some wonderful people in Long Beach, people I still keep in contact with. This is a first. I don't have friends that I can go visit up to this point. I give leagues a shot again, joining a bowling league, a dart league, and two beach volleyball leagues. This could be my connection to place I've been searching for. Then my older brother shows up on my front stoop; he tells me he has AIDS. I care for him until I get to the point of needing assistance. I make the difficult decision to leave Long Beach and return to Virginia; I have to help my brother.

After my brother's death, there's no reason for me to stay in Virginia. I go back to California, but I've been away for over a year. Things aren't the same. I thought I could just step in at the point where I left, but my absence changes my relationships there. I still love Long Beach, still have a sentimental connection of place, but it never becomes the strong connection I had before I left for Virginia. Instead of trying to reconnect with what I had, I focus on my career, which takes me to Denver, Colorado. The position I receive is 100% travel taking me all over the USA, and eventually all over the world. Due to the travel, I'm never around long enough make the connection to place I'm still seeking. The travel was a great experience, but connections are difficult when the longest one stays "home" is nine days in a year. I suppose my position was perfect for a person experiencing placelessness. However, I've now reached a point where I want to find the connection and interactions that will create a lifelong attachment to place. It's not until my move to Tampa, Florida that I find a connection to *place*.

* * *

The connections that are strengthened over time as I remain in the Seminole Heights neighborhood of Tampa create a network of close friendships that have been the longest lasting relationships-of-choice in my life. These are not vague and ambiguous geographical (Gravenkemper, 2007), political (Bowler, 1991), or theoretical (Bickford, 1996; Epstein, 2006) friendships, but rather bonded friendships (Rawlins, 2009; Tillmann-Healy, 2001). Spencer and Pahl (2006) affirm that friendship bonds create an emotionally-close environment free from judgment. This freedom from judgment allows me to finally be vulnerable. The close bonds break down my defenses and create not only strong attachments to place, but also close bonds of friendship that have become familial.

FINDING PLACE THROUGH CONNECTIONS

I finally arrive home; I have a connection to place. The sense of place doesn't simply appear; it strengthens with each passing day. Throughout my solitary existence in placeless places, I had seen myself as taking up space in the world. In order to adjust, I conformed to the expectations of others (Goffman, 1959). However, in finding a sense of place, I participate in and create my own story.

Attachment, interaction, reciprocity, and belonging all develop over time—forged through bonds of trust. The moving from place to place resulted in a lack of understanding of the importance of place. I think I had to experience placelessness to know the sense of place that I now have among my chosen family (Spencer & Pahl, 2006). This connection affords me the comfort and security I had that first day I sat in my grandfather's forest green leather chair with its wooden claw armrests. I may not have Grandpa's chair, but I am home.

* * *

I am not trying to offer a grand narrative of discovery. Instead I offer the fluid nature of connecting, and how we traverse in and out of these connections. I am trying to offer the contradiction of finding place, but not always fitting in. Through my personal experience and the (re)construction of my narrative, I am telling one story. However, my story is not the only story. Readers can apply events given to reflect on other aspects or problems of placelessness to which they can develop meaning and perhaps even change. Eisner (1991) makes it clear that for qualitative works to be helpful to the reader, the work must bring the reader to an understanding, make future applications of the reading, and serve as a guide for the reader to notice aspects of life that may go unnoticed.

Interactions with and within place(s) allow us the ability to apply a sense of connection/belonging (Peace, Holland, & Kellaher, 2005). If we do not make connections, the sense of placelessness can render one's perception of self as invisible, so we do not know who or what we are. I think Wendell Berry rightly reminds us that "[i]f you don't know where you are, you don't know who you are" (cited in Stegner, 1992, p. 199). Connections to place are formed through interactions developed over time. These interactions influence attachment to and emotional involvement with place. My use of evocative autoethnography enables me to "bypass the representational problem by invoking an epistemology of emotion, moving the reader to feel the feelings of the other" (Denzin, 1997, p. 228). I employ the evocative approach by inviting others to share their standpoints as well as to see how connection to place is developed from a series of (mis)connections to a more salient attachment of place through interactions. As such, I operate from the vantage point of my lived experiences. The interpretations I have provided are contingent. Other researchers with different standpoints are likely to provide different interpretations, which I hope will inspire readers to share their narratives and begin a dialogue regarding placelessness and finding place.

NOTES

[1] Harold L. Purnell, Jr. died at the age of 34 from complications related to AIDS.
[2] A historical dive bar which changed ownership in July 2015. It is now called The Hole in the Wall.

REFERENCES

Altman, I., & Setha, M. L. (1992). *Place attachment.* New York, NY: Plenum Press.

Bickford, S. (1996). Beyond friendship: Aristotle on conflict, deliberation, and attention. *The Journal of Politics, 58,* 398–421. doi: 10.2307/2960232

Bochner, A. P. (1994). Perspectives on inquiry II: Theories and stories. In M. L. Knapp & G. R. Miller (Eds.), *Handbook of interpersonal communication* (2nd ed., pp. 21–41). Thousand Oaks, CA: Sage.

Bowler, S. (1991). Contextual models of politics: The political impact of friends and neighbours. *Political Geography Quarterly, 10*(2), 91–96. doi: 10.1016/0261-3794(90)90004-R

Denzin, N. K. (1997). *Interpretive ethnography: Ethnographic practices for the 21st century.* Thousand Oaks, CA: Sage.

Dewey, J. (1984). *The collected works of John Dewey: The later works, 1925–27* (Vol. 2, J. A. Boydston, Ed.). Carbondale: Southern Illinois University Press.

D. PURNELL

Eisner, E. (1991). *The enlightened eye: Qualitative inquiry and the enhancement of educational practice*. New York, NY: Macmillan.

Eliot, T. S. (2015) *The T. S. Eliot collection: Collected poems and essays*. e-publisher: Biblyiotech.

Ellis, C. (1991). Sociological introspection and emotional experience. *Symbolic Interaction, 14*, 23–50. doi: 10.1525/si.1991.14.1.23

Ellis, C. (2004). *The ethnographic I: A methodological novel about autoethnography*. Walnut Creek, CA: AltaMira Press.

Ellis, C., & Bochner, A. P. (2000). Autoethnography, personal narrative, reflexivity. In N. K. Denzin & Y. S. Lincoln (Eds.), *The handbook of qualitative research* (2nd ed., pp. 733–768). Thousand Oaks, CA: Sage.

Epstein, J. (2006). *Friendship: An expose*. New York, NY: Houghton Mifflin.

Gieryn, T. F. (2000). A space for place in sociology. *Annual Review of Sociology, 26*, 463–496.

Goffman, E. (1959). *Presentation of self in everyday life*. Garden City, NY: Doubleday Anchor Books.

Goodall, H. L., Jr. (2000). *Writing the new ethnography*. Walnut Creek, CA: AltaMira Press.

Gravenkemper, S. (2007). Building community in organizations: Principles of engagement. *Consulting Psychology Journal: Practice and Research, 59*(3), 203–208. doi: 10.1037/1065-9293.59.3.203

Hayden, D. (1995). *The power of place: Urban landscapes as public history*. Cambridge, MA: MIT Press.

Kunstler, J. H. (1993). *The geography of nowhere: The rise and decline of America's man-made landscape*. New York, NY: Simon & Schuster.

Kyle, G.T., Mowen, A.J., & Tarrant, M. (2004). Linking place preferences with place meaning: An examination of the relationship between place motivation and place attachment. *Journal of Environmental Psychology, 24*, 439–454. doi:10.1016/j.jenvp.2004.11.001

Milligan, M. J. (1998). Interactional past and potential: The social construction of place attachment. *Symbolic Interaction, 21*, 1–33. doi: 10.1525/si.1998.21.1.1

Peace, S., Holland C., & Kellaher, L. (2005). Making space for identity. In G. J. Andrews & D. R. Phillips (Eds.), *Ageing and place: Perspectives, policy and practice* (pp. 188–204). London, England: Routledge.

Purnell, D. (2013). Breathing back my life. *Journal of Loss and Trauma: International Perspectives on Stress and Coping, 18*(2), 91–102. doi: 10.1080/15325024.2012.679118

Relph, E. (1976). *Place and placelessness*. London, England: Pion.

Rawlins, W. (2009). *The compass of friendship: Narratives, identity, and dialogue*. Thousand Oaks, CA: Sage.

Rosenwald, G. C., & Ochberg, R. L. (Eds.). (1992). *Storied lives: The cultural politics of self-understanding*. New Haven, CT: Yale University Press.

Russo, M. (1994). *The female grotesque: Risk, excess, and modernity*. New York, NY: Routledge.

Seamon, D., & Sowers, J. (2008). Place and placelessness, Edward Relph. In P. Hubbard, R. Kitchen, & G. Vallentine (Eds.), *Key texts in human geography* (pp. 43–51). London, England: Sage.

Spencer, L., & Pahl, R. (2006). *Rethinking friendship: Hidden solidarities today*. Princeton, NJ: Princeton University Press.

Stegner, W. (1992). *Where the bluebird sings to the lemonade springs: Living and writing in the west*. New York, NY: Random House.

Tilley, C. (1994). *A phenomenology of landscape: Places, paths and monuments*. Oxford, England: Berg.

Tillmann-Healy, L. (2001). *Between gay and straight: Understanding friendship across sexual orientation*. Walnut Creek, CA: AltaMira Press.

David Purnell
Department of Liberal Studies
Mercer University

MOLLY WIANT CUMMINS

17. LEARNING TO CARE[1]

If I'm honest, I know what it means to have caring teachers. As a privileged (White, middle class, U.S. American) student who attended funded schools, I knew what it felt like to be cared for and to make connections with teachers. These positive experiences are what made the pain of moments of non-care that much more distressing. When I became a teacher, I realized I now held the possibility of caring or not caring for my own students. I needed critical care—the nexus of care theory and critical communication pedagogy (see Fassett & Warren, 2007)—to reflexively consider how I care. Cooks (2010) defines critical communication pedagogy (CCP) as "a space for self-reflexivity and critique in one's teaching and research .... CCP is critical pedagogy *in, of,* and *for* communication" (p. 295, emphasis in original). Critical care necessitates reflexively caring in pedagogical spaces; it requires investigating how power imbues how and for whom we care. Critical care asks me to consider how non-caring moments reify a system that privileges the mind and numbs or deadens the body and soul in the classroom.

In this chapter, I offer five moments of my pedagogical history. These stories are representative of my evolving understanding of how teachers do and do not care for students, as grounded in care theory. As I continue to learn from these moments, they influence my relationships with my own students.

I write this autoethnography in response to a call from Warren (2011), who argues that tracing our pasts helps elucidate what we believe and how we came to believe it. Warren encourages readers/pedagogues to consider what experiences we have had that inform our teaching philosophies. Specifically, Warren engages his own autoethnographic pedagogical history to explain, in part, how he developed an ethic of teaching in which he cares "deeply about what it means to encounter the student as a person, as a whole being that has a history, a story of how they too arrived in this pedagogical moment" (p. 140). By acknowledging that both he and his students bring histories into the present pedagogical moment, Warren embodies his belief in critical communication pedagogy. This is my autoethnographic experiment of mining my pedagogical history based on Warren's model.

GROUNDING IN CARE

Writing extensively on care as a moral act and orientation, Noddings (1984, 2005) frames care as an encounter between two parties: the *one-caring* and the *cared-for*. Both parties must contribute to the relationship in order for care to be complete. The one-caring sees the best possible self in the cared-for, and works with the

S. L. Pensoneau-Conway et al. (Eds.), Doing Autoethnography, 163–171.
© *2017 Sense Publishers. All rights reserved.*

cared-for in an effort to actualize that best self. The cared-for completes the caring relationship by responding with the "happy and confident pursuit" of their projects in addition to "occasional smiles, shared comments, appreciative gestures or eye contact that conveys understanding" to the one-caring (Noddings, 2007, p. 43).

Noddings helps me ground myself in pedagogical care, but I know I don't come to this understanding without experience. Caring teachers emphasize Noddings's (2005) call that teachers have a responsibility to help students develop the skill of caring. In other words, teachers should care for their students, but they should also work to teach their students how to care.

Moment One: A Grounding in Care

My high school senior year is particularly tough for me. I date someone whom a close friend likes. As a result, friends view me as manipulative, a backstabber, and call me "bitch" and "slut." Although I try to mend these friendships, many friends see this relationship as either a moment to support me or to recall every possible time they have felt jilted by me. They even consider forming a group called FOBMA (Fucked Over By Molly Association), a support group to air grievances about me. My friends draw battle lines.

During Mrs. Walsh's English class, on an especially rough day, a friend begins using the story of my new partner and the subsequent breakdown in friendships as an example. I feel ashamed of the situation, frustrated with myself that I have hurt people, and frustrated with friends who I read as vicious. I don't want to talk about the situation in front of classmates I don't trust; I fear I will be judged, and I think this is a situation that should only be between the friends directly involved. Exhausted by the relational struggles, I begin to cry. Sitting at my desk with tears streaming down my face, I look to Mrs. Walsh, hoping she will save me the embarrassment of having to explain the story to classmates. I look up to see that she, too, is crying. I can only assume it's out of compassion. As we both take tissues from the box she hands me, letting this moment permeate a room full of my classmates, I think I know her tears come from a big heart that wants what's best for all her students. She demonstrates in a simple emotional act that I matter, someone cares about me, and my struggles with my friends are felt. I don't remember her exact words, but her reaction to my situation offers visceral support in a moment of self-doubt. Through her tears, she shows a caring teacher.

While I don't believe teachers *must* cry with their students, I believe caring teachers embrace emotional aspects of classroom teaching; they don't deny the body is present and alive in the classroom. Mrs. Walsh's tears may have had nothing to do with me. Still, I choose to read her tears as an empathic response to my own, and it's my reading of her tears that matters. As Noddings (1984) makes clear, care is fulfilled in the receiver—what matters is I read her crying as care. For me, Mrs. Walsh embodies Camangian's (2010) notion that "teachers can nurture caring relationships with and among students by creating a curriculum of concern for their lives outside of the classroom, tapping into social emotions rarely shared in academic spaces" (p. 182). In this way, Mrs. Walsh engages with me by sharing my life in and out of class, sharing an emotional response often considered outside the realm of classroom decorum. Maybe what I most need in this moment has to be felt and not said. This moment with Mrs. Walsh teaches me the power of eros (Garrison, 2005, p. 94), allowing us to be "whole in the classroom" (hooks, 1994, p. 193). Mrs. Walsh embodied erotic passion that made space for our selves to be present in the classroom.

As I consider what this moment teaches me in relationship to my students, I find I can't ignore how my body reacts to them. I can trust my body's intuition as a way to form an empathic and humanizing response. Mrs. Walsh connects with me in a moment of care, and it serves as a reminder of how a simple gesture can make a big difference.

Moment Two: A Lesson in Writing

During my junior year of college, Dr. Piero offers a course on women in philosophy. I'm excited for the course and, through it, I meet scholars like bell hooks who change my life. At the beginning of the semester, Dr. Piero informs us that although all our work would be turned in to him, his graduate assistant, Kate, would grade it. Kate never attends class. Few of us ever even meet her.

For one of our written assignments, I work hard to fulfill the requirements, spending hours trying to complete it as well as I can. When I receive my assignment back, I'm a bit shocked at what I see. Written in Kate's purple ink is a "C." The grade surprises me because I'm unaccustomed to C's, but also because I can't understand, given the feedback, the reason for the grade. I notice her few suggestions throughout the paper, but I don't see any major errors. Even after reading her comments at the end, I wonder why my paper warrants a C. She suggests using different words and proofreading better, but then adds, "Otherwise, this is well-written, and you have an acceptable grasp of the concepts." Confused, I schedule an appointment to talk with her.

When I hand her my paper, she sees the C she has written on the front page. She looks at me with annoyance; perhaps because this is an Honors course, she makes an assumption as to why I've come to see her. She begins to read my paper and snaps, "Don't worry, you'll get your A!" I'm surprised. Although the grade admittedly bothers me, this isn't about "getting an A." I want to understand why I have earned a C in order to improve as a writer. As she scans my paper again, her tone eases. I ask questions about what I hadn't done well, and she counters by reiterating that what she has written makes sense as is. Because most of the class didn't fulfill the requirements of the assignment according to Dr. Piero's standards, we were all given the chance to revise our papers. The only comment I receive on my revised paper from Dr. Piero says, "Much improved." I still can't see where I've failed or succeeded previously to understand what I've improved. Even though I'm allowed to edit the paper for a better grade, I never forget feeling belittled.

I pause here to acknowledge that Kate's reaction may have had nothing to do with me. Still, this moment demonstrates the power Kate has in our relationship as well as the necessity of dialogue for care to occur between teachers and students.

Noddings (2005) explains dialogue as "the common search for understanding, empathy, or appreciation" (p. 23) and positions dialogue as a powerful way to teach care to students. But I don't get to experience dialogue to understand or dialogue that might have produced something greater than Kate's and my individuality (Simpson, 2008). I don't find myself positively changed by the interaction. Instead, I find little chance for dialogue. To be fair, this moment isn't only on Kate's shoulders; we both could have engaged one another differently.

This moment with Kate teaches me that caring teachers must do their best to avoid interacting with students in ways that preclude dialogue. It's the difference between caring *about* and caring *for* a student. While caring about demonstrates concern for someone else, caring for is actively working to positively affect someone else (Gay, 2010). Because anti-dialogical moments are all-too-common in educational experiences, it's imperative that teachers engage in an ethic of care that works with students to actualize the best possible self.

Moment Three: Valued Feedback

I meet Dr. John T. Warren the first day of my Master's orientation. He is young and energetic, with a sharp mind and quick wit. I learn so much from him during the few years I am blessed enough to call him my advisor, teacher, mentor, and friend. When I begin my Ph.D. program, I know that I want John to serve as my advisor again. I take "Critical Communication Pedagogy" with him my first semester as a Ph.D. student. It's a class, like others I have taken with him, that makes me think, learn, and grow by pushing me to more deeply consider issues we study. As challenging as they sometimes are, I walk away from his classes feeling I have worked hard and become a better person for it. I spend time making sure my final paper is one I can be proud of.

John's feedback on this paper encourages the budding scholar in me to keep pushing while helping me to see growth in my writing. With comments, thoughts, and suggestions throughout, his overall feedback ends with, "I'm just noting that I'm noticing the shift from M.A. to Ph.D. student and I'm very excited to see it. Kudos on pushing yourself and your ideas." John sees a better self for me, sees me working toward that better self, and encourages me to keep pushing toward that goal. He engages me through his feedback as one-caring (Noddings, 1984; 2005). John's words teach me the importance of honesty with students, as well as how far a little encouragement can go. I treasure these written words now in his very-present absence. He followed Rawlins' (2000) "truism," which claims teachers who care about their students take time to evaluate and comment on student work (p. 13). Partially because of this lesson, when my students turn in papers, I try to mark what I see as strengths in their writing to encourage them as John encouraged me toward a better self.

In all of his feedback, John takes my work seriously without lowering his standards (Gay, 2010; Rawlins, 2000). He shows me that teachers "who really care for students honor their humanity, hold them in high esteem, expect high performance from them, and use strategies to fulfill their expectations" (Gay, 2010,

p. 48). He teaches me how necessary it is for teachers to ask students to continue to do the difficult work of becoming better selves. In this way, John teaches me how to care authentically (Valenzuela, 1999, p. 61) for my students, inside and outside the classroom as one-caring. In other words, John demonstrated and embodied authentic care that highlighted a relationship of reciprocity between us.

Moment Four: Demanding Vulnerability

At first, I'm excited to take an anthropology class called "Theorizing the Body" because I think that the additional literature might further what I know about the body within communication. The feeling dissipates when, during the sixth week of class, the professor gives us verbal feedback about our proposals in front of our classmates—without warning and without us knowing what others are writing about. When he arrives at my project in his pile of papers, he makes a confused face and tells me—and the class—that he is disappointed by what I've proposed.

Initially, I want to write about embodied knowledge I gained through performance work, and had previously written about in another paper. I'm honest with my professor in the proposal, saying that I want to "revamp" this old paper. He declares, "Surely, coming all the way across campus, you could come up with a new idea." I feel he misunderstands my proposal to be that I'll simply turn in a paper I have previously written for another class. Even as I try to explain the miscommunication, he continues: "I've been so impressed by what you've said in class; surely you can come up with something new."

I feel like someone has sucked the air out of me, that all eyes are on me, and that there is a blinking neon sign above me that says, "disappointment." I'm astonished that this is actually happening, and I'm struck still in the moment, unsure of what to say in response. I already feel vulnerable about him publicizing our projects in front of classmates who haven't heard us describe our ideas. I feel humiliated as he tears apart my project, and no one is able to defend me, including myself. Try as I might, I can't seem to defend my work. He must be able to read the emotions on my face because he begins to backpedal: "Well, I guess the paper will be fine." I try to respond, "I don't want to write a paper you don't want to read." I eventually end the moment by asking if I should talk to him outside of class.

When I meet with him in his office, he lectures me for a half-hour about other topics. As he begins to talk about the class, he tells me that he feels he has to "walk on eggshells." After a few minutes, he decides it's probably inappropriate to share this with me. I couldn't agree more. When I try to return the conversation to what happened in class, he finally apologizes to me in a sweeping gesture, "Well, sorry if I offended you in class." After that, there's no further talk about what happened. I'm frustrated, but not shocked. Reflecting on the situation, I didn't ask him for more than that. I didn't have the courage to ask if we could more deeply consider the moment that happened in class, even as I expect him to offer a better apology.

He has become, for me, a symbol of pedagogy that makes students vulnerable without reciprocity, of professors who demand vulnerability by enacting authoritative power. Still, I have to wonder about the moment from his point of

167

view. Perhaps talking with me about his concerns for the class was his way of being vulnerable. Perhaps in that moment he was hoping that I might meet him as one-caring to process with him how to change the direction of the class. Perhaps hoping he'd engage in reciprocal vulnerability was asking too much of him.

Because care necessitates responsiveness from both the one-caring and the cared-for (Gay, 2010; Noddings, 1984, 2005), a relationship of care requires reciprocity. To enter into a relationship where care is possible requires vulnerability to openness, to allowing oneself to be seen and known (Palmer, 1993). If I had entered the moment as one-caring, open to the possibilities of reciprocal vulnerability, my experience of the conversation in this professor's office would have been different, which, ultimately, might have helped me differently understand the moment in his classroom. However, considering the power imbalance inherent in teacher-student relationships, it's difficult to feel that I should be anything but the cared-for in his office. Having a relationship not previously situated in trust and vulnerability impeded my entering his office open to the possibility of caring for him.

This experience teaches me to reflexively consider how I engage my students. It reminds me care is Freirean (1970/2000) praxis, as reflection and action upon the world in order to transform it. While I wish to enter relationships with my students in vulnerability and reciprocity, I must reflexively understand that I will sometimes fall short of this goal. I understand this moment now as a falling-short when care was not completed, as a moment where vulnerability was miscommunicated. As I move forward in my own pedagogical relationships, I take this moment as a painfully learned lesson of the importance of entering in care.

Moment Five: Dialoguing Vulnerability

My first interactions with Dr. Sandy Pensoneau-Conway come in the "Dialogue and Pedagogy" class she teaches. She allows us to choose what assignments might individually be beneficial for us as part of her commitment to critical communication pedagogy. For a semester-long project, I want to attempt letter-writing in a class centered on dialogue. When I meet with Sandy to propose the idea of writing letters with me, she immediately agrees. For some reason, this surprises me. I don't expect that she'll be so willing to take on this project. Still, I'm elated that this new professor willingly invests in me and my project.

Throughout the semester, our dialogical letter-writing space becomes a place for me/us to vent, to work through struggles, and to celebrate, knowing there's someone who'll respond with empathy and encouragement to whatever I/we write. I write a letter to Sandy explaining my experience of the event in Moment Four. While others had listened to the story and tried to offer their advice about how to handle the situation, Sandy offers kindness, empathy to my hurt and frustration, and support that no one else could.

She writes an elegant, eloquent, time-intensive response for which I'll be forever grateful (see Pensoneau-Conway & Wiant Cummins, 2016). She helps me consider the experience through theory, and name my experience as violent by connecting to Freire (1970/2000) that violence interferes "with the individual's ontological and historical vocation to be more fully human" (p. 55). Sandy's able to articulate different layers of this experience, even pointing out how my professor's and my own "dialogue" was useless because, as she writes,

> He embodied his role as *professor*, as one who professes rather than embodying that respecification of the teacher-student relationship .... He could not live up to the call for reflexivity, the call to acknowledge his own unfinishedness, the call that he remain vulnerable and not have all the answers.

Near the end of her letter, Sandy also comments that she knows I can take this experience and "turn what he did into a more compassionate response in the sense of how you respond to others."

Sandy's willingness to engage with my project suggests that she cares about me as a student, she cares about my future success, and she is willing to help me work toward that. I know that her vulnerability with me came from care because she offers the space of our letters as a place where we can engage one another as fully human (Freire, 1970/2000; hooks, 1994). She doesn't keep a distant, "teacher-only" perspective. Rather, she enters the space open about her struggles as a fellow human in the world. This reciprocal vulnerability allows me to be both the cared-for and the one-caring in our relationship, effectively teaching me how to better engage my own students in care. Sandy shows me that pedagogues who want the utmost from their students are willing to invest the energy to help students feel that their work matters (Gay, 2010). This space of vulnerability becomes a place where we can grow, learn, and care together.

Sandy embodies in these letters what Noddings (2005) has identified: the need for teachers to not only engage in care with their students, but to help their students learn to care as well. Rawlins (2000) argues for care that is conveyed through teacher-student friendship, and calls for dialogue that is at the center of sharing knowledge. By engaging me in dialogic, reciprocal vulnerability, Sandy helps me see that dialogue allows us to "create richer and more complete knowledge" (Simpson, 2008, p. 140) together. As she enters this dialogic space with me, Sandy also demonstrates care by becoming involved in my life, viewing teaching and learning holistically (Gay, 2010).

CARE THROUGH EXPERIENCE

If autoethnography is about the meanings we attach to our experiences (Ellis & Bochner, 2000), I understand that the way I narrate these stories influences how they are read by the reader and how they continue to influence me. As representative examples of a (privileged) student's experiences, the knowledge from and connections to my stories that readers make influence how we interact with our students. Even as I reflexively reconsider these moments, I don't feel less touched by them—positively or negatively. These feelings aren't isolated to one story. To reflexively reconsider these stories means I must attempt to understand

169

the layers of meaning present in each. I try to understand that what I read as non-care may have felt like an attempt at care from my instructors' points of view. The emotions that I continue to experience with each of them remind me why these are some of the most significant moments of my pedagogical history. Furthermore, these moments matter because they ultimately affect how I treat my students, which, in turn, affects my students' pedagogical histories.

As I write the positive moments in which I experience care, I reflect on Calafell's (2007) words that "these small acts of love mean so much. These small acts of love sustain us" (p. 435). When I consider these moments, I realize that even in their complexity, they are small. I can imagine that these teachers, being the wonderful people they are, may not connect the deep significance to these moments in the same way I do. However, like Griffin (2012), I believe these teachers "beckoned me into a compassionate space and validated my humanity which left me ready, willing, and able to communicatively do the same" (p. 218). While these moments may have been routine responses to students for these particular teachers, they meant the world to me. These moments have strengthened my pedagogy, and helped me learn how to better respond to students in kind.

Critical communication pedagogues not only recognize the inequities that exist in society; they seek to bring about possibilities for the future (Fassett & Warren, 2007). These moments help me believe in the power of care in education as a possibility for bringing about a better future. Critical care recognizes the complexity of humanness. If we don't work to actively and critically care for our students in ways that acknowledge their full humanity in the classroom, we risk creating spaces where they don't feel care at all, a dehumanizing pedagogy where students are disengaged and disenchanted (Freire, 1970/2000). As critical communication pedagogues who are committed to making the world more equitable through our pedagogy, examining the moments in our own lives where we have experienced non-care and where we have felt cared-for is vital to caring for our own students. Further, caring about our students influences their possibilities for success (Gay, 2010).

When we don't actively try to grow in our caring for students, we risk falling into the trap of not-caring, of becoming another classroom in which students feel like numbers. We risk becoming a moment in a student's pedagogical history that is identified with non-care, rather than a moment that is hopeful in its remembering when students experience moments of care (e.g., dialogue or reciprocal vulnerability). Students who leave our classrooms fulfilled by care become those who understand that the world and the classroom, even with their limitations, remain spaces of possibility and hope (hooks, 1994). It is in the space of possibility that our future for a better world awaits.

NOTE

[1]   Throughout this chapter, I use the real names of my caring teachers with permission, although I name John T. Warren without his explicit permission due to his death. I name these teachers to

honor their pedagogical care as I believe teachers rarely receive credit or gratitude when they have impacted so many lives. For the moments of non-care, I use pseudonyms to protect the teachers.

REFERENCES

Calafell, B. M. (2007). Mentoring and love: An open letter. *Cultural Studies ⇔ Critical Methodologies, 7*, 425–441. doi: 10.1177/1532708607305123

Camangian, P. (2010). Starting with self: Teaching autoethnography to foster critically caring literacies. *Research in the Teaching of English, 45*, 179–204. doi: 10.2307/40997089

Cooks, L. (2010). The (critical) pedagogy of communication and the (critical) communication of pedagogy. In D. L. Fassett & J. T. Warren (Eds.), *Handbook of communication and instruction* (pp. 293–314). Thousand Oaks, CA: Sage.

Ellis, C., & Bochner, A. P. (2000). Autoethnography, personal narrative, reflexivity: Researcher as subject. In N. K. Denzin & Y. S. Lincoln (Eds.), *Handbook of qualitative research* (2nd ed., pp. 733–768). Thousand Oaks, CA: Sage.

Fassett, D. L., & Warren, J. T. (2007). *Critical communication pedagogy.* Thousand Oaks, CA: Sage.

Freire, P. (2000). *Pedagogy of the oppressed* (M. B. Ramos, Trans.). New York, NY: Continuum. (Original work published 1970)

Garrison, J. (2005). Ameliorating violence in dialogues across differences: The role of eros and lógos. In M. Boler (Ed.), *Democratic dialogue in education: Troubling speech, disturbing silence* (pp. 89–103). New York, NY: Peter Lang.

Gay, G. (2010). *Culturally responsive teaching: Theory, research, and practice* (2nd ed.). New York, NY: Teachers College.

Griffin, R. A. (2012). Navigating the politics of identity/identities and exploring the promise of critical love. In N. Bardhan & M. P. Orbe (Eds.), *Identity research and communication: Intercultural reflections and future directions* (pp. 207–221). Lanham, MD: Lexington.

hooks, b. (1994). *Teaching to transgress: Education as the practice of freedom.* New York, NY: Routledge.

Noddings, N. (1984). *Caring: A feminine approach to ethics and moral education.* Berkeley, CA: University of California Press.

Noddings, N. (2005). *The challenge to care in schools: An alternative approach to education.* New York, NY: Teachers College.

Noddings, N. (2007). Caring as relation and virtue in teaching. In R. L. Walker & P. J. Ivanhoe (Eds.), *Working virtue: Virtue ethics and contemporary moral problems* (pp. 41–60). New York, NY: Clarendon.

Palmer, P. J. (1993). *To know as we are known: Education as a spiritual journey.* New York, NY: Harper One.

Pensoneau-Conway, S. L., & Wiant Cummins, M. (2016). Towards epistolary dialogue. *Critical Education, 7*(10). http://ices.library.ubc.ca/index.phb/criticaled/article/view/186128/185373

Rawlins, W. K. (2000). Teaching as a mode of friendship. *Communication Theory, 10*, 5–26. doi: 10.1111/j.1468-2885.2000.tb00176.x

Simpson, J. L. (2008). The color-blind double bind: Whiteness and the (im)possibility of dialogue. *Communication Theory, 18*, 139–159. doi:10.1111/j.1468-2885.2007.00317.x

Valenzuela, A. (1999). *Subtractive schooling: U.S.-Mexican youth and the politics of caring.* Albany, NY: State University of New York Press.

Warren, J. T. (2011). Reflexive teaching: Toward critical autoethnographic practices of/in/on pedagogy. *Cultural Studies ⇔ Critical Methodologies, 11*, 139–144. doi: 10.1177/1532708611401332

Molly Wiant Cummins
Independent Scholar

IGOR VINICIUS LIMA VALENTIM

18. ACADEMIC PIMPING

Is Anyone Afraid of Researching Academic Relationships?

UNIVERSITIES, SUBJECTIVITIES AND ACADEMIC RELATIONSHIPS

We live in and are part of a capitalist logic that is centered on the production of behaviors and aims to naturalize in ourselves some values instead of others. Values, ways of thinking, feeling, seeing oneself, and establishing relationships with others are all (re)produced in/with universities. The university context produces subjectivities, which are here understood as the ways subjects make experience of themselves (Foucault, 1999).

Guattari and Rolnik (2007, p. 33) identify the central position occupied by subjectivity as a subjectivity with a "machinical" nature. That is, it is fabricated, modeled, received, consumed. It is important to reflect on the ways these modes or styles of living and existing are produced. "[T]he production of modes of existence or lifestyles" is what Deleuze (1992, p. 142) names as subjectivation. There are several subjectivity production "machines," like companies and media, just to cite two examples. And universities function as an increasingly important machine.

Among the few classic theorists who described aspects related to the importance of academic relationships, Weber (1989) points out that the scientist is part of a "science factory" in which the passion and personalities of professors can influence academic beginners. Bourdieu (1984) states that the scientific field is constituted by forces that aim for either the conservation or transformation of the *status quo*. The interesting aspect here is that knowledge amounts to just a part of the numerous productions that take place in Academia.

Despite their differences, most higher education undergraduate courses increasingly prepare human beings to dream about winning and thriving in an individualistic and wild "market" that preaches values which create and deepen misery, competition, and social unfairness. As I consider that "subjective forces, especially those of knowledge and creation" fundamentally feed the capitalist regime (Rolnik, 2006a, pp. 13–14), it seems to be difficult not to admit the important role universities play in contemporary societies.

While some values spread across all dimensions of our lives and get naturalized by most of us, to what extent can they be stimulated by/in the relations established between academics? Uberti (2006, p. 110) suggests that we need to think about what problems Education has historically answered and the ones it needs to answer now. She considers it a task of us all to fight for a fairer and more humane world.

S. L. Pensoneau-Conway et al. (Eds.), Doing Autoethnography, 173–185.
© *2017 Sense Publishers. All rights reserved.*

In academic relations, bodies, souls, spirits, and minds of everybody are objects of experience (Ferreira, 1996). It is possible to consider that Pedagogy is implicated in the fabrication of human beings as it exerts "a type of power that excludes, impedes, limits, prohibits, imposes; or that impels, incites, induces, stimulates, favors and extends" individuals' possibilities of being one way or another and of acting in one or other direction (Foucault, 1995; Garcia, 2001). What subjectivities are produced in/by academic relations and what values are stimulated and naturalized in/by these relationships? It is not an exaggeration to consider that the academy shows great ability to analyze external entities but still investigates very little about itself, its *modus operandi*, relationships, behind-the-curtains situations, silences, and non-saids.

Latour and Woolgar (1982) have investigated the practices inside a research institute, but it is rare to find investigations that center academic relations as objects of analyses. Bourdieu (1984) has written his classic *Homo Academicus*, dedicated to investigating the academic world from a sociology of education standpoint. Brazilian professor Marcelo Diversi's position is interesting when he sees "the university classroom and the traditional sites where the production of knowledge takes place, like journals, books, and academic conferences" as his new battleground in academic work (Diversi & Moreira, 2009, p. 208). In a book about her life, Laurel Richardson (1997, p. 53) considers that "[i]ntellectual labor is accomplished in social institutions and through particular social relationships."

While an assistant professor in a Brazilian Public University, I submitted a research project focused on the subject of academic relations to an institutional competitive call. The successful proposals would receive one undergraduate student research initiation scholarship. With the help of autoethnography, I consider the received report as a space/locus of academic relationships in order to build this chapter's analysis. I put Academia and its ways of functioning as research focuses. I write this chapter to question and reflect on the academic relations we establish, with a special attention to the subjectivities they produce.

AN AUTOETHNOGRAPHY IN THE UNIVERSITY

Autoethnography has to do with stories and histories—with narratives. One of its main characteristics is that it may surpass some aspects of "traditional" ethnography, such as the separation between the observer and the observed, supposed neutral descriptions of already-there (*déjà-là*) objects, and detachment.

It seems important to consider that autoethnographic narratives do not necessarily have the objective of telling stories the way they happened, or representing a static and sequential, linear past, accessible by memory. This is why in this autoethnographic text I do not worry about the narrative's supposed veracity or facticity, but about its credibility, which is related to aspects such as the story's cohesion and the senses readers build from it. Richardson (1997) remarks that "[c]redibility is accomplished, in part, through the artistry of the teller—the selection of details, the tone, the images, metaphors—and, in part, through locating the story within a larger context" (p. 77).

A text with autoethnographic inspirations may have the aim of stimulating reflections on questions such as: "[w]hat story are you telling about yourself and your fieldwork?" "What does your experience suggest about culture?" It is always important to note that "[a]ny story we construct is partial, privileged, and rhetorically crafted for an audience" (Adams et al., 2015, p. 82). Autoethnographies may include thoughts, ideas, desires, feelings, and narratives derived from our or others' experiences. These pieces may destabilize us and also "make us question, reconsider, and reorder our understandings of ourselves, others, and our worlds" (Adams et al., 2015, p. 47).

Adams considers autoethnography "a method that allows us to reconsider how we think, how we research and maintain relationships, and how we live" (Adams, Holman Jones, & Ellis, 2015, p. 8). Versiani (2005) suggests that this method has potential to change the ways we perceive subjectivities' construction processes, especially because of the way autoethnographic narrative is built, as "an extension of life and of the movement that exists in what is alive" (pp. 224–225).

To write in accordance with these principles also has to do with Larrosa's thought (2015): "to read and to write (to listen and to speak) is to put oneself in movement, is to always go beyond oneself, to always keep open the interrogation about what oneself is" (p. 40). Autoethnographers "intentionally use personal experience to create nuanced, complex and comprehensive accounts of cultural norms, experiences, and practices" (Adams et al., 2015, p. 33), as well as to reflect about the ethical, aesthetic, and political characters that are present in these dimensions; we need to use the stories we write and tell in order to break silences related to power and relationships (Adams et al., 2015, p. 103).

Autoethnography is a method that makes it possible to build knowledge about "particular lives, experiences, and relationships rather than general information about large groups of people" (Adams et al., 2015, p. 21). Inspired by autoethnography, in this text "I tell a situated story, constructed from my current position, one that is always partial, incomplete and full of silences, and told at a particular time, for a particular purpose, to a particular audience" (Ellis, 2009, p. 13). This method is related to our scars, to what we live, to what we feel. It has to do with what *marks us* and not necessarily with what marks.

SUBMIT A PROJECT, SUBMIT YOURSELF!

As I briefly mentioned, the main objective of the research project I submitted to BPU was to critically analyze the university itself and the relationships between its members. The 12-month limit imposed by the call presented the need for a delimitation. More specifically, the project would focus not on the whole university, but on BPU's Management 4-year undergraduate program. It aimed to reflect on/build together with students, faculty and staff, points of view and affections about academic doing, academic relationships, and the subjectivities built in/within the university. Interviews, collective meetings, and anonymous online questionnaires would help the proposal to fulfill its objectives.

I had all the bureaucratic requisites in order to participate in the call. Each faculty was allowed to apply for one 12-month scholarship, for a student under their supervision that would collectively develop the research project with them. Since I had been already working with a volunteer student in the same project, I decided to submit the proposal to BPU's call.

After 40 days I received an email informing me that the results were available in BPU's electronic platform. The proposal had scored 34 out of 60 points: 56%. To receive one student scholarship, the proposal needed at least 35 (or 60%). Just one point more and I would have made it!

I was curious to read the reviews in order to understand the reasons why the project was rejected. My surprise came when I noticed that there were not multiple reviews—the project had been evaluated by a single reviewer. The qualitative feedback I received from the anonymous reviewer, reproduced below, provides an interesting point of analysis:

> The proposal would only be relevant if it comprised other universities. The development inside the institution's walls points to a fragility, possible embarrassments and a very limited and circumstantial perspective. It will be difficult for the methodology to allow an impartial and neutral analysis. Yet, important theoretical references are missing, like Durkheim, Weber and Bourdieu, among others. The evaluation is not favorable to the project.

Shock. Surprise. Frustration. I cannot believe they denied the proposal claiming *these* reasons.

The statement that "the proposal *would only be relevant if it comprised other universities*" caused me shock and perplexity. It seems undeniable that the more places investigated in a project, the richer a research about academic relations has the potential to become, in terms of amplitude. However, this was neither a comparative project. I keep wondering if the reviewer has really read the proposal and its theoretical background.

At least two more aspects are worth reflecting upon.

First, I recognize that the project's theme—academic relationships—is largely absent and rarely investigated in contemporary Brazilian academia, but it is difficult to comprehend the argument that the proposal should only be relevant if conducted in other universities. If it was suggested to expand the project and make it wider, I would fully understand and agree. But to simply deny the project inside BPU, where nothing has been investigated about the subject yet, by saying that only other places would bring relevance seems very strange. The neighbor's yard is always greener, is it not?

Many voices
I like your work, but I never meet a junior faculty doing this.
People might be moved by your prose, but they will not hire you.
You have to be flexible as scholar.
Don't let the anger get the best of you.
It's nice, but why do it here in academia?

[…]
What is this? Am I not able to land a job because I do not behave, do and think, do not ask/answers, and do not write/research/perform the same questions like the others? (Diversi & Moreira, 2009, p. 168)

Second: An analysis that only sees validity and relevance in an investigation which is related to quantity, numbers, and statistical significance, belongs to a determined and well-known way of thinking and seeing the world, which is defended by many, with strong influences since the Enlightenment project. But this point of view is not the only one to exist. I consider that it is when we feel each context's singularities that the research gets built and enriched. Truths are circumstantial (Barros, 2008, p. 75) and I try to be alert to singularities, affects and subjectivities, to what runs through myself.

It is not difficult to notice that a single university, alone, already encompasses and builds uncountable different worlds. Even a single department may show huge diversity concerning the relationships established and the stimulated values.

With an evaluation report like the one I received – which considers the number of researched universities as criteria for evaluating the project's relevance, it is possible to envision several clues about the kind of science (and scientific knowledge) we are producing, as well as about the one that is considered relevant. How can we consider an investigation as relevant only if developed in other places when we have not studied the (multiple) settings of the own university we belong to? Is the relevance of research merely quantitative and statistical? It could also be just an excuse for a university not to investigate itself and not to analyze its attitudes, relationships, and values.

I continue analyzing the feedback: the "very own *development inside the walls* points to a fragility, possible embarrassments and a very limited and *circumstantial* perspective." I question the embarrassment that could occur in investigating what we do in the academy, in our academic practices and relationships, and in being auto critical and stimulating auto critics. Are the university members building so many absurd situations in their daily activities that they would get embarrassed at looking at themselves? It seems strange to consider research as "strong" when it is devoted to investigate others, but fragile when it looks at the relations we build and the institutions we belong to. As I already mentioned, the opinion that the proposal is limited and circumstantial because it only looks at the university I belong to is also connected to a point of view that understands statistics as a synonym of validity. But the intriguing aspect is that according to the proposal's theoretical background, this is exactly how I see things: truths are always circumstantial and temporary. I question if a project would only have merit if it shared the same principles and world view of the reviewer.

In academia, a supposed guardian of autonomous investigations and freedom of thought and knowledge, it gets even more difficult to understand how a proposal can be disqualified for not reflecting the beliefs of a single reviewer. I keep looking for the stimuli to diversity, multiplicity, and different methods, visions, and theoretical bases.

It does not seem to be a mere coincidence that the reviewer stated that the project would have difficulties, with its methodology, to achieve a neutral and impartial analysis. This kind of argument reinforces the considerations mentioned in the paragraphs above and amounts to a science conception linked to absolute and verifiable truths, aligned with a search for neutrality, impartiality, and with a desired separation between the researcher and the researched. It portrays a world view that fosters dichotomies such as right/wrong, good/evil, and that is present since a time in which a study needed to be anchored in the precepts of mathematical and biological sciences—experiments, positivism etc.—in order to be considered scientific.

The evaluation received may also indicate that academic research liberty/autonomy could be increasingly threatened. Threatened? Or has it always been more rhetorical than effectively lived in our practices? While I easily recognize that freedom and autonomy are always present in media and institutional discourses about the university, it is important to question to what extent they are present in academic practices and relationships.

Most academic infrastructure, material resources, and even scholarships to students and researchers are currently allocated to areas like engineering and health sciences. Would it be a coincidence that in a 2003 editorial, Nature Materials already criticized "whether funding priorities should be so heavily skewed towards a few so-called strategic areas"? The journal even asked: "Should researchers be forced (even indirectly) to change the aim of their research so that it better complies with so-called strategic priorities?" (p. 639). To give another concrete example, in Portugal, in 2014, the Portuguese public funding foundation mapped (FCT, 2016) that 41% of the country's research institutions were dedicated to Social Sciences and Humanities but they just received 21.9% of the national budget. At the same time, 35% of the institutions were related to Engineering and Technologies and they got 37.4% of the national budget.

But this is not an exclusive matter of knowledge areas/fields. Although some scientific fields have bigger shares of the available resources than others like arts, social sciences, and humanities, even in these marginal areas there are intense disputes between different perspectives that are not always capable of stimulating and respecting multiplicities. So, it seems urgent to reflect on what kind of autonomy we are talking since some values and world visions are privileged over others, especially in evaluations and competitions.

We should ask what a neutral and impartial analysis is when it is made by people and inseparably built by values, ways of feeling, thinking, being, seeing, and working. Impartiality only seems possible to those who internalize and (re)produce beliefs in the mentioned neutrality and in absolute truths which use validity indicators and bet on control as a means of quality assurance, preferring proofs and verifications instead of trust and openness. Only to those who treat people who are considered to be more competitive as truly superior to the others, who criticize others more than themselves and who, for this reason, prefer to embarrass others than themselves.

I remember Richardson's words (1997) when she says that "the new discourses threaten not only the quaint seventeenth-century notion of a purely objective science, held by many in administrative ranks, but also the actual power (prestige/salary) of the entrenched within the university. New mines have been set. As in real war fields, the young, inexperienced, and adventurous are the most vulnerable to detonations" (p. 208). How not to play these games? Or how to play them differently?

Do I need to salute? Is it necessary to act like the masters do or expect?

TOWARDS ACADEMIC PIMPING?

I wonder about the implications of an academia based on evaluations like the one I received and what it implies in terms of attitudes, daily routines, relations, desires, and subjectivities. I keep thinking about what I should do after receiving the feedback. In having denied a scholarship to a student who is interested in participating in a research project like this, maybe I should give up and not research about the proposed subject and look for a more accepted and recognized topic. Or maybe research alone.

The message implies that a project focused on analyzing the academic *modus operandi*, looking at the same institution, will not be supported. And the message goes not only to professors but also to students: *You can't do what you want, dear academic aspirant! Follow the leaders, act like the masters!*

A discourse that considers public universities as sacred temples of autonomy also seems to be difficult to be seen in practice, since those who want to research about some subject may do it, but without any support. In other words, either we investigate what the institutions (or the sponsors) desire or all the responsibility to find support and resources rests solely on our shoulders. Would this be a price for us to pay to "succeed"?

> If I want tenure, I must not complain about anything and always accept whatever classes they assign me, even if I get 20 hours of teaching a week and my colleague is given only 4.

Stimuli for people to autonomously build their own objectives and invent ways to achieve them are increasingly rare in academia. In order to be considered scientific and/or academic work, it is expected that the authors cite the most famous and prestigious names in the field. And most times this is more valued than the content of what is invented by the authors. Creativity does not not seem to be well recognized in Academia if the famous, if the "owners" of the fields are not there—cited in the texts—giving legitimacy to the "autonomously" written words. First and foremost, you are stimulated to behave like a parrot, that is, to reproduce a series of famous/prestigious/recognized references to look "more truthful."

> If I want to be a Doctor, I have to cite A, B, and C in my dissertation.

In a pastoral education, people do not think in singular, autonomous ways, with their own problems. "Deleuze (2006, pp. 227–229) affirms that we need to 'have the right to our own problems,' since we will continue to be slaves as long as we are obliged to 'think' problems of others" (Carvalho & Gallo, 2010, p. 296). Most pathways seem to follow Bourdieu's (2006) heteronomy in science production, since investigations and researchers' (and aspirants') subjectivities have been framed so they have objectives—and ways of achieving them—aligned with the establishment and considered valid according to mainstream logic and values. We are stimulated to an almost hypnotic identification with the images of the world broadcast by advertising and mass culture (Rolnik, 2006b, p. 5). And the academy is great in developing and propagating models of success which seduce us.

If we think about contemporary productivity metrics that guide most academics' performance assessments, we will be tempted to get convinced that anything is valid to achieve recognition by institutions and by other academics. One must have many high impact publications, approve externally financed research projects, among others. And most important: it does not matter either the means used to achieve these objectives or the ways by which our academic relationships are built, not even the values we (re)produce and stimulate. Only the results we achieve according to the cited "quality" and "recognition" indicators matter.

> If I want to be a professor, I have to publish in the journals X, Y, and Z, even though I do not like to read any of them.

Moreira comments that he feels trapped in a "Foulcaltian power system that disciplines and punishes whose name is Higher Education" (Diversi & Moreira, 2009, p. 46). We must question these positions so we do not become mere followers of traditional "academic religions." Sometimes I question myself if we are imprisoned. Are we destined to create only inside the "market's fence"? Rolnik (2006a) questions: "How and where does the vital strangulation which imprisons us inside the intolerable and that asphyxiates us?" (p. 22).

It is no use to just write wonderful highly critical texts and then act in an autocratic way. *Do what I say, not what I do.* It seems fundamental to reflect about the patterns, images, and behaviors of success that guide us in academia. What are we willing to do in order to achieve these goals? In this sense it is also important that we question what values and images of success our daily attitudes help to produce in the others we relate to in academia.

Rolnik discusses the geopolitics of pimping (2006b), thought by her as initially linked to art. Still, according to Rolnik, several of the inventors of earlier decades' transformations got dazzled by

> the rise to power of their transgressive and experimental force of creation which was now thrusting them beneath the glamorizing spotlights of the media, launching them into the world and lining their pockets with dollars [and] fell into the trap. Many of them surrendered themselves voluntarily to their pimp, becoming the very creators and constructors of the world fabricated by and for the new-style capitalism. This confusion undoubtedly stems from the politics of desire that characterizes the pimping of subjective and creative forces—a kind of power-relation that is basically exerted

through the sorcery of seduction. The seducer conjures up a spellbinding idealization that leads the seduced to identify with the seducer and submit to him: that is to say, to identify with and submit to the aggressor, impelled by an inner desire, in hopes of being recognized and admitted into the seducer's world. (p. 6)

What a concept to the academic world: *academic pimping.* In relationships established between academia members, academic pimping amounts to situations in which one academic voluntarily surrenders to another academic's (person or group) desires, wishes, and/or expectations, even to the point of (re)producing once criticized world views, values, and senses. Academic pimping has to do with acting, working, thinking, like the pimp wants and/or expects one to.

Academic pimping is usually motivated by desires of recognition and admission to the pimp's world: one wants to be admitted to the pimp's world! *It is important to consider that academic pimping is usually based on seduction, worship, and admiration.* What I mean is that the seduced academic sometimes identifies with the pimp (and/or the pimp's world), but even in the cases in which this identification does not occur, the will to belong to the pimp's world is still present.

If I research/write/publish about this, no other professor in the department will want to work/publish/research with me anymore.

If I research this topic, no one will want to supervise me and no Doctoral Program will accept me.

If I want to research this topic, no department/college/university will want to hire me.

We are dealing here with the pimping of forces and desires that are related to the invention, creation and production of worlds, values, and subjectivities. We are discussing the processes of pimping which operate by means of seduction. It is not a matter of the use of brute force. Some academics must allow themselves to be directed (Carvalho & Gallo, 2010, p. 293); they must find advantages, justifications, and even pleasure in being told what do to, in doing what others want them to do, in acting like others want them to act, in researching, writing, teaching, and asking what other academics want them to.

Academic pimping is less related to requisites which are present in norms and regulations and more linked to the construction of desires in the seduced ones, transforming them into "aspirants." Academic pimping, then, does not necessarily involve coercion, but the identification and seduction by images and even promises and the consequent reproduction of behaviors, desires, and attitudes. Ellis (2009) says she felt she had "to learn to think and talk like other academics if I wanted to be a full member of this [academic] tribe" (p. 64). This is a de-potentialization of differences: one is seduced and/or surrenders oneself to act as the pimp wants or expects in order to have more chances to be accepted into the pimp's world.

It is important to consider that academic pimping is not always connected to long-lasting identifications. What I mean is that there is not necessarily one that always acts like a seducer/pimp and others that always behave like the seduced/pimped. These binary oppositions do not necessarily last long here. These are not fixed identities. In a situation one can be the pimp and in another, the same person can be seduced and voluntarily surrender oneself to what seems to be necessary in order to access the idealized worlds. The roles are always changeable. Identities are fluid, circumstantial, ephemeral.

We all face a risk of being pimped and also of becoming pimps. What are our images and goals of success in academia? What worlds do we daily build by means not only of the subjects and authors we discuss but mainly of our actions and the relations we establish? To what extent have we already been pimped? To what extent do we float between moments and situations in which we act like academic pimps and others in which we are seduced and pimped?

I, too, want to be a famous and recognized professor, with at least ten papers published per year like professor XYZ!

Ten per year? So are you going to copy some passages from students' assignments or maybe repeat your writings several times in different articles? Or are you going to tell your masters and PhD students that good academic behavior considers that everything they write while under your supervision will have to have your name included as co-author?

CONSIDERATIONS

It is important to point out the need for other research dedicated to critically analyzing academic relationships and the values, ways of seeing, feeling, working and living constructed by them. Thinking about Brazilian academia in particular, and Higher Education in general, how can we build forms of socialization, of feeling, thinking, working and desiring more linked to life potentiation without critically looking at what we do, at how we act and to what we stimulate with our attitudes and relations?

I will only do this after I finish my undergraduate program. I will only do this when I finish Masters. I will only do this when I am a Doctor. I will only do this when I become a professor. I will only do this after I get tenure. I will only do this when I have this project financially supported. I will only do this when I retire.

Nietzsche (2008) affirms that everything we call truth until now ends up being acknowledged as a harmful, and subterranean form of a lie, "the sacred excuse of making humanity 'better' appears as the astuteness to exhaust life, to make it anemic. The moral as vampirism" (p. 109). The vampiric moral of academic pimping.

Every paper that I write during my dissertation needs to have my supervisors as a co-author, even if they did not write, review, or read a single word of it.

Today, while concluding this text, I remember when I was called by a university colleague as "the pimping guy," after having approved a research project which is linked to the themes developed here. It is not mere coincidence that Adams et al. (2015) remark, while writing about autoethnographic method, that you become the stories you write.

As my narratives show, the assessment I received can be linked to several facets of academic pimping: an assessment that operates stimulates, inspires, fosters and directs others to act like and/or do what the reviewer wants or expects.

My rejected proposal calls me to reflect on the process. Where did I go wrong? Where can I improve? But do I have to address all these suggested modifications until the next submission? If I do as the reviewer told me to, would not it be another proposal? If I have to behave like the reviewer expects me to, what would be the use of being an academic, anyway? Where would be my autonomy and freedom of thought?

Academic pimping is based on seduction, worship, admiration. Models of academic success. Desires to be like the pimps. This is Academia. This is how it works. What do I have to do because of the fear of not being accepted? I have to fix my proposal if I want to have it approved; if I want to succeed and be a prestigious academic. But is there only a single way of succeeding as an academic? What are the images of successful academics that I have?

Academic pimping only gives merit to what shares the view of the evaluators/reviewers/supervisors/etc., and disqualifies those who think, act, or write differently. Academic pimping stimulates others to think with the problems of others and not with their own problems, and puts autonomy in jeopardy. Academic pimping seduces others to behave like the pimps expect, criticizes others but does not look to what the pimps do: *do what we tell but not what we do!*

Dear reviewer, I cannot do what you want without feeling I am being pimped.

It is easy to criticize others in Academia. Lots of books, chapters, articles and reports on… others! Let me begin with myself. What do I consider to be a successful academic and what are the prices I am willing to pay to build my own paths and problems and not just follow others' footsteps?

This text is not only an answer to a situation I have lived, but a call to our attention and reflection on similar situations daily faced by students, professors, and staff in their academic relationships which somehow usually get silenced. The possibility of pimping is always present. We need to fight against becoming academic pimps or, still, being pimped by others. In case we care about that, of course. Numerous appeals to servilism, to pimping, to conformism. To the identification with images of success derived from the *status quo*

While thinking about production of subjectivities … the assessment … to research, to write, to act like it is expected. To cite who wants to be cited … or to have proposals denied … and to be left outside the elite academic clubs. Aspirations. Desires. Voluntarily submitting oneself. Myself? Not this time!

I. V. L. VALENTIM

NOTE

[1] It is important to acknowledge the support received by Federal University of Rio de Janeiro, Rio de Janeiro's Carlos Chagas Foundation (FAPERJ) and by the Portuguese national funding agency for science, research and technology (FCT), under the Project UID/SOC/04521/2013.

REFERENCES

Adams, T., Holman Jones, S., & Ellis, C. (2015). *Autoethnography*. New York, NY: Oxford University Press.

Barros, R. (2008). Crítica científica e modelos interpretativos em Nietzsche. *Trans/Form/Ação, 31*(2), 61–77.

Bourdieu, P. (1984). *Homo academicus*. Paris, France: Minuit.

Bourdieu, P. (2006). *Para uma sociologia da ciência*. Lisboa: Setenta.

Carvalho, A. F., & Gallo, S. (2010). Do sedentarismo ao nomadismo: Intervenções para pensar e agir de outros modos na educação. *Educação Temática Digital, 12*(1), 280–302.

Clareto, S. M., & Oliveira, M. E. (2010). Experiência e dobra teoria-prática: a questão da formação de professores. In S. M. Clareto, & A. Ferrari (Eds.). *Foucault, Deleuze e educação* (pp. 65–89). Juiz de Fora: Ed. UFJF.

Deleuze, G. (1992). *Conversações*. São Paulo: Ed. 34.

Deleuze, G. (2006). *Diferença e repetição*. Rio de Janeiro: Graal.

Diversi, M., & Moreira, C. (2009). *Betweener talk: Decolonizing knowledge production, pedagogy, and praxis*. Walnut Creek, CA: Left Coast Press.

Ellis, C. (2009). *Revision: Autoethnographic reflections on life and work*. Walnut Creek, CA: Left Coast Press.

FCT. (2016). *Estatísticas da Fundação para a Ciência e Tecnologia*. 4 January 2016. Retrieved from https://www.fct.pt/estatisticas/unidades/ResumoEstatisticasInstituicoes.pdf.

Ferreira, J. M. C. (1996). Pedagogia libertária versus pedagogia autoritária. In M. O. Pey (Ed.). *Educação Libertária: Textos de um seminário* (pp. 109–133). Rio de Janeiro/Florianópolis: Achiamé/Movimento.

Foucault, M. (1995). O sujeito e o poder. In H. Dreyfus & P. Rabinow (Eds.). *Michel Foucault, uma trajetória filosófica: Para além do estruturalismo e da hermenêutica* (pp. 231–249). Rio de Janeiro: Forense Universitária.

Foucault, M. (1999). *La creación de modos de vida. Estética, ética y hermenéutica*. Barcelona: Paidós.

Garcia, M. M. A. (2001). O sujeito emancipado nas pedagogias críticas. *Educação e Realidade, 26*(2), 31–50.

Guattari, F., & Rolnik, S. (2007). *Micropolítica: Cartografias do desejo*. Petrópolis: Vozes.

Larrosa, J. (2015). *Pedagogia profana: Danças, piruetas e mascaradas* (5th ed.). Belo Horizonte: Autêntica Editora.

Latour, B., & Woolgar, S. (1982). The cycle of credibility. In B. Barnes & D. Edge (Eds.). *Science in Context: Readings in the Sociology of Science* (pp. 35–43). Cambridge, MA: MIT Press.

Nature Materials (2003). Research funding: The problem with priorities. *Nature Materials, 2*(10), 639. doi: 10.1038/nmat992

Nietzsche, F. (2008). *Ecce homo. Como se chega a ser o que se é*. Covilhã: LusoSofia press.

Richardson, L. (1997). *Fields of play: Constructing an academic life*. New Brunswick, NJ: Rutgers University Press.

Rolnik, S. (2006a). *Cartografia sentimental: Transformações contemporâneas do desejo*. Porto Alegre: Sulina; Editora da UFRGS.

Rolnik, S. (2006b). Geopolítica da cafetinagem. *Núcleo de Estudos da Subjetividade*. Retrieved from http://www.pucsp.br/nucleodesubjetividade

184

Uberti, L. (2006). Estudos pós-estruturalistas: entre aporias e contra-sensos? *Educação e Realidade, 31*, 95–116.

Versiani, D. B. (2005). *Autoetnografias: conceitos alternativos em construção*. Rio de Janeiro: 7Letras.

Weber, M. (1989). *Sobre a universidade*. São Paulo: Cortez.

Igor Vinicius Lima Valentim
Faculty of Education, Federal University of Rio de Janeiro, Brazil
CSG, SOCIUS, ISEG, University of Lisbon, Portugal

CLAIRE SMITH

19. A GHOSTLY PRESENCE

(Un)Belonging in Spaces on the Peripheries

Ghosts are unsettled creatures, moving between worlds as they seek a place
to belong.
—Jessica White (2014, p. 116)

Ghostlike, I move between the worlds of traumatic brain injury, Dystonia, and
academia, seeking a place to belong. Badalotti (2014) suggests that the "notion of
boundaries, of belonging and not belonging … is thrown into sharper relief and
magnified through personal experience" (p. 134). Her observation lends credence
to my story; I suspect my ghostlike feelings of (un)belonging were initiated by a
life-changing personal experience. On September 13, 1997, I sustained a severe
traumatic brain injury when I fell from my horse.

For the first couple of years after the head injury, I was determined to resume
life as it had been. During that time, I performed as Dziura (2015) credits
Shakespeare (1996) for predicting: "newly disabled people often try to stay their
old self and to feel as ordinary as possible" (Dziura, 2015, p. 34). Both echo
Frank's (1995) description of the restitution stage in his typology of illness
narratives: "Yesterday I was healthy, today I'm sick, but tomorrow I'll be healthy
again" (p. 77). When I finally realized that my equestrian self, the only self I'd ever
consciously known, had been ripped from my being, I was heartbroken. For years
after that awful time, I often dreamt of my equestrian past. Now, albeit
infrequently, yearning still "engulfs me at unexpected moments … [serving] as a
reminder of the irrevocable loss" (Dutta, 2015, p. 162).

As my healing journey progressed, and as I gradually regained self-awareness, it
became apparent that the life-altering experience of head injury was the source of
the feelings of which I was slowly becoming cognizant, tangled feelings of
(un)belonging. My head injury was invisible and ghostlike (Mullins & Preyde,
2013) so, for many years, I felt situated "in between" the abled and disabled
(Stone, 2005, p. 295). But, although physically invisible, the brain injury did, for
the first few years after I was injured, cognitively hinder my day-to-day
functioning. Thankfully, as the years went by, I noticed these interferences less and
less often. My friends and family may disagree, but today, almost twenty years
after that moment, I think that I'm cognitively fine. Nevertheless, I wonder if the
fact that I sustained a head injury, even if the accident happened long ago, means
that I belong in the world of survivors of head injuries.

S. L. Pensoneau-Conway et al. (Eds.), Doing Autoethnography, 187–196.
© *2017 Sense Publishers. All rights reserved.*

* * *

Nine years after the head injury, my life got even more complicated. In 2006, I started dragging my right foot while I was walking, the first troubling indication that all was not as it should be. I was terrified, having no idea what was going on. Doctors finally diagnosed that the chronic illness Dystonia, its symptoms being rigidity and muscle spasms in the affected parts of the body, had begun to seize control of my right leg. In all likelihood a consequence of the head injury, the illness insidiously invaded my leg over the course of the next few years. I now wear a noticeable brace that runs the length of my right leg, fitting only over my pants. It's very visible, so the impairment is not at all ghostlike (White, 2014). Dystonia is, however, ghostlike in its own way: there's nothing wrong with my leg. The illness originates in the brain, its source far removed from its manifestation.

I was in denial of the impact of Dystonia for the first few years after it began intruding into my life. However, once I'd successfully defended my Ph.D. thesis in November of 2010, I no longer had any choice but to stop sticking my head in the sand like the proverbial ostrich, pretending that there was nothing wrong. It was time to stare Dystonia in the face and acknowledge the changes it was forcing me to make to my lifestyle. However, even with much needed professional help, it took me a couple of years to put Dystonia in perspective.

Because it's a proper noun, Dystonia is capitalised. However, as my story evolved, I realised that I could choose to allow only a lowercase "d": I won't let dystonia be more than a bit player when I describe who I am. Living life to the fullest, I've worked hard to put dystonia in perspective (Good, 2009). Now, more than ten years after dystonia first reared its ugly head, I use a wheelchair to navigate through life. Fortunately, I'm still able to walk a few steps. Modifications to my life help enormously: a wheelchair lift in my van, a stair-lift to reach the second floor of my house, a golf-cart to use in the garden.

I wonder though, how my experiences with dystonia have contributed to shaping the confusion in my mind about where I belong? Because I had to eventually acknowledge that dystonia wasn't going to go away, does that make me a member of its community? Do I belong in its world?

* * *

When I affixed "Ph.D." to my name, I questioned whether I would ever belong in academia. Since my graduation almost seven years ago, I haven't used my degree, and I find that I have little desire to do so. I finally decided that my academic years had come to a natural end when, in April 2016, my colleague Derek Bolen invited me to write a chapter for this book. The offer was hard to resist. Although the ghost metaphor has probably run its course, I'm going to use it once more: I had to haunt my academic self until it gave in and let me compose this contribution.

What follows is an autoethnography that delves into the concept of (un)belonging. I'll slip into and out of, across and in between, the cultures of traumatic brain injury, dystonia, and academia to explore the

uncertainty I feel,
brought about by
head injury,
chronic illness,
and a Ph.D. I wonder
who am I?
where do I belong?

THEN

Twenty years ago, I was a member of the Canadian Equestrian Team at the 1996 Olympics in Atlanta, Georgia. Gazing through a narrowly focused lens that was precisely tuned to my privileged equestrian life, I felt secure with where I belonged in the world. At the opening ceremonies of those Olympics, the participating countries' athletes, some teams consisting only of the flag bearer, marched alphabetically, country by country, into the arena. Waving enthusiastically as they flowed down the ramp that led into the enormous stadium, the athletes paraded around the track, then gathered in the infield to celebrate the opening of the Games. Standing shoulder to shoulder with athletes from around the world, I laughed and I danced. For that brief time, we just enjoyed ourselves. Not thinking about our impending competitions, we all seemed to be so in the moment, so proud of what we'd accomplished getting to the Olympic Games.

At what I now realize was, for me, a defining moment, the party paused.

Holding our breaths,
we all watched as
Muhammad Ali
shakily lit the Olympic flame.
Unashamed of his Parkinson's,
he revealed his disability
for the world to see.

I was so honoured to be representing my country, so in awe of the enormity of the Olympic Games, that I didn't understand the significance of what I was witnessing.

JUNE 3, 2016

When I heard that Muhammad Ali had died, I relived the moment when I'd watched him light the Olympic flame at the Opening Ceremonies. Twenty years ago, I'd been clueless as to the real reason why the event was so amazing. I just thought that it was wonderful that such a champion was lighting the flame. I hadn't yet grasped that the athletes had been given the unique opportunity of watching a champion stand up to his Parkinson's and display it unashamedly to the world.

Now, almost two decades later, the memory remains razor sharp in my mind; it means so much more to me than it did at those Olympics. How I then understood disability and chronic illness was, I now know, uninformed. At that time, I had

189

thought of them as things that some people suffered from and were forced to live with. I didn't pay them any mind. For me, disability was something that afflicted other people.

However, during the years following that evening in Atlanta, I've come to understand what I'd witnessed firsthand: Ali showing the world that he acknowledged his own disability and illness. By doing so, he became an exemplar for everyone who struggles with uncertainty about loss and disability. When he lit the Olympic flame, Ali let a huge audience know that "disabled" was part of his identity. Swimmer Janet Evans had passed the Olympic torch to Muhammad Ali just before he lit the cauldron. Afterwards, she said that, as Olympians, "our role is to inspire others to achieve their dreams, and no person has ever lived that role more than Muhammad Ali" (Associated Press, 2016).

Dave Zirin, Sports Editor of *The Nation* magazine, was interviewed after Ali's death. He underscored the widespread impact of Ali's actions:

> Any time anyone ever stands up under difficult odds or conditions, they can say in their mind that they stand in the legacy of the champ…you can't underestimate what that meant to people who felt like they had to live with stigma or shame or daily challenges. (CBC Radio, 2016)

* * *

Why does Ali's lighting of the flame at the 1996 Olympics now resonate with me? I've no doubt that it's because the words *disability* and *loss* have come to be in the forefront of my life. At the opening ceremonies of those Olympics I didn't understand what I was seeing, but I can now relate. My story has evolved into one that speaks of facing many challenges that have been brought about by injury and illness. These days, head injury and dystonia have ensured that I know a lot about the words *disability* and *loss*, as well as about the uncertainty that both have invited into my world. I'm also sensitive to words with which *disability* and *loss* tend to coexist: words like *stigma*. And *difference*. And *(un)belonging*.

WHEN WILL IT RAIN?

It's the middle of a Canadian July, and it's hot. We need rain desperately; the lawn is parched, straw-like in texture and appearance. I don't even consider its well-being, but I'm intent on watering the myriad of young trees and immature shrubs on my property. Short, fifteen minute stints in front of my computer are all I get, my time broken up by trips outdoors. There, I climb into my electric golf-cart so that I can drag the hose over to the next grateful shrub.

Were you to take a closer look at the sessions that I spend at my desk in between the gardening interruptions, you'd see that I'm in the process of searching for academic articles. Deciding on the ones I'd like to read, I ask a friend to procure them—I no longer have access to the university library—in hopes that they'll add new ideas to the mixture of information I'm trying to absorb as I struggle to understand if and where I (un)belong. When my wonderful friend emails them to me, my thoughts fly as I read about belonging and the many interpretations of its meaning.

Levett-Jones, Lathlean, Maguire, and McMillan (2007) succinctly describe belonging as "the human need to be accepted, recognised, valued and appreciated" (p. 211). When I move yet again to the outdoors, I mull over their definition. After slipping into my electric golf cart, I drive across the lawn towards my precious, babied Seven Son Flower. Spraying the shrub with the hose when I get there, I think about whether I feel accepted, recognized, valued, and appreciated. I sense that the understandings these authors have of belonging is too simple, too clear for me. I'm not sure. I see "belonging" as having fuzzy, qualitative edges: there's no clear answer, especially when disability and illness are thrown into the mix. I relocate again, dragging the hose over so that I can water the Dwarf Willow.

* * *

How do I understand belonging? When I return to my desk, the question percolates in my mind. I also wonder what I think about belonging's relationship with illness and disability. According to Gill (1997), a sense of belonging in the world is the first step towards incorporating illness and disability into one's self-concept. The idea jars me: I think that inviting dystonia into my self-concept would imply that it's a larger part of me than I want it to be, and I don't feel I need to be polite to dystonia. I refuse to incorporate the chronic illness into my life.

I can, however, work with the disability that dystonia has created. But, when I consider Gill (1997), I find myself wondering if the reverse is possible. Wouldn't individuals only begin to feel a sense of belonging *after* they'd included their disabilities into their self-concepts? For me, the opposite makes more sense and follows my experiences with becoming disabled. After I had begun the journey of incorporating disability into my self-concept, I started to feel a sense of belonging.

My situation is probably too much of an influence, but I firmly believe that, even though I've come to an uneasy understanding with dystonia, I'll never incorporate the disease itself into my self-concept. The chronic illness and I now icily tolerate each other—I'm just able to stand it. I have, however, come to terms with being disabled, with using a wheelchair, as well as with all the socially and personally imposed meanings that come with it. So although disability has become part of my self-concept, dystonia has not. I'm left feeling addled; Gill (1997)'s ideas of illness and disability, as well as their relationships with belonging, remind me of chickens and eggs. Which came first?

* * *

How does impairment differ from disability? When I look up the meanings of *impairment* and *disability*, I learn that dystonia is an impairment because it results in a loss of physiological, or anatomical, structure or function. A disability refers to the function of the individual: any restriction or lack of ability to perform an

191

activity in the manner considered normal for a human (WHO, 2016). Handicaps become apparent when social, economic, and cultural circumstances disadvantage individuals with impairments and disabilities, limiting or preventing the fulfillment of their roles in society. If there's no wheelchair ramp so that individuals with disabilities can enter a building, they're handicapped in that location.

Smith (2013) shows the devastating impact that disability can have when he describes the experiences of several individuals who have impairments in the form of spinal cord injuries. When those individuals returned to the places where they had exercised before they were injured, Smith found that these once psychologically positive places were now limiting and harmful to their psychosocial health. Because the individuals were physically impaired, they could no longer exercise as they had before their injuries. The facilities were not accessible, so the individuals were handicapped.

DISABILITY'S MARGINS

More often than not, when describing someone who has an impairment and uses a wheelchair, "disability is the most salient feature, more salient than gender" (Rohmer & Louvet, 2009, p. 80). After my disability became visible with the onset of dystonia, it "sharpened [my] sense of the margins" (Hallahan, 2013, p. 231), margins that outline the gap between the disabled and the abled. Along the disabled edge, belonging is too often the exception, unbelonging too often the rule. Felt inequality and oppression accentuate the gap between these margins, leaving a wide cultural space between the disabled and abled (Barnes & Mercer, 2001).

For the first couple of years after I was injured, I wasn't cognitively well enough to notice, let alone deal with, the cognitive and emotional changes that everyone around me was observing. I was oblivious to the margins that had been— unconsciously?—constructed by the equestrian community. Now, all these years later, I wish that I'd only imagined their presence. I fear, however, that that isn't the case. As I slowly became more self-aware, these margins became more and more defined.

Murray and Harrison (2004) remark that unseen emotional changes are often more disabling than are physical impairments. They recognise that after a life-changing injury, such as a head injury, activities and skills that were once "interwoven with participants' sense of identity" (p. 811) may no longer be possible, resulting in a "profound loss of self" (p. 810). In my case, the harsh reality was that I could no longer ride competitively. My equestrian self, the only self that had ever been apparent to me, had been ripped from me. Its loss was heartbreaking: being a competitive rider was an inextricable part of my identity before the accident.

The pain became almost unbearable when, at the same time as I was gradually realizing that I could no longer live as I had before the injury, I became cognitively aware enough to feel that the margins of inequality and oppression had become greatly magnified. These days, I give the equestrian community the benefit of the doubt, optimistically hoping that its members were unaware that they had drawn these margins.

* * *

The puzzling symptoms of dystonia appeared nine years after the head injury. However, although these symptoms foreshadowed that the chronic illness was about to move in, I wasn't at all ready to deal with them. Nor was I ready to cope with dystonia when it was eventually diagnosed. Although uninvited, dystonia forced reflection as I tried to understand what was happening to me. When it was first diagnosed, I refused to acknowledge the illness. However, since then, I've put my loss in perspective (Good, 2009). At the same time, I've stayed resentful of dystonia's visibility, holding it accountable when I feel (un)belonging.

Initially, I denied that the illness was accentuating the margins that had already been imposed by head injury. However, I eventually acknowledged that, by emphasizing the margins and widening the gaps of my life, dystonia was causing heartache by calling attention to my previously invisible head injury. These days, I'm finally able to emotionally cope with the fact that dystonia has made it evident to all that I have a disability.

Although I may be imagining things, it seems that people's unconscious reactions to the visible deficits that are now part of me have accentuated the margins that I've been trying to minimalize.

THE EVOLUTION OF MY (UN)CERTAINTY

Three hours later, I finally finish watering—will it ever rain?—so I roll up the hose, plug in my electric golf cart. Once inside, I settle back into my chair in front of the computer and ponder the role that dystonia has come to play in my life. I've never let dystonia "move in": I've always maintained that dystonia can seek a place to belong all it wants, but it will never find a home here. Although it inhabits my right leg, it'll never be a part of me. I despise dystonia, but I've made peace with it. That doesn't mean it belongs though, does it? I still find myself unsettled as I try to determine how dystonia fits in my life. When your mind simmers while you're doing something unrelated, Wallas (1926) maintains that you're incubating. In my case, I incubate while I'm swimming, feeding the dog, or listening to a song on the radio as I drive home.

After many hours of unconsciously mulling over the problem, suddenly, while I'm making a sandwich, the light goes on. I recall Barbara Paterson's (2001) "Shifting Perspectives Model of Chronic Illness." The model has resonated with me since I first read about it; I've previously used it to describe my life (Smith, 2012). Paterson thinks that it's important to consider how individuals cope when they live with chronic illness; she proposes that the significance of a person's chronic illness continuously fluctuates because "people with chronic illness live in the worlds of both the well and the sick" (p. 988). She notes that when these individuals feel that illness is in the foreground, their attentions are focused on their illnesses. Their lives revolve around them; their illnesses have great influence on everything they do. Then, when their illnesses are in the background, the illnesses are not ignored or forgotten, but these individuals' lives are not being constantly overshadowed by them.

Paterson's model does not just apply to illness. For example, if you are planning a wedding, your life is consumed by the wedding. Afterwards, the wedding fades into the background of your life. A few years later, if you separate, the wedding and all it signifies may come back into the foreground.

The onset of disability can railroad one's life: its physical impact can be unusually cruel, its consequences often hard to stomach. When dystonia was in the foreground, my life revolved around the chronic illness. What I perceived, what I believed, and how I felt about my illness was central to my world. It overshadowed everything else; it seemed that I made sense of everything in terms of my illness. Dystonia was controlling my life. As luck (or good therapy) would have it, dystonia moved to the background a few years ago. Wellness is now in the foreground; since it's been there, the gap between the margins of disability and ability has become almost imperceptible, at least to me. On so many different levels, the illness doesn't matter to me now. When I became able to put wellness in the foreground, I was able to modify my perceptions of what is "possible and normal" now that dystonia is bent on being part of my life (Paterson, 2001, p. 23).

* * *

Now that my losses are in perspective, I realize that life is OK. Dystonia will never find a home with me; I'll never let it belong. However, I've discovered that, despite this adamant refusal, I might belong in the world of disability. I try to help others with disability; I'm on the Disability Advisory Committee for my County. A remnant of my equestrian days is my compulsive exercise routine. I'm a regular, three or four times a week swimmer; dystonia is much less noticeable when there's no weight on my foot. I'm on the Board of Directors at the YMCA where I swim. I see my biggest contribution there being that I can advocate for the disabled and, because I've fairly recently become disabled, I can see "both sides of the fence." I'm on the board of a local head injury group. With these volunteer efforts, I feel that I'm giving back, trying to smooth the path for others faced with disability.

Although I've reconciled myself with being disabled, and I'll always use a wheelchair, it's only a small part of who I am. I manage dystonia in other innovative ways: my preferred method of locomotion is skating quickly on a smooth floor by pushing my portable wheelchair with my left (good) leg. I move along more rapidly than people walk; it's a lot easier than using the lift in my van to take out the real wheelchair.

I'm not afraid to ask for help.

"Excuse me, hello!" I shout at the man I see walking thirty feet in front of me into the entrance of an unfamiliar store.

"Could you please push me up the slight incline leading to the door?" When I propel my portable wheelchair with my left (good) leg, I go really fast on the level, but it's impossible for me to navigate up any sort of incline. This unfamiliar store, appealing for its promise of canisters for my seltzer water, has an incline outside the front door. The man seems happy to help me.

"Thanks so much. I should be fine once I'm inside." Once in the store, I skate quickly on the smooth floor.

* * *

When President Obama reflected on Ali's passing, he observed that, at the 1996 Olympics, we "watched a hero light a torch, and fight his greatest fight of all on the world stage once again; a battle against the disease that ravaged his body, but couldn't take the spark from his eyes" (Dailymail.com, 2016). I feel the same way: being visibly disabled doesn't rob me of my spark. I won't let it change the meaning of my life.

Swimming,
volunteering,
and writing
have put
dystonia
in its place.

Dystonia is one reason why I struggled for a long time to come to terms with where I belong, where I'm comfortable, where I'm happy. Now that I'm content, I refuse to give dystonia any attention; I've found ways to work my way around it, to put it in perspective. I don't attend support groups; in no way do I give dystonia a chance to raise its voice. I grudgingly acknowledge it: do I accept it? Never. I'm not held captive by dystonia. The disability is not why I do—or don't do—things. Instead, I do things because of what they mean to me.

REFERENCES

Associated Press (2016, June 4). Reaction to the death of "The Greatest" Muhammad Ali. Retrieved from http://www.cbc.ca/sports/olympics/summer/muhammad-ali-dead-reaction-1.3616442

Badalotti, F. (2014). This is my home now: Multilingualism and belonging as a choice. *New Scholar: An international journal of the humanities, creative arts and social sciences, 3*, 133–144. Retrieved from http://www.newscholar.org.au/files/journals/1/articles/144/attachment/144-720-1-AT.pdf

Barnes, C., & Mercer, G. (2001). Disability culture: Assimilation or inclusion? In G. Albrecht & M. Bury (Eds.), *Handbook of disability studies* (pp. 515–532). Thousand Oaks, CA: Sage.

CBC Radio. (2016, June 6). *Remembering Muhammad Ali.* Retrieved from https://www.facebook.com/radiocbc/posts/10154255777001913

Dailymail.com. (2016, June 4). "Muhammad Ali was the Greatest: If you just asked him, he'd tell you": Barak Obama pays powerful tribute to his hero, thanking the fallen Champ for "gracing our time." *Daily Mail Online.* Retrieved from http://www.dailymail.co.uk/news/article-3625232/Muhammad-Ali-Greatest-just-asked-d-tell-Barack-Obama-pays-heartfelt-tribute-hero-thanking-fallen-Champ-gracing-time.html#ixzz4Bli2Zzcg

Dutta, U. (2015). The long way home: The vicissitudes of belonging and otherness in Northeast India. *Qualitative Inquiry, 21*, 161–172. doi:10.1177/10778800414542703

Dziura, J. (2015). Psychological adaptation and identity change after the aquistition of a physical disability in adulthood, a critical analysis of an autobiography. *Gallaudet Chronicles of Psychology, 1*(3), 31–42.

Frank, A. (1995). *The wounded storyteller*. Chicago, IL: The University of Chicago Press.

Gill, C. J. (1997). Four types of integration in disability identity development. *Journal of Vocational Rehabilitation, 9*, 39–46. doi: 10.3233/JVR-1997-9106

Good, M. (2009). Elvin Semrad (1909–1976): Experiencing the heart and core of psychotherapy training. *American Journal of Psychotherapy, 63*, 183–200.

Hallahan, L. (2013). Down the rabbit hole: Reflections on thirteen narratives of living with the "disabled" label. *Narrative Inquiry in Bioethics, 3*, 229–234. doi: 10.1353/nib.2013.0070

Levett-Jones, T., Lathlean, J., Maguire, J., & McMillan, M. (2007). Belonging: A critique of the concept and implications for nursing education. *Nursing Education Today, 27*, 210–218. doi: 10.1016/j.nedt.2006.05.001

Mullins, L., & Preyde, M. (2013). The lived experiences of students with an invisible disability at a Canadian university. *Disability & Society, 28*, 147–160. doi: http://dx.doi.org/10.1080/09687599.2012.752127

Murray, C. D., & Harrison, B. (2004). The meaning and experience of being a stroke survivor: An interpretive phenomenological analysis. *Disability & Rehabilitation, 26*, 808–816. doi: 10.1080/09638280410001696746

Paterson, B. (2001). The shifting perspectives model of chronic illness. *Journal of Nursing Scholarship, 33*, 21–26. doi: 10.1111/j.1547-5069.2001.00021.x

Rohmer, O., & Louvet, E. (2009). Describing persons with disability: Salience of disability, gender, and ethnicity. *Rehabilitation Psychology, 54*, 76–82. doi: 10.1037/a0014445

Shakespeare, T. (1996). Disability, identity and difference. In C. Barnes & G. Mercer (Eds.), *Exploring the divide* (pp. 94–113). Leeds, England: The Disability Press.

Smith, B. (2013). Sporting spinal cord injuries, social relations, and rehabilitation narratives: An ethnographic creative non-fiction of becoming disabled through sport. *Sociology of Sport Journal, 30*, 132–152. doi: 10.1123/ssj.30.2.132

Smith, C. (2012). (Re)discovering meaning: A tale of two losses. *Qualitative Inquiry, 18*, 862–867. doi: 10.1177/1077800412456962

Stone, S. D. (2005). Reactions to invisible disability: The experiences of young women survivors of hemorrhagic stroke. *Disability and Rehabilitation, 27*, 293–304. doi:10.1080/09638280400008990

Wallas, G. (1926). *The art of thought*. New York, NY: Harcourt, Brace, & Wold.

White, J. (2014). Ghostliness and un/belonging as a hard-of-hearing writer. *New Scholar: An International Journal of the Humanities, Creative Arts and Social Sciences, 3*, 109–118. Retrieved from http://www.newscholar.org.au/files/journals/1/articles/136/public/136-729-1-PB.pdf

WHO. (2016). *Disabilities*. Retrieved from http://www.who.int/topics/disabilities/en/

Claire Smith
Independent Scholar

AMY ARELLANO

20. ARE YOU LEGAL?

A Question of Citizenship

You will not find them easily in the hallway, the union, or the dorms. Despite your diligent screening some will slip through the cracks and infiltrate…or rather infest the classroom with tongues that are unruly, bodies that are nonconforming, and minds that only Hollywood claims are beautiful. The rejection letters missed some that flew under the radar. The ones struggling after hours to pass as normal. You will not know they are there usually … that is until you are given an official envelope marked confidential requesting what some believe is "special treatment." The emphasis on "special" as a euphemism for euphemisms that never extend the circumference out enough to include rational or able. An emphasis that continues to ignore that we do not all learn the same and reduces the seven intelligences down to conformity.[1]

Within the academy, scholars and students are still paying for the residuals of the Modern era, where rationality was established as a precedent and criterion to evaluate the mind. This mentality has motivated a chilling effect within academic dialogue and research regarding the treatment of students and professors who have been documented with learning disorders. The purpose of this manuscript is to reframe the vantage point in which we understand how individuals with learning disorders are treated within the academy. Margaret Price (2011) suggests there is a "theoretical and material schism between academic discourse and mental disabilities" (p. 8). Simply put, learning disorders and academic thought are assumed to be mutually exclusive identities that never intersect. Despite this mentality, academic minds are still confronted with what some would consider to be "impairments." Price asserts that passing as a "rational mind" becomes a condition of surviving within the academy (p. 33). Specifically, Price establishes that "the necessity of passing for survival perpetuates the conventional view of academe as an 'ivory tower'—an immaculate location humming with mental agility and energy, only occasionally threatened (from the outside) by the destructive forces of insanity" (p. 7). Price recognizes an inherent side effect of passing is identity erasure, thus Price turns to disabilities studies as a venue to engage in academic understandings of mental disabilities. Relying on the work of Simi Linton, Price constructs a framing of disability studies "best understood in terms of variety and difference rather than deviations from an imagined norm" of the mind (p. 5). Essentially, disability studies acts as a form of theoretical understanding and activism that seeks to appreciate and advocate for alternative

S. L. Pensoneau-Conway et al. (Eds.), Doing Autoethnography, 197–203.
© 2017 Sense Publishers. All rights reserved.

learning styles. This focus becomes imperative to achieve both institutional criticism as well as opening new spaces of access for marginalized groups.

I turn to analytical autoethnography as a method of further understanding what is at stake regarding how we currently address learning disorders within the academy. Leon Anderson (2006) established the following guidelines for analytical autoethnography:

> The researcher is (1) a full member in the research group or setting, (2) visible as such a member in the researcher's published texts, and (3) committed to an analytic research agenda focused on improving theoretical understandings of broader social phenomena. (p. 375)

Through the use of analytic autoethnography, I acknowledge that as a critic I am challenging how we construct the idea of "expert researcher." Arguably, in order to meet the tenets Anderson offers, researchers may be required to realign from "expert" to transparent and at times vulnerable. This shift in positionality most likely will occur when a researcher directly addresses how they meet the standards of analytical autoethnography.[2] Anderson notes this methodology should expose a new way of understanding social phenomena through experience. In order to offer an alternative perspective regarding how we treat and respond to learning disorders within the academy I utilize Kenneth Burke's "perspective by incongruity."

Perspective by incongruity serves as a methodology exploring the benefits of metaphors. Specifically, Burke (1984) posits, "it is precisely through metaphor that our perspectives, or analogical extensions, are made — a world without metaphor would be a world without purpose" (p. 194). This position comes from Burke's belief that through placing understood metaphors onto new objects we develop a new perspective of understanding. Perspective by incongruity, or gauging situations by verbal "atom cracking," allows for a dramatic vocabulary to emerge that challenges normative assumptions (Burke, 1959, p. 308). That is to say, through planning the researcher utilizes beliefs or customs applied to a certain category of identity and metaphorically applies these beliefs or customs to a different category of identity. Methodologically, perspective by incongruity is the revelation of something that is traditionally unseen being revealed by placing two things together that are not typically found in comparison. Through violating the typical convention of understanding, a new perspective is garnered by the researcher and audience. It is crucial to note that Burke (1959) asserts the knowledge garnered from perspective by incongruity should "introduce new principles while theoretically remaining faithful to the old principles" (p. 229). Thus, I begin at the intersecting narratives of two of my marginalized selves: Latin@ and a student with learning disorders. This comparison allows a convergence of experience to occur rooted within metaphor as a means to adjust how we treat those with alternative learning styles. I turn to the following key themes that develop from the intersecting identities: illegal, documentation, and deportation as a pushback against the academy for who/what counts as academic.

ARE YOU LEGAL?

I spent 4 days doing timed testing, organizing blocks, writing, spelling, math... all as a means of screening to determine if I would need a passport for the classroom. I went home to learn it was the same testing my partner went through in 3rd grade to determine if she should be in the gifted and talented program. I sob becoming concerned with whether or not I could finish a program where I had spent my first year struggling to tread water, not ever really finding my footing in my sophomoric writing or disjointed grammar. Reluctantly I gave into the wet foot/ dry foot clause the academy offers to the intellectual illegals like myself, accommodations.

The narrative and normative identity constructed around "intellectual" needs to be confronted if we hope to close the gap between practice and application concerning identity politics. Annamarie Jagose (1997) notes, "identity politics are eviscerated not only by the differences *between* subjects but the irresolvable differences *within* each subject" (p. 83). By requiring a student to be registered with the College's Office of Student Services and/or disabilities, a precedent of documentation highlights the difference between bodies...of who belongs. As a body that has obtained documentation for my diagnosis, feeling like an imposter within the university has increased creating an identity crisis of whether or not I belong within the walls of the "ivory tower." Following my diagnosis, I started talk therapy because I could not silence the internal doubt of not properly performing graduate student. This crisis mirrors the same tensions I had upon starting college as a first-generation Latin@ college student.

WHERE IS YOUR DOCUMENTATION?

I grew up not far from south Texas in that middle ground where college is seen as a luxury for the Latin@ that has been gentrified into a coconut through education. My acceptance letters came with the burden of selling out, forgetting my roots, or worse—not immediately joining the workforce to help provide for my family. My grandpa never had papers, never saved up enough green to afford a green card or apply for citizenship. This wasn't my story; when La Migra would visit construction sites in the hill country my brother never had to run. I never had to worry about providing a social security card when applying for a job. My story was always, are you Latin@ enough? That was until I was 33 and entered a classroom where we would have written exams that mirrored the comprehensive exam process. There were three tests, five questions per test, and we were expected to handwrite our answers with no spell check in one hour and 15 minutes. When I went to talk with the instructor, she referred me to the small paragraph many instructors, including myself, have in their syllabus: If you require special accommodations, please contact Student Services for Disabilities (SSD) in order to obtain proper documentation.

The idea of needing documentation to exist within academic space and the price of accepting/requesting accommodations becomes a loaded rhetorical and embodied act producing a space of immanence to witness and examine.

Immanence should be seen in opposition with transcendence. Gilles Deleuze (2001) clarifies that immanence can be viewed conceptually as the collision between social disciplining and an individual's embodied experience where specific research can be conducted. Within this convergence, I extend my understanding of how "documentation papers" function as a tool for biopolitics.

The previously noted experience birthed this metaphor project grounded in autoethnography and critical rhetoric. George F. McHendry et al. (2014) suggest scholars extend the circumference of rhetoric to include immanent participation: where the researcher grounds one's body in a matrix of relationships, affect, vulnerability, and options of resistance. Through trying to find calm in the borderlands of this experience, immanent participation became necessary. This requires me to publically out the invisible learning disorders with the risk of otherization and possibly being labeled as defective by the academy, or this research disqualifying me in future job searches.

WHY AM I BEING DEPORTED?

I would like to say the hardest conversation I ever had about my learning disorders came from being asked for documentation for class assignment extensions. However, that was not the case. The hardest conversation came when I needed to "out myself" to my supervisory committee and inquire how my diagnosis would impact comprehensive exams. As I scheduled each meeting, I was afraid one of them would tell me that maybe I should just quit. I never heard that, which I know is a luxury many of us are not afforded.

I spent the summer before my comprehensive exams in countless meetings trying to figure out the "adjusted rules." In June, I got an email that said I needed to see if the SSD office could administer my exams because the accommodations of reduced noise and double time could not be met in the department, on the floor where the rest of my cohort would be taking their exams. I knew through watching the exam process the last two years that space and silence were limited. I tried not to be offended. But the first morning when I started my exams across campus, 923 footsteps away from my department, a week before my colleagues would start writing their own answers, I never felt more alone. I was in a place I did not grow up in, a land I did not call my home. In order to try and secure a better future, a higher level of education, I left my home for what seemed to be another country. Where I could not understand why I felt deported, punished for coming out.

* * *

Perspective by incongruity allows me to partner the treatment of Latin@ bodies within the political sphere with the treatment of learning disorders within the academic sphere. The choice of this pairing was based on acknowledging that many individuals have a stronger understanding of how we treat Latin@ bodies within the public sphere as opposed to how we recognize those with learning disabilities. As a researcher, I hope individuals explore this practice to rethink how we discuss learning disorders within the academy. With that said, I explore the role of rhetorical disciplining within the academy and how perspective by incongruity can also shed light on the methodological practice of autoethnography.

First I explore how rhetoric functions as a disciplining tool. Foucault (1979) asserts that language serves as a tool of social disciplining to mark the other. Specifically, this perspective accounts for how both "documentation" and "deportation" serve as methods to socially discipline learning disorders within the academy. As a disciplining tool, the ability to afford the testing required to document learning disorders benefits those with financial privilege. I was not "documented" prior to graduate school so I often had to struggle within courses. The only reason I was able to access documentation of my learning disorders occurred because my university provided free testing. The role of being able to afford documentation plagues both the identity of immigrants and academics with learning disorders. This acknowledgement extends the fit between the metaphors.

Additionally, Foucault (1979) asserts that opposition to existing order occurs through the specific intellectual rather than the universal intellectual. Within this chapter, I am only able to give an account of how I understood the experience of academic accommodations. I was told the use of deportation would be seen as offensive and non-palatable; I respond by noting how the ways we treat those in academia that do not fit our vision of the intellectual are equally offensive and non-palatable. As I place my body here for scrutiny we can determine how we treat and talk about learning disorders in the academy, so that students and professors do not live in fear of deportation if they are unable to provide proper documentation.

I would be lying if I said this chapter is not imbedded with risks. Much like family members are concerned that ICE will turn their pursuit of the "American dream" into a nightmare resulting in deportation, I am concerned that outing myself as an alternative learner may impact my pursuit of the "Academic dream." This concern grows stronger based on our current socio-political environment. Right now, there is a concern not only regarding visibility, but also whether documentation papers will matter to the current administration. While several political respondents and civic advocates fight against the "wall" along our imagined borders, there is another wall being built to block out academic access. As an educator, I was concerned with the appointment of Betsy DeVos as Secretary of Education. I know the concern was replicated by many of my colleagues regarding school choice, the collapse around church and state, and the dismal reality of Michigan's schools under her leadership. Though valid concerns, my worry is rooted in the treatment of alternative learning students under a charter school model. What some may not know is that for-profit charter schools have consistently failed to satisfactorily meet ADA standards for their students. An investigative report completed by Capital and Main regarding the infrastructure and support for alternative learning students found that high teacher turnover rates, less experienced teachers, and student screening processes underserved the ADA student demographic (Failing the test, 2016). Additionally, in Los Angeles school districts, students requiring ADA accommodations were often turned away from charter schools. These charter schools argue that based upon the students' specific learning needs, ADA seeking students should seek public schools that are better equipped with resources to house alternative learning style students. Ana Martinez, single-mother of a 15-year-old daughter with a learning disability, enrolled her daughter at Alliance Morgan McKinzie High School, a charter school in East Los Angeles (Failing the test, 2016). Ana explains how her daughter was discriminated against on her first day of school when Ana was told her daughter's learning disabilities could not be accommodated with the charter school resources. Despite her daughter having the expensive ADA documentation for services, Ana's daughter was removed from the charter school that day. Because of this, it is vital for individuals to determine the risk associated with either "passing" or "outing" oneself based on the marginalized identity of alternative learning. Her daughter was diagnosed with severe dyslexia, ADHD, and two non-specified learning disorders—a diagnosis almost mirroring my own. It is not difficult to imagine what happens to bodies (and minds) caught by border patrol. It is slowly becoming reality in our current educational system.

The part of my narrative that has not been as easy to negotiate has been acknowledging that at some point, regardless of dual citizenship, one becomes a naturalized citizen, and as such risks losing their mother tongue. Some individuals will deny their origins as the education system has painted their learning styles as something shameful and requiring secrecy. Others, like myself, become lost in the assimilation of likeness, slowly cleansing my tongue of colloquialisms and slang to learn the most recent style guide. In order to produce academic articles for publishing opportunities, I turn to copy editors which straighten out the spirals of my ADHD ideas into straight formattable lines. Each time that I surrender to this academic cleanse, I tell myself this is necessary collateral damage regarding academic production. On the days that I can feel myself losing some of my mother tongue, I turn to autoethnography so that I can imbed the personal narrative that goes along with this type of work. The rough and sometimes brutal negotiation between publications and the grammatical gridlock of my multiple learning disorders at times causes me to question if the academy is where I belong. In fact, I question if receiving my doctorate degree will serve as the "green card" I have been applying for over the last three decades within the academy. This tension, the same tension I feel when returning home for the holidays, makes me feel as if I no longer quite fit regardless of my desire and dedication to break down walls. I view the witnessing of this tension as creating a possible new origin of research; specifically, I am interested in examining the possible tensions negotiated within code-switching and authenticity. Additionally, there may be a need to study the potential intrapersonal and interpersonal costs associated with the assimilation of marginalized bodies to better fit within the academy. Our borders will never be as clean as we may have once hoped, but that does not mean we should not continue to honor and listen to the stories of those trying to negotiate the tightrope between real disabilities and ideal performances.

NOTES

[1] I purposely frame this chapter to look at the widespread institutional practice of requiring students with alternative learning styles to be registered with student services for disabilities to obtain documentation for educational accommodations. This criticism is rooted in the practice of accessibility and treatment of students with learning disorders. I would like to note that I am criticizing the system of accommodations as opposed to my particular institution. Unlike some students, I had a supportive advisor to help me with negotiating this new ground.

[2] Analytical autoethnography requires the researcher to disclose positionality and identity either within the text or a footnote. In order to provide transparency, this manuscript emerged from realizing the rhetorical power "documentation" has in disciplining marginalized bodies. As a member of the Latin@ community and having learning disorders, I find myself occupying and oscillating between these two identities. As a researcher I have taken up projects that account for struggling with an alternative learning style within the academy. Additionally, I believe that it is vital to note that it is from the intersection of two of my marginalized identities that I first identified how documentation was being used as a tool to discipline bodies with learning disorders. I am not confident this discovery would have happened without my commitment of addressing Latin@ rights.

REFERENCES

Anderson, L. (2006). Analytic autoethnography. *Journal of Contemporary Ethnography, 35*, 373–395. doi: 10.1177/0891241605280449

Burke, K. (1959). *Attitudes toward history*. Los Altos, CA: Hermes Publications.

Burke, K. (1984). *Permanence and change: An anatomy of purpose*. Los Altos, CA: Hermes Publications.

Deleuze, G. (2001). *Pure immanence: Essays on a life*. New York, NY: Zone Books.

Failing the test: Charter schools' winners and losers. (June 1, 2016). *Capital and Main*. Retrieved from http://capitalandmain.com/failing-the-test-charter-schools-winners-and-losers-0601

Foucault, M. (1979). *Discipline and punish: The birth of the prison*. New York, NY: Vintage Books.

Jagose, A. (1997). *Queer theory: An introduction*. New York: New York University Press.

McHendry, G. F., Middleton, M., Endres, D., Senda-Cook, S., & O'Byrne, M. (2014). Rhetorical critic(ism)'s body: Affect and fieldwork on a plane of immanence. *Southern Journal of Communication, 79*, 293–310. doi: 10.1080/1041794X.2014.906643

Price, M. (2011). *Mad at school: Rhetorics of mental disability and academic life*. Ann Arbor: University of Michigan Press.

Amy Arellano
Department of Communication
Boise State University

LEE MURRAY

21. SECRETS

To Tell or Not to Tell?

I am very good at keeping secrets. I have come by it honestly as they say. I have learned how to keep secrets. I have been told not to tell. I am confused by secrets, and I am in awe of secrets. I remember reading Sissle Bok's (1989) discussion of this dichotomy of secrets:

> We are all, in a sense, experts on secrecy. From earliest childhood we feel its mystery and attraction. We know both the power it confers and the burden it imposes. We learn how it can delight, give breathing space, and protect. But we come to understand its dangers, too: how it is used to oppress and exclude; what can befall those who come too close to secrets they are not meant to share; and the price of betrayal. (p. xv)

Secrets remain a mystery to me. I am interested in an inquiry into secrets, and in particular, secrets related to mothering. Maybe mothering and being mothered has taught me to keep secrets. Is my secret-keeping connected to learned behavior, socialization, or hiding behind a mask? Is it about projecting a certain image, not burdening others with problems, or avoiding exposure to possible criticism and judgment? Is it about keeping family matters private and tightly enclosed within the family and working hard not to let them seep out? Or is it about protecting not only myself but also others? I want to explore my Mom's secrets because I have a sense they are related to mine: "Behind all [my] stories is always [my] mother's story because hers is where [mine] begins" (Albom, 2006, p. 194).

A MOTHER, A DAUGHTER, AND SECRETS

Mom[1] seemed to have many secrets from her family of origin. I found out about them from the wrong people usually, and I found out much later than I felt I should have. My friend in high school told me Mom was married once before she married my dad. She was married briefly to her high school sweetheart before he was killed in the Royal Navy. I told Mom about what I had heard from my friend and she seemed so upset ... So even after I knew, I was reluctant to ask questions or talk about it with her. Even as an adult when I had children of my own, I was still hesitant to talk about her first marriage.

I remember the time I gave her the book that opened the dialogue about this particular secret.

S. L. Pensoneau-Conway et al. (Eds.), Doing Autoethnography, 205–215.
© *2017 Sense Publishers. All rights reserved.*

* * *

I wake up in the night and can't go back to sleep. I have a dreaded sense of loss and emptiness. My stomach feels hollow and empty. I hurt all over and feel incredibly sad and alone. I wonder, "Is this related to the book? Have I been dreaming about it? Is this what it feels like to lose a husband? To know you will never see him again? To say good-bye without ever dreaming you would not be reunited soon?"

Lost at sea. It sounds so dark, alone, distant, and scary. I feel cold and hot at the same time, and it seems difficult to breathe. I am confused for a moment; I don't know where these feelings are coming from. Is it the book? It must be the book. I felt the same way when I first read the passage in the book:

Morelli, J.L., Salt Royal Navy
Sub-Lieutenant (HMS Merganser RN pilot). John Louis Morelli of Plunkett died 19451115 and is commemorated on the Lee on Silent Memorial, Portsmouth, Hampshire, England, for members of the Fleet Air Arm who died with no known grave. Morellis' family came to a farm northeast of Plunkett from Sondrio in northern Italy near the Swiss border in 1912. John was educated at Badger school and Plunkett and enlisted in the RCAF in 1943. He was released just before the war's end, but re-enlisted in the Royal Navy as a flying instructor. Morelli was married just before returning to England, and died with two students when their Barracuda aircraft stalled joining a formation just off the coast of Scotland. (Barry, Chisholm, & Parsons, 2005, p. 325)

I don't know if I should give Mom the book. I don't know how she will react. "Will she be upset with me? Will it upset her?" I worry.

I bought *Age Shall not Weary Them: Saskatchewan Remembers its War Dead* (Barry et al., 2005) as a Christmas gift for her, but I can't decide what to do. "Am I afraid of what her reaction might be Christmas morning? Or am I afraid I may not have an opportunity to give it to her if I wait?" I wonder.

My Dad died suddenly just before Christmas last year, and I didn't get to give him the gift I was so excited about. I know things can happen without warning, and I don't want to take a chance. I decide to give it to her early.

She is pleased when I read it to her. She says, "I was afraid that because he had joined the British Navy he would not be remembered in Canadian history."

I ask her, "Did you know he had been discharged and, yet, re-enlisted?"

She looks at me as if I have two heads, "Of course I knew; I was his wife." She explains, "Of course we talked about it. He wanted to return and join the British Navy so he could fly and land planes on an aircraft carrier."

"Was his plan to stay in the Navy and you would join him?" I ask.

She responds, "No, he was planning on coming back and becoming a dentist. He always wanted to be a dentist, and his parents would have been able to help him. He was their only son, and he had four sisters."

As Mom says this, a memory is triggered. I remember visiting Mom's first husband's family when I was younger. I didn't know who they were (although I was old enough to), and I couldn't understand why everyone was crying and why they were hugging Mom so tightly. They were Italian and had a small vineyard in British Columbia. I don't remember much else. We sat in the backyard on the patio that had a surrounding trellis with grape vines. It was hot that day, and it seemed like Mom didn't want to leave.

* * *

I wonder, "Was she trying to hold onto something that she had lost? Did she feel connected to him there with his family?" I didn't even know about him then, so I wonder this now. I didn't know Mom was married before. I didn't know anything about it, and I have always wondered why.

I wish I could remember what my dad was doing during that visit and how he was reacting. However, although I felt a strong connection to John Morelli when I read the passage to Mom, I also felt some kind of betrayal of my dad. It was strange because I never did understand how Mom talking about her first marriage was a betrayal to Dad, yet I felt it, too. Are mothers and daughters so connected? Do I feel the same need to keep secrets as a way of protecting others or myself?

The sharing of this secret creates a new bond between Mom and me. As I come to understand more details of her story and her secret, I begin to understand that the keeping of her secret may not be so much about the secret itself as about the effects of telling on others, particularly those close to her. I also wonder if my own secrets are locked in a similar box of protection, betrayal, and perceived shame.

* * *

I say to Mom, "Life is funny; different roads and sliding doors." She agrees and we're silent, thinking about how different her life could/would have been if John hadn't died at sea.

She says, "You would have liked him; he was lots of fun, and a good dancer, too." Too, meaning a good dancer like my Dad. Dad was an incredibly smooth and fabulous dancer. "I wish you could have seen your dad and I do the jive in our prime," she laughs.

"Me too," I reply.

I think to myself, "Who was this John Morelli?" I like saying his name.

I wonder, "Why do I want to know? Why am I so curious about this man? Why do I want to know what their relationship was like? Was it different from her relationship with Dad? Was he a gentler man than Dad? Did Mom love him more or just first? Did she know Dad when she married John?"

She continues, "I was young, only 19. Mom wanted me to wait until John got back from overseas to get married."

"I'm glad you didn't wait," I tell her.

"He was supposed to be home for Christmas. Another sad Christmas," she sighs.

John died November 15, 1945. Dad died December 4, 2004.

"Another sad Christmas," I lament.

She continues, "I got a letter saying John was missing. I had an uncle in England, and I contacted him and asked him to investigate. After a period of time, I received a letter from John's friend, and he told me what had happened. John's plane had gone down over the North Sea."

I think of the irony. The war was over, and his plane stalled. How cruel. What was he thinking about as the plane went down? Mom, I'm sure.

She tells me, "John had visited my relatives in Wales and England—relatives I had only written to but had never met. I didn't meet them until many years later. It was probably close to twenty years before I met them, and they met me with a different husband and two of our children. A few years after John died, I had an opportunity to go to Wales with my mother. She wanted me to go with her and get married when I returned to Canada. I stayed home and married your dad."

I look at her and smile, "I'm glad you did."

* * *

I look back now on that time Mom and I shared in my kitchen one Saturday afternoon. I look back on the sharing of the secret and the new understanding it brought for both of us. I think about my hesitation to show her the book. I was not sure what her reaction would be. I was concerned she would be upset. I was worried she would think I was prying. I hesitated to show her the book, but I couldn't wait. I told her about finding the book and my reaction when I read it.

* * *

"Mom, I was in a bookstore looking around one day, and I noticed this book. I don't know why I was drawn to it, but I picked it up and began to read part of it. I was disappointed to find that it seemed to contain only obituaries of the men and women who had died in the war. I went to set the book down again when the name 'John Morelli' went through my mind." I reveal, "I don't know why."

Mom nods her head but doesn't comment.

I continue, "I wondered if John would be in this book. I slowly turned to the 'Ms,' and there it was: 'J.L. Morelli.' My heart was pounding, and I had a sense of being totally alone in the busy bookstore. I could hear voices, music in the background, and the hum of shoppers milling around, yet I felt like I was standing alone as I stared at his name. It was hard for me to understand that this was your first husband. I began to read the passage. I read that he was from Plunkett, your hometown. I don't know why, Mom, but I felt overwhelmed and almost panicky when I read that. I wanted to sit down, yet I couldn't stop reading until I read 'Morelli was married just before returning to England.'(Barry et al., 2005, p. 325). Then my eyes filled up, and I couldn't read any further for a long time." I look at her. Her eyes are full now, too.

"I can't imagine what it must have been like for you; to be a newlywed at 19 and find out that your husband is 'lost at sea,' never to return," I murmur quietly.

I stand there staring at the passage and looking at Mom. My eyes are misty. I am unable to focus. My chest feels tight, and I feel such a sense of loss, loneliness, and connectedness all at once. There is no picture of him in the book, but I can picture him on his wedding day with Mom. Should I tell her about the wedding picture?

* * *

The wedding picture is yet another secret. Mom's lifelong best friend, Kathy, gave me a wedding picture of John and Mom—making me promise that I would not tell Mom. I agreed but I wondered why the secret. Kathy attempted to explain. She seemed to understand Mom's need to keep the secret, but she was unable to articulate it or help me understand. Kathy also understood that she was to remain a keeper of the secrets, but something was different that day.

My sister Rae and I had gone to visit Kathy while in Calgary. Kathy seemed very nostalgic that day, and as we sipped tea, she began reminiscing about growing up in Plunkett and all the experiences she and Mom had shared. She had many funny stories about catching gophers and selling their tails, or waiting for the train to come with the big barrel of ice cream, and about all the various characters who contributed to life in Plunkett. Both Mom and Kathy had lost their fathers at a young age. Hearing all their stories suggested that they had formed a close bond the moment they met or as far back as they could remember. Listening to Kathy that day, I also got a sense of how important they were to each other's happiness, contentment, and survival.

Rae and I were always curious about some of the things that happened to Mom while growing up because we had only heard little pieces of the stories. We were always afraid to ask more in case it upset Mom. I felt safe to ask Kathy a few questions that day about other family secrets. Mom's older brother committed suicide when she was quite young. Rae and I had never heard any explanation of what happened or what it was all about. Kathy told us her recollection of that day, and things began to make a little more sense. The losses my mom endured—how strong she had been—became so obvious that day.

Mom's father had died in a car accident when she was only 9 years old, and her mom never got over it. Kathy said that my grandmother functioned well, worked outside the home, provided for her family, and was involved in the community, but she really struggled in her role as a parent after her husband died. I have heard bits of other stories, and my sense is that my grandmother may have been emotionally distant in many of her relationships. Perhaps it was a way of protecting herself. Parts of the stories I have heard Mom tell give me a sense that her and her brothers were very protective of my grandmother and never fought or disagreed in front of their mother. They never wanted to upset her and didn't get to be normal kids in that sense. I imagine that they never discussed the details or their feelings around these family losses. The message may have been clear that any talk or discussion would upset their mother, and as a result, all hurtful events became secrets.

As I reflect on these family secrets, I acquire some realization of how and why secrets developed in Mom's family. She never grew up with the experience of sharing and discussing grief. She never learned how to share and discuss grief, and maybe I didn't either. I keep things quiet, rather than sharing them with people who could support me. I believe I was socialized to keep those things a secret. Maybe that is part of the reason why it is so difficult to tell my own stories.

My reluctance to share personal parts of my life seems connected to Mom's reluctance to discuss things that were traumatic or hurtful and may have reflected badly on her or her family. I have been quite reluctant, even avoidant, to think about some of my secrets. I believe Mom felt that digging up her past served no purpose, or all the loss and grief she experienced were better left behind. I have a similar sense that maybe my traumas and secrets don't need to be shared. Perhaps they are better left alone, untouched, and undisturbed. Maybe the leaving behind is a form of dissociation and not wanting to remember the pain, not wanting to re-experience it. I wonder if that may be true for Mom—that in telling her secret stories she would relive the experience. If she told her stories and repeated the telling, would it force her to relive not only the pain but also the story itself? Would she then re-story it in a different way? Does dissociating and leaving it behind to avoid the pain get in the way of developing an alternative perspective?

A MOTHER, A SON, AND A SECRET

I can certainly relate to the experience of dissociation. It has happened to me at different times in my life, and I realize it has contributed to my keeping of secrets. Dissociation often allowed me to tolerate pain, to escape pain momentarily, to continue with life responsibilities and obligations, and more importantly, it allowed me to survive. However, I realize that dissociation is not always healthy. It may help me to survive, but it also helps me to avoid. Prolonged avoiding gets in the way of dealing with the issues, the trauma, and the pain, and it leads to my secrets being kept.

When my son Jordan was involved in a car accident, 18 months after his disclosure of sexual abuse, I wanted to separate from the emotional mom and be the rational nurse—but I couldn't. I was stuck in the role of mom because I could not leave that role. It seemed the most important role at the time. If I had been able to separate, it might have been more helpful to Jordan's well-being. I would have insisted on certain medical procedures and processes being done. But the emotional response to the accident was not only appropriate to have but also appropriate to share. As a result, all the pent up emotions that were related to the abuse came pouring out when the accident happened. It may have appeared to others as an atypical or extreme emotional response from me but it was accepted and understood. Instinctively, I knew the normative discourse allowed this type of sharing in the public domain. The discourse implies that it's okay to talk in great detail about accidents but not about abuse.

When Jordan told me that he had been abused, I involuntarily separated to another space to hear and respond to his disclosure because the lived emotional experience would have overcome my abilities to respond appropriately and support him. I wonder now how my separation in the moment contributed to my later "not telling" of this painful experience. Perhaps my dissociation created a space that got in the way of my telling. By the time I put the pieces together, I felt as if it was too late to tell.

Thinking about this experience, I continue to struggle with the "why" of information keeping and holding secrets. Now, in my present space, I want to recognize what holds me back from telling my secrets, and I want to understand my motivation when I do tell. Estes (1992) helps me understand such an impulse to some degree:

> All women have personal stories ... but there is one kind of story in particular, which has to do with a woman's secrets, especially those associated with shame; these contain some of the most important stories a woman can give her time to unraveling. (p. 374)

I was exhausted holding the secret of Jordan's sexual abuse. I continued questioning myself over and over: Why is this story so difficult to tell? What am I afraid of? Why is it a secret? Who does the secret benefit? Perhaps me and mine, for a while, but I wonder when the keeping of a secret becomes more damaging than the telling of a secret. Why do we keep things secret when they are about the bad behavior of others and not ourselves? Or do we think that, had we had better behavior, we could have prevented someone else's bad behavior? What do we choose to tell? What do we choose not to tell? Why do we talk about difficult knowledge, certain challenges, and experiences more easily than others? Why do people respond the way they do to the telling of difficult knowledge? How does that shape our future telling? How do we learn to talk about difficult topics?

We all live with secrets, big and small, shameful and harmless, terrifying and humorous. Why do we choose to tell certain people and not others? What do we want to happen when we tell? Do we have a certain expected response that we want from others? Do secrets lose their power in the telling, or do they gain power? As I begin to tell my stories and share these secrets, I gain an appreciation of the tension between telling and not telling. I often wonder if there is healing in the telling. Jung (1954/1957, 1963/1965) supports the telling of secrets as a way toward healing, as does Estes (1992). Jung believed that, when we hold a secret related to shame or injustice, we cannot be healed unless we tell the secret to at least one person we trust. He referred to these secrets (sorrowful errors) as having themes including betrayal, rejection, disapproved interest or lifestyle, unplanned pregnancy, loss of courage, inability to do something, and neglect and abuse. Estes maintains that it is good to tell our shameful secrets, to open the secrets up, to tell someone we trust, to write a new ending, to examine one's part in it and one's attributes in enduring it.

There is a time of decision-making, a moment or perhaps an eternity, before a secret is revealed. There are many thoughts and feelings that are a part of that decision. For example, my past experiences of telling or not telling and the assumed or expected consequences of telling are all considerations before I tell. However, I remain surprised that the same secret can elicit such different reactions.

* * *

I call her to see why she left Jordan and her son alone at her home while she got groceries. I decide to tell her about Jordan's disclosure of being sexually abused as a way of clarifying my concern for Jordan and her son. I think she has a right to know this information if Jordan and her son are going to play together. She is appalled and doesn't think they should get together in the future ... and they don't.

* * *

I feel so warm and comfortable in this home. I can't explain it. It is beautiful yet unassuming. Every room is more beautiful than the one before and the backyard is a dream. It seems like it has been raining forever and now the sun has finally decided to come out. I tell Sherry, "I am a prairie girl, and I could never live in Vancouver with all the rain." She agrees. The mountains make her claustrophobic, and the humidity makes her sick.

I am having coffee with Sherry because she overheard I was planning to renovate, so she invited me to see her newly renovated kitchen. We are acquaintances from being at the same Special Olympics functions, and we have one very important thing in common: we are both moms of special needs sons. We also have something else in common, but neither of us are aware of that at the moment as we share the warmth of the fireplace and view the serenity of the backyard. I don't know her story when I tell her mine. And I don't know why I tell my story of Jordan's abuse on this particular day, at this particular time. But it feels right, and I receive the warmest, most caring, and sincere response to my secret from anyone I was brave enough to tell. It feels as though we are isolated in time for that moment. She cares for me, then is appropriately outraged, and then she tells me her story.

* * *

Sometimes I wanted to tell. Often I felt I needed to tell, but the response to the telling was sometimes not ideal or what I expected. This type of response, once again, perpetuated the keeping of the secret.

* * *

She calls to say that Jordan was inappropriate with a girl at teen club. We discuss the issue, and there appears to be a lack of supervision. I explain my concern for the girl and for Jordan. Hesitantly, I decide to tell her about Jordan's sexual abuse. She is silent for a moment then responds, "Are you telling me *that is why* Jordan is perverted? I don't think he should come to teen club anymore."

* * *

The mother of one of Jordan's friends calls. I can tell she is upset. She explains that she does not want her son to visit at our home anymore. Although Jordan is welcome in their home, on occasion, where there is adequate supervision. She explains that her son does not have the same vocabulary as Jordan and there is no need for her son to know about intercourse, sexual orientation, or sexual relationships at this point. I try to explain that I think this information is important to our sons but also that Jordan learned much of this vocabulary at an early age because of his sexual abuse. And I try to help her understand that I wish I had told Jordan more about these issues and topics, in the hope that it may have prevented the abuse. She is not interested in discussing it further.

* * *

The response of these mothers reflects the possible "costs of breaking the silence" (Zingaro, 2009, p. 179). So I cannot be reassured that revealing will bring healing. I cannot predict the consequences of telling. From my experience, when Jordan disclosed his sexual abuse, there was an overwhelming feeling of failure to protect my child—failure to protect Jordan from the abuse, failure to respond to the disclosure in the most supportive way possible to prevent further harm, and failure to address the social and political environments that allow childhood sexual abuse to continue to happen. There was a need to be a caregiver, a mom, an activist, and an advocate when my world was crumbling. My responsibilities were overwhelming at a time when my sheer revulsion about the abuse and overpowering empathy for Jordan rendered me silent and immobile.

Disclosure of secrets is often about speaking out (Zingaro, 2009). It is often about finding the courage to tell without knowing the consequences of telling. The decision to tell is a mystery that is not easily explained. I would like to say that the telling of Jordan's abuse has brought healing, and perhaps it has in some ways. I have told others, until now, mostly on an individual basis, but a public telling has its own consequences. Sometimes the struggle continues or increases with a public telling. Often, the telling is only the beginning. And I realize that healing takes time and there are "disclosure consequences" and "a price to pay to tell the truth about ourselves" (Zingaro, 2009, p. 180).

TO TELL OR NOT TO TELL?

Mom's secrets and my secret about my child may seem very different, but at the root of those secrets lies shame, self-blame, and guilt. I still feel all those emotions when I think about Jordan's abuse. I blame myself for not teaching him more about sexual health and how to protect himself. I blame myself for not recognizing the signs of abuse, especially when I have the knowledge, education, and practice in the area of adolescent mental health. I am a Clinical Nurse Specialist and I missed it! Once Jordan told me, I did due diligence. I reported the abuse to the police, and they initiated an investigation. There were several errors in the investigation and concerns about Jordan's ability to testify. Although physical examination confirmed sexual abuse, there was limited evidence to identify the abuser and no witnesses. Ultimately, no charges were laid. As a result, the alleged perpetrator is still working in the school system with adolescents who have developmental disabilities. I frequently go to the school board to remind them of the case and encourage them to "watch this guy" and "to do something," because I am terrified he will abuse another vulnerable child. And I struggle nearly every day with the fact that he probably has and will.

I feel so frustrated and at a loss as to what to do next. I also know the statistics related to the sexual abuse of people with developmental disabilities are staggering and I recognize the gap in services. I have developed and deliver a program promoting healthy sexuality and healthy relationships in an attempt to prevent abuse of this particular population. This program has given me the most hope. Perhaps if I was unable to prevent the abuse of my own child, I can prevent the abuse of other very vulnerable children and adolescents. Hopefully my story and the program will begin to make a difference.

I also begin to understand how Mom's silence is also due to the shame and guilt that she feels related to her secrets. She continues to hold her thoughts and feelings very close and only wants to talk about the "fun times" of her past. She is 91 years old, still spunky and still living in her own home. I think she should be able to talk about whatever she wants at this point. I see her as frequently as I can. Each time I say good-bye, I wonder if it will be the last. She looks so tiny and frail, and it is difficult to leave sometimes. And each time, after I leave, I wonder to myself, is there something I should say to her, something I should ask her, something I may regret not saying or not asking? And sometimes I wonder what we don't know about each other (those protected secrets), and I also wonder what we know about each other and yet don't talk about (another kind of protected secret).

I have often thought that if I begin to share my secrets with Mom it will open up the discussion—we will understand each other more and it will bring us closer. On one such occasion, I started to talk to Mom about this "lonesome feeling" she often describes. She hates the feeling and says it often signifies something bad is going to happen. It is not an "alone feeling" or a "lonely feeling." It is not missing someone or something but an emptiness. And there is a lot of nostalgia wrapped up in that sense of lonesomeness. I have felt it too. I explain to Mom how it feels for me, and I find myself choking up. She looks at me empathetically. Then she pulls back and says, "Aren't the flowers out the window beautiful?" I pull back, and I am stuck with a huge lump in my throat that I struggle to swallow.

The silence and withholding may be more about avoiding the emotions than it is the protecting of the secret. Perhaps Mom can't talk about her lonesome feeling, the loss of her first love, her father's death, or her brother's suicide without being overcome with emotion. Perhaps it is the packing away of memories and emotions rather than the protection of secrets. And perhaps that is true for my secrets and the reluctance to talk about Jordan's disclosure of sexual abuse. The memories and emotions can be overwhelming at times. Sometimes I still can't believe it happened. So is emotional avoidance, the keeping of secrets, and dissociation all part of surviving trauma? Is there a need to tell? A time to tell?

Today
Then the day came
When the risk to remain
Tight in a bud
Was more painful than the risk it took
To blossom
(Benton, as cited in Blue Sky Press Editor, 2013)

NOTE

[1] Excerpts from this autoethnographic narrative were adapted from my unpublished PhD dissertation (Murray, 2010). My identity, my son's identity, and my mother's identity are therefore already available in the public domain. All other names are pseudonyms. The autoethnographic dissertation proposal was approved by the Research Ethics Board at the University of Saskatchewan.

REFERENCES

Albom, M. (2006). *For one more day*. New York, NY: Hyperion.

Barry, W. R., Chisholm, D., & Parsons, B. (2005). *Age shall not weary them: Saskatchewan remembers its war dead*. Regina, Canada: People Places Publishing.

Blue Sky Press Editor. (2013, March 5). Who wrote "Risk"? Is the mystery solved? [Web log]. Posted to http://anaisninblog.skybluepress.com/2013/03/who-wrote-risk-is-the-mystery-solved/

Bok, S. (1989). *Secrets: On the ethics of concealment and revelation*. New York, NY: Vintage Books.

Estes, P. E. (1992). *Women who run with the wolves: Myths and stories of the wild woman archetype*. Toronto, Canada: Random House.

Jung, C. G. (1957). *The practice of psychotherapy: Essays on the psychology of the transference and other subjects* (Vol. 16). (C. G. Adler & R. F. C. Hull, Eds. & Trans.). Princeton, NJ: Princeton University Press. (Original work published 1954)

Jung, C. G. (1965). *Memories, dreams, reflections*. (A. Jaffe, Ed., R. Winston & C. Winston, Trans.). New York, NY: Vintage Books. (Original work published 1963)

Murray, B. L. (2010). *Secrets of mothering*. (Unpublished doctoral dissertation). Saskatoon, Saskatchewan: University of Saskatchewan.

Zingaro, L. (2009). *Speaking out: Storytelling for social change*. Walnut Creek, CA: Left Coast Press.

Lee Murray
College of Nursing
University of Saskatchewan

DEVIN COLLINS

22. THE ART OF FAKING A SMILE

A Layered Account of Mental Illness and/in Relating

As I write this essay, it is my hope to bring the voices of mental illness out from their silence. Through (re)writing my past, I describe my experiences living with depression, attention deficit disorder, and anxiety. This essay navigates moments within my life where "disruptions" have occurred—encounters with people where actions come to be understood as hurtful or incompetent (Frank, 2000). These moments of disruption are prime spots to submerge myself within the reflexive process of doing autoethnography in order to better understand my own mental illnesses and how my mental illness has affected and has been affected by my interactions with family and others.

In 2015, the National Institute of Mental Illness (2015) estimated that 16.1 million adults aged 18 or older in the United States (U.S.) had experienced at least one major depressive episode in the previous year. They further estimated that 40 million people suffer from anxiety disorder, and post-traumatic stress disorder affects 7.7 million people. These figures do not represent those suffering from attention deficit hyperactivity disorder, autism-spectrum disorders, bipolar disorder, borderline personality disorder, eating disorder, obsessive-compulsive disorder, schizophrenia, and social phobia. The wide range of disorders is further complicated because many do not have a definite known cause—even diagnosis can be troublesome.

When a person is suffering from a mental illness, the communication process requires considerable resources in order to communicate effectively. Fisher et al. (2012) note, "when those resources are taxed by a clinical problem, in many cases people no longer have the wherewithal to encode and decode messages to their full potential" (p. 540). Young (2009) describes a person with mental illness as "someone who internalizes the cultural ideology about mental illness, and then expresses that ideology symptomatically" (p. 53). That individual must construct symptoms of what they are feeling. Those ideas must be interpreted by another social construction of terms to identify what the symptomatic experience of that person might be.

THE CALL OF OUR STORIES

Beyond the national health care system, there is a growing need for narratives on how patients interact on an interpersonal level. Scholars continue to call for patient narratives in the field of interpersonal communication and point to a history of

S. L. Pensoneau-Conway et al. (Eds.), Doing Autoethnography, 217–227.
© *2017 Sense Publishers. All rights reserved.*

others doing so too (Caplan, Haslett, & Burleson, 2005; Knobloch & Delaney, 2012; Ness, Borg, Semb, & Karlsson, 2014; Nimrod, 2013). Although telling personal narratives might not heal physical wounds, it can work toward reducing stigma by possibly healing one's self-image (Bochner, 2001).

As narrators, individuals assign symbolic meaning to experiences, thus creating a sense of self and how we view the world (Harter & Bochner, 2009). "The struggle is personal, cultural, and political" (Bochner, 2001, p. 147), and, in order to give narrative the room it needs, notions of researcher neutrality and objectivity must be re-evaluated so that the self is written along with others (Ellis & Bochner, 1999). In writing narratives and putting the self at risk, locations of vulnerability become available for the significant reworking of thought and action (Denshire, 2014). Writing illness narrative aids the journey for authenticity (Bochner, 2001).

MY EMBODIMENT AND ENGAGEMENT IN/OF AUTOETHNOGRAPHIC WRITING

I inquire into the ways that narrative vignettes, layered accounts, and messy texts come together—constructing my mental illness so that it is seen as a relational accomplishment.

Narrative vignettes. Narrative vignettes use representation and reflexivity as an alternative approach to qualitative research (Humphreys, 2005). I attempt to create a window in my autoethnography where the reader can view my pleasure and pain—connecting me to the reader as both writer and subject. Embedding vignettes—short personal narratives—in this way creates a space where the reader vicariously experiences my memories as if they had been there in the moment. Narrative vignettes comprise the spaces, the layers of the layered account—strengthening each as they build upon or against each other.

Layered accounts. My autoethnographic approach draws on the layered account (Rambo Ronai, 1992, 1995; Rambo, 2005) to show a reader the blurred lines and intertwined voices that occur within the communication of lived experiences (Bochner, 2002). Layered accounts challenge the telling of my life from only one viewpoint (Denshire, 2014), allowing data, abstract analysis, and research to simultaneously engage with personal experience (Ellis, Adams, & Bochner, 2011) and unite the voices of personal experience and the academy in unobtrusive ways (Bochner, 2002). The process of layering accounts allows me to be reflexive about how I leave and take impressions of others, developing and changing identity formation because "every identity we have experienced is neither fully present nor fully erased" (Rambo, 2005, p. 567). Layered accounts challenge the telling of my life from only one viewpoint by opening up the future to the proliferation of juxtaposed multi-voiced narratives (Denshire, 2014). Adding to this ensemble of voices, I locate my writing in one final genre—messy texts.

Messy texts. Messy texts are often systemic modes for writing against hegemonic discourses (Marcus, 2007). I use the license that messy texts offers in order to write through reflexive tales. I use messy texts not as a model to follow, but as a way to represent substantive personal styles of thought and writing (Marcus, 1994). When I write into my messy text, I bring out the "experiential, interpretive, dialogical, and polyphonic process at work" (Marcus, 2007, p. 1128). Messy texts ask for readers to read their authors' experiences the way that the author experienced and re-experienced their memories—messily.

An account of mental illness. By showing/telling personal stories of mental illness, my layered narratives present an image of living with mental disorders. While it is tempting to just accept that mental illness is simply a neurochemical issue, medical narratives (i.e., the stories of medicine) do not provide a full story (Frank, 1995). In showing/telling my story, I write my experiences, interactions, and influences—the social and cultural.

Mental illness as a relational accomplishment. My goal for this essay is to tell/show stories of relating. Through my narratives, I recount a desire to connect and understand. I scribble the ways the self is seen by others and how the self is seen in others (Frank, 1995). I rewrite the ways in which I see myself as living with mental illness—engaging in creative acts of storytelling that help reveal myself to my self (Ellis & Bochner, 2006). In working through my autoethnographic narratives, I creatively show my self at work (Goodall, 2004).

Relational communication. I use this essay to give my body's voice equal importance where it too often has not had the privilege of speech. My contribution to relational communication is the addition of my dyadic body—a body that gives itself up to others (Frank, 2000). By embracing myself as a storyteller, I create a space where the construction of the self is navigated—weaving itself through interrelated others, languages, cultures, and histories (Spry, 2011).

My narrative layers present an image of my mental illness that will not translate to a survey or experiment (Ellis et al., 2011) because to do so would remove the relational support columns that make my authorship a voice of somebody (in particular) from somewhere (in particular) (Bochner, 2002). I construct my essay aware that I am standing on the shoulders of those who wrote before me—informing the ways that I write, paint, dance, or perform my self through personal experience (Douglas & Carless, 2013). I use their toolsets to creatively show personal experience in ways an audience will find accessible (Adams, 2012). This writing enables my personal narratives to drift outward from the self (Holman Jones, 2013), making writing perform (Pollock, 1998). Every relationship I have experienced is unavoidably embedded in my written text. As I sprawl my written self upon the page, my sense making process directly contributes to the relational essence of communication (Gannon, 2013). I place life on a stage where I perform and speak to and for others (Richardson, 1992). I use the privilege of authorship to choose the character motivations of others—annunciating their values.

I *do* autoethnography to break from the traditional ways that research is conducted. I become, through autoethnography, self and other focused (Hernandez & Ngunjiri, 2013) and show how lives are shaped by experiences (Adams, Holman Jones, & Ellis, 2014). By showing experienced life, I reduce stigma and eliminate silence through acts of writing (Holman Jones, Adams, & Ellis, 2013).

I embed personal experience through aesthetically pleasing and relational experiences written through stories (Ellis et al., 2011)—embracing uncertainty and emotionality to release silences at work (Holman Jones et al., 2013). I write to acknowledge a position that is not neutral (Gannon, 2013). In seeking to make life better, I provide stories to think about, but more importantly, creative stories to live with (Bochner, 2001). I reflexively layer accounts (Rambo Ronai, 1992) through narrative vignettes (Humphreys, 2005) to write against hegemonic discourses in messy texts (Marcus, 2007).

Writing has made my life better, so I must let my words radiate out. I must join the reader in carrying the stories of my mental illness narratives through academic journals, classrooms, and conversations with friends, family, and strangers (Harter & Bochner, 2009). Together, we will continue "creating space for dialogue with silenced others" (Denshire, 2014, p. 845) by allowing our bodies to be the bodies for those willing and ready to listen (Frank, 1995)—reducing and, ultimately, eliminating the silence of mental illness through communication.

* * *

Chad is riding shotgun as I drive down the steep hill that put me through my paces when I was learning to drive my manual stick shift. I stare at the road, but not really paying attention, the drive is muscle memory by this point. My ex-girlfriend's face is running through my head as the street lines blur and drift away. My heart pumps faster and faster. I feel like I am running at full sprint. Except, I am not breathing. I begin to gasp for air. I have never felt my body lose control like this.

Breathe in: At the very top of my head, I feel a numbing sensation begin to radiate from my skull.

Breathe out: I feel the creature pulling my essence out. I can feel the energy leaving my fingertips—numbing to the point that they feel like they are swelling. My mouth begins to feel like it was shot with Novocain, and I move my jaw around to get feeling back. I want desperately to keep my cool.

Breathe in: I no longer have feeling in my feet, and I feel like my chest is seizing. I can no longer focus my eyes on the road. Traffic pushes its way past me on my left.

Breathe out: I am unable to describe what is happening. No one ever told me things like *this* could happen. I want to tell Chad that I am worried about my safety, yet completely unobservant of his danger in this situation. I don't have the words that I need right now. All I know is that for some reason, I am dying.

No breath: The lights go out. I am driving 30 miles per hour down the road, and I can no longer see or breathe. The only action I can think is to pull the truck to the right and hope I don't fall into some ditch hidden in the tall grass.

"Take deep breaths," Chad is telling me.

"I can't breathe, I am dying," I yell back at him.

I frantically search in the dark for the manual window crank. The humid Texas air fills the truck. I breathe a little slower, and the vision begins to return. The blur fades, and the front of my truck is just feet from a telephone pole. I wipe the snot from my nose and try to stop the flow of tears.

"I think you had a panic attack," Chad says, his hand on my shoulder.

We never talk about it again. Why has no one warned me that this could happen?

* * *

Her head tilts up toward me, and I see her body slowly begin to rotate. Just as her legs are about to tip over, they stop and stick straight up in the air. I look at the dirt on her belly, then back into the eyes of this tiny, yet dense, little German Shepherd puppy. As her legs relax spread eagle, I say, in an Irish accent, "You're a fuckin' mess, dag."

Switching to a motherly, Midwestern accent, I continue, "Close your legs! I can see your hoo-ha spread out to the world like a puppy porn star."

She makes the most adorable, heart-melting, and expressive little howl—looking me in the eyes. The trust that this dog is placing in me. Why? Why me? Of all the people you could have found on the street, it was my jacket that you began nuzzling in. You are everything I have been fighting to keep myself away from in my depression ... happy things.

In this moment something begins to happen that hasn't happened in a long time. Water leaks from my eyes. My voice cracks as I say to her, in my best Michael Caine impression, "Look what you've done. I bring some un-tagged, mystery dog in from the cold, and what do I get? Sad, leaky face, that's what I get!"

The tears roll down my cheeks, I realize just how fucking alone I have felt for a long time and how alone this dog must have felt abandoned on the street. As if cameras were filming, I make sure to use all of my super powers of acting so that this little dog and I have more honest and genuine acting beats than a *House of Cards* episode.

I forget how nice it is to say something and have a response—not worrying if she is going to judge me when my mouth gets ahead of my thoughts and I forget whatever linguistic game plan I had originally planned for myself.

Wiping the tears from my cheek, I lean my head down toward her face, sniffling snot loosened by my previous leaking episode.

"I fuckin' love you, Boo-Boo," I say, in my own voice.

It is then that she can suppress her teething urges no longer. She bites my finger.

"Ow! I'm trying to have a moment with you, dammit!" I whimper.

* * *

We arrive at Walmart and walk through the aisles not really talking. I watch people go about their shopping, checking off lists. I leave her not saying a word—looking for the section where I am bound to find something, the toy aisle. I can't go wrong finding happiness there.

I rummage through the baskets filled with squishy, indefinable toys. These baskets are filled with the misfit toys, the ones that don't fit any other category. The toys squeezed for their texture, fiddled with, and then placed back in the bin because no one ever really wants to buy this shit. Sometimes I feel like these toys. People don't want the misfits.

I stare deeply at the higher shelf toys. The action figures, Ninja Turtle flashlights, the extremely ripped wrestler wearing nothing but tiny black undies and multi-colored neon arm ribbons. I stare and think of my father lying in the hospital bed. He is a broken toy, and I might not see him ever again.

I am aimlessly adrift in toy land when I hear a voice, but it sounds faint or muffled. The pictures in my mind become wavy as the static starts to consume everything. I open my eyes, and I am standing back in the toy aisle. Just as I lock my eyes onto her, she lets out two small whistles, points to the ground by her feet and hollers, "C'mon."

She takes the little bit of steam I've mustered. My shoulders slump, and I slowly shuffle my body in her direction. "I'm not a fucking dog," I quietly say.

"Then stop looking like a sad dog that knows it peed on the carpet," she chides.

I feel insulted and reduced to something lower than shit. I want to respond with something smart/cold/hurtful, but there are too many thoughts rushing through my head to focus. I choose to say nothing as I drag behind her with my ears folded back in submission. I feel like a burden.

* * *

It has been three months since my grandmother died, and I am not able to process why my mother isn't done with her grieving. I blame my mother for only hurting herself by drinking all the time. When I walk through the house from my room to the back door, I stop to see how my mother is doing. She gives standard responses as she keeps her face tucked in a book. I lean down to give her a hug, hoping it might cheer her up.

When I reach my arms over her, I can smell the booze. She is hiding her alcohol from me, which makes me furious. She is becoming an alcoholic. When I speak with my brother, he patiently listens as I describe how she is hiding a bottle somewhere and that she buries empty bottles at the bottom of the trash. I can't calm my blood pressure because I just can't figure out how she is doing it.

I want to say something, but I stay silent and storm off to my room. I grab my weed and one hitter pipe, huffing and puffing as I walk out into the backyard where it's pitch black. I flick the lighter, igniting the end of the pipe. I inhale/exhale the smoke, easing into my high, still furious that she will not just be honest with me. I think I see a shadow, and with a burst of speed, I hide my pipe. Am I just imagining this alcohol problem?

* * *

This is your moment, relish it. Careful. One step at a time. Remember to breathe, and as you walk forward to the mic, just play it cool. Grab your pick, set your guitar, and begin to play … nice. Hear each note 100 different ways as it travels through every individual and out into the cosmos. Feed on their energy, and enjoy the texture of this delicacy.

Now, ease into the chorus on the downbeat ... now.

* * *

One Mississippi.

My heart stops as I catch the guitar around my knees. Time distorts and this is unfamiliar. Throughout my body, it just feels uncomfortable. I am hunched over, desperately holding on to my guitar as if it's the only safety net I have.

Two Mississippi.

Holding my guitar with the strap hanging limp, my heart feels like it makes twenty beats between every second. My eyes adjust to the lights, and I look out among an absolutely silent crowd. An ocean of blue caps and gowns unmoving—completely still waters.

Three Mississippi.

There are 506 graduates holding their breath and fighting the uncomfortable urge to squirm in their seats while they watch your train wreck. People can't turn their head away from smoldering wreckage and bright emergency lights. This is fucked! You are fucked. Each student brought family, friends, and any other yokel with a blow horn to the Freeman Coliseum for this ceremony. Two thousand people, possibly more, just watched your guitar drop off your shoulder. This will be your legacy.

Four Mississippi.

* * *

When I look back on high school graduation, I am thankful that smart phones were invented several years later.

* * *

I close my eyes and take a deep breath as I begin to shake. My fingers feel like they are moving through half dried cement. The tremble finds its way to my diaphragm and vocal chords, and I don't know if I have enough physical strength to keep my voice on pitch, remember all the words, and play guitar all at once.

My body physically rejects the choice I've made to play. I am conscious not to keep my knees locked, and it's probably the only thing keeping me from crumbling to the floor. Nothing feels like the feeling when your body deceives you, especially in front of others.

I miss having my Ladybird on my left shoulder to ease the nerves.

* * *

I fantasize my death scene frequently during my senior year of high school. The voice in my head likes to remind me that, if using a razor, I need to cut vertically and not horizontally across my wrist. I search the junk drawer for anything resembling a razor—only finding old batteries, chip bag clips, and a plug adapter.

Having chosen a plastic bag, I return to my room and quietly close the door. I sit and begin to tie the bag around my neck. I imagine the faces of my family as they discover my body. Right now, I don't matter and this is how I will show people that they should have cared more about me. Fortunately, my obsession with death is balanced with my anxiety towards dying.

As my oxygen begins to deplete, I panic. I rip a whole in the bag that wraps around my head, but I don't burst through exclaiming, "I want to live!" The only thing going through my head is that I am a fucking failure.

* * *

I look into her eyes and she doesn't recognize who I am. She looks at me unblinking, as I am sure she is trying to process why I would drop this on her now. The movie *The Tao of Steve* plays in the background and my friends sit on the couch staring intently at the TV trying to not acknowledge the awkward situation I have unleashed upon the living room.

"I'm not doing this now!" she says.

"I tried to fucking kill myself!" I shout with all of the strength in my lungs.

The silence makes the moment feel like it lasts hours, as she finally turns, lights her Swisher Sweet cigar, and exits to the back porch.

* * *

I push my fork into my Chuy's burrito, cutting it up and moving it around my plate. I look up and get lost in the various hubcaps, license plates, and general car stuff adorning the ceiling and walls. As I actively avoid eye contact with my mother, I am silent while my mother and brother talk in between eating chips and dip.

I wish I had stayed home. Had I stayed home, I could be smoking weed, cuddling with the dogs, and, in general, not feeling as bad for not being able to afford a gift for my mother. I lock eyes accidentally and watch tears gather at the bottom of her eyes. One tear escapes the rest.

"I just wish I knew how to help you," she says, crunching a chip in her mouth.

I can't tell her about the things that have been going wrong this summer. I can't tell her about my eviction notices, electric bill, or bounced check. I am ruining her birthday because she blames herself for my depression. I am ruining her birthday because I let her think she is to blame by never speaking up. Too often, I fake a smile and continue going about life as if nothing is wrong. I had to do that when my grandmother died. I had to be the strong one in the house.

* * *

I watch my mother with confusion. She is overwhelmed with emotion—upset to tears because Jack in the Box didn't put mayo on her burger. This is unnecessary.

"Why are you so upset over this little issue? Just let it go!" I say, ignoring the amount of misery she has collected and bottled up over the years. This isn't about mayo. The mayo simply popped the cork. This is about the fight we had. This is about my grandmother's death. This is about the four pets we lost in the last year. This is about being single and alone. This is about the world pressing her down to the point that she has no strength. I can't be around others who are depressed. Sadness is a contagion, and some days that's too much to risk.

* * *

She looks at me with a smile of empathy as her blue eyes tell me she has seen more than I know. She grabs a cocktail napkin, scribbling the lyrics, "You desire my attention, but deny my affection." She barely knows me, but she understands how to handle me. She looks back at me, staring into my eyes while she thinks of what to say next.

* * *

The note reads, "Dev, don't be an idiot by making life harder than it needs to be." It's signed, "–R."

REFERENCES

Adams, T. E. (2012). The joys of autoethnography: Possibilities for communication research. *Qualitative Communication Research, 1*, 181–194. doi: 10.1525/qcr.2012.1.2.181

Adams, T. E., Holman Jones, S., & Ellis, C. (2014). *Autoethnography.* London, England: Oxford University Press.

Bochner, A. P. (2001). Narratives virtues. *Qualitative Inquiry, 7*, 131–157. doi: 10.1177/107780040100700201

Bochner, A. P. (2002). Perspectives on inquiry III: The moral of stories. In M. Knapp & J. Daley (Eds.), *Handbook of interpersonal communication* (3rd ed., pp. 73–101). Thousand Oaks, CA: Sage.

Caplan, S. E., Haslett, B. J., & Burleson, B. R. (2005). Telling it like it is: The adaptive function of narrative in coping with loss in later life. *Health Communication, 17*, 233–251. doi: 101207/s15327027hc1703_2

Denshire, S. (2014). On-auto-ethnography. *Current Sociology Review, 62*, 831–850. doi: 10.1177/0011392114533339

Douglas, K., & Carless, D. (2013). A history of autoethnographic inquiry. In S. Holman Jones, T. E. Adams, & C. Ellis (Eds.), *Handbook of autoethnography* (pp. 84–106). Walnut Creek, CA: Left Coast Press.

Ellis, C., & Bochner, A. P. (1999). Bringing emotion and personal narrative into medical social science. *Health, 3*, 229–237. doi: 10.1177/136345939900300206

Ellis, C., & Bochner, A. P. (2006). Analyzing analytic autoethnography: An autopsy. *Journal of Contemporary Ethnography, 35*, 429–449. doi: 10.1177/0891241606286979

Ellis, C., Adams, T. E., & Bochner, A. P. (2011). Autoethnography: An overview. *Forum: Qualitative Social Research, 12*(1). Retrieved from http://www.qualitative-research.net/index.php/fqs/article/view/1589

Fisher, C. L., Goldsmith, D., Harrison, K., Hoffner, C. A., Segrin, C., Wright, K., & Miller, K. (2012). Communication and mental health: A conversation from the cm café. *Communication Monographs, 79*, 539–550. doi: 10.1080/03637751.2012.727284

Frank, A. W. (1995). *The wounded storyteller: Body, illness, and ethics.* Chicago, IL: University of Chicago Press.

Frank, A. W. (2000). Illness and autobiographical work: Dialogue as narrative destabilization. *Qualitative Sociology, 23*, 135–156. doi: 10.1023/A:1005411818318

Gannon, S. (2013). Sketching subjectivities. In S. Holman Jones, T. E. Adams, & C. Ellis (Eds.), *Handbook of autoethnography* (pp. 228–244). Walnut Creek, CA: Left Coast Press.

Goodall, H. L. (2004). Narrative ethnography as applied communication research. *Journal of Applied Communication Research, 32*, 185–194. doi: 10.1080/0090988042000240130

Harter, L. M., & Bochner, A. P. (2009). Healing through stories: A special issue on narrative medicine. *Journal of Applied Communication Research, 37*, 113–117. doi: 10.1080/00909880902792271

Hernandez, K. C. & Ngunjiri, F.W. (2013). Relationships and communities in autoethnography. In S. Holman Jones, T. E. Adams, & C. Ellis (Eds.), *Handbook of autoethnography* (pp. 262–281). Walnut Creek, CA: Left Coast Press.

Holman Jones, S. (2013). The performance space: Giving an account of performance studies. *Text & Performance Quarterly, 33*, 77–80. doi: http://dx.doi.org/10.1080/10462937.2012.746215

Holman Jones, S., Adams, T. E., & Ellis, C. (2013). Coming to know autoethnography as more than a method. In S. Holman Jones, T. E. Adams, & C. Ellis (Eds.), *Handbook of autoethnography* (pp. 17–41). Walnut Creek, CA: Left Coast Press.

Humphreys, M. (2005). Getting personal: Reflexive and autoethnographic vignettes. *Qualitative Inquiry, 11*, 840–860. doi: 10.1177/1077800404269425

Knobloch, L. K., & Delaney, A. L. (2012). Themes of relational uncertainty and interference from partners in depression. *Health Communication, 27*, 750–765. doi: 10.1080/10410236.2011.639293

Marcus, G. E. (1994). What comes (just) after "post"? The case of ethnography. In N. K. Denzin & Y. S. Lincoln (Eds.), *The handbook of qualitative research* (pp. 563–574). Thousand Oaks, CA: Sage.

Marcus, G. E. (2007). Ethnography two decades after writing culture: From the experimental to the baroque. *Anthropological Quarterly, 80*, 1127–1145. doi: 10.1353/anq.2007.0059

National Institute of Mental Illness. (2015). *Major depression among adults.* Retrieved from https://www.nimh.nih.gov/health/statistics/prevalence/major-depression-among-adults.shtml

Ness, O., Borg, M., Semb, R., & Karlsson, B. (2014). "Walking alongside": Collaborative practices in mental health and substance abuse care. *International Journal of Mental Health Systems, 8*, 82–97. doi:10.1186/1752-4458-8-55

Nimrod, G. (2013). Online depression communities: Members' interests and perceived benefits. *Health Communication, 28*, 425–434. doi:10.1080/10410236.2012.691068.

Pollock, D. (1998). Performing writing. In P. Phelan & J. Lane (Eds.), *The ends of performance* (pp. 73–103). New York: New York University Press.

Rambo, C. (2005). Impressions of grandmother: an autoethnographic portrait. *Journal of Contemporary Ethnography, 34*, 560–585. doi:10.1177/0891241605279079

Rambo Ronai, C. (1992). The reflexive self through narrative: A night in the life of an erotic dancer/researcher. In C. Ellis & M. Flaherty (Eds.), *Investigating subjectivity: Research on lived experience* (pp. 102–124). Newbury Park, CA: Sage

Rambo Ronai, C. (1995). Multiple reflections of child sex abuse: An argument for layered account. *Journal of Contemporary Ethnography, 23*, 395–426.

Richardson, L. (1992). The consequences of poetic representation: Writing the other, rewriting the self. In C. Ellis & M. G. Flaherty (Eds.), *Investigating subjectivity: Research on lived experience* (pp. 125–137). Newbury Park, CA: Sage.

Spry, T. (2011). Performative autoethnography: Critical embodiment and possibilities. In N. K. Denzin & Y. S. Lincoln (Eds.), *SAGE handbook of qualitative research* (4th ed., pp. 497–512). Thousand Oaks, CA: Sage.

Young, E. (2009). Memoirs: Rewriting the social construction of mental illness. *Narrative Inquiry, 19,* 52–68. doi: https://doi.org/10.1075/ni.19.1.04

Devin Collins
Department of Communication Studies
Southern Illinois University Carbondale

DESIREÉ D. ROWE

23. AUTOETHNOGRAPHY AS
OBJECT-ORIENTED METHOD

On my desk sits the well-worn stapler I smuggled in an old printer paper box from my last job. "This is MY stapler," I thought as I tucked it into a back corner of one of the non-descript boxes that lined my office wall. The dull black paint is worn away where the space between my thumb and pointer finger holds it. It's not like the new one that sits in my desk drawer; this one is a well-oiled relic from the past that moves smoothly and requires very little attention. I feel a kinship to Stephen Root's character "Milton" in the 1999 movie *Office Space*. The red Swingline he dearly protected and ultimately lost was a comic device that marked the ways in which our workplace, sometimes, forgets us. Forgets that we are people, too.

* * *

There is potential in bringing an object-oriented perspective into autoethnography. When marking the potential of object-oriented autoethnography, I am framing objects as non-human entities. Physical objects, or the material *things* that make up our everyday world, become the focus of the narrative. Like Wiegman (2012), my use of *objects* "is not, then, a theoretical commitment to a distinct body of psychoanalytic thought, but...that objects of study are as fully enmeshed in fantasy, projection, and desire as those that inhabit the more familiar itinerary of intimate life, such as sex, lover, parent, sibling, friend" (p. 20). Unlike Wiegman, I am not interested in pointing to the particular usefulness in ideological formulations that do not reveal an immediate materiality (discourse, ideology, love). In this moment, I stay with objects that are the immediate material representations (worn pages of tired books, the cracked paint in the bathroom, the frayed end of a shoelace). I am inspired by the simplicity that Bogost and Schaberg (2017) use in describing their *Object Lessons* book series "about the hidden lives of ordinary things."

Autoethnography is already well-versed in linking personal narrative to larger ideological forces through vivid storytelling. Berry (2013) describes autoethnography as "a discursive accomplishment, a spinning whose rotations personify a commitment to experimentation, evocation, and scholarly voice" with reflexivity at its core (p. 211). These few pages seek to advocate for an increased theoretical unpacking of the power of objects within autoethnographic writing. To do this, I will discuss the construct of what a *thing/object* is and then work through

S. L. Pensoneau-Conway et al. (Eds.), Doing Autoethnography, 229–232.
© *2017 Sense Publishers. All rights reserved.*

how this can, and does, appear within autoethnographic writing. Spliced within, I offer my glimpses of this object-oriented autoethnography.

* * *

It's chilly and I pull my hoodie over the top of my head as I walk a bit quicker to the parking garage on my university campus. The fabric of the hood cuts off a bit of my peripheral vision but doesn't mask my whiteness. As the sun sets and the temperature begins to dip I don't feel threatened or unsafe, just a little cold. My scalp has been feeling exposed and bare since the surgery and I need this sweatshirt. In *Hood,* Kinney (2016) gives us an object lesson on the cultural locations of the hood from the dark ages executioner to the Klansman, and most movingly, to the ways in which the sweatshirt hoodie has become an emblematic symbol of the Black Lives Matter movement. The simple hood. It's an object storied by a past and present that makes it more than a simple piece of fabric.

* * *

An object-oriented autoethnography allows for a broader sense of the multiple critical trajectories that are possible within a single, tangible, *thing.* In working through, carefully, the relationship of self to a particular object, we engage in a mapping of that object into a sociopolitical location. Mapping through writing allows us to explore the multiple dimensions of the object, and its place within our own narrative. This *thing,* then, brings into sharp focus the multiple meanings it embodies and the how it intersects with identity, self, and politics. The object is a prop to our lived experiences, a prop that aids us on our continued quest to perform an embodied expressive epistemic. The autoethnographic mapping of the object, then, allows for us to unfold the intersections of stories and bodies. In "Thing theory," Brown (2001) began opening the conversation about the intersections of things and critical theoretical engagement when he notes, "The story of objects asserting themselves as things, then, is the story of a changed relation to the human subject and thus the story of how the thing really names less an object than a particular subject-object relation" (p. 4). The thing/object intertwines with our lives in ways that simultaneously embody and allude to articulation. The analysis in this way does not ignore the material relations of theory but, rather, places critical theoretical considerations in conversation with the actual materiality of lives, asking: what objects create/sustain/destroy our lives? What are the stories of those objects in relation to the subject?

* * *

I have spent years writing about scum. Well, S.C.U.M. as the Society for Cutting Up Men and its founder, Valerie Solanas. Solanas disavowed the transference of scum to S.C.U.M., claiming that her publisher, Maurice Girodias, created the acronym to make her look crazier and sell more books after the shooting of

Warhol. The real story, for me, was always about scum itself. The murky, floating liquid that moves silently across black water. Solanas didn't haphazardly choose to mark her relationship with that object. Through poetry, non-fiction, and short stories, she intertwined herself with the abject waste of scum. With each opaque wave, a cluster of white bubbly froth dissipates and reappears. Back and forth. Fort and da. As object, scum becomes more than just a metaphor when it appears in your own life and you have to do the work of cleaning it up. Scrubbing the scum from in-between the tiles, from the ring of the toilet, underneath the water bottle lid. Getting rid of the ring of scum. I spent years scrubbing. And still it moves. Back and forth. Dissipate and reappear. I pick at the scab on top of my head, wanting to scrub it. It feels unclean.

* * *

In turning towards an object-oriented autoethnography it becomes important to mark what autoethnography is seen as, in this moment, and how those functions can be best served and expanded through this approach. Autoethnographers are not just writing stories about their lives. As Adams (2011) clearly parses out, autoethnographers interview cultural members, participate in and observe "cultural events and rituals," examine "members' ways of speaking and relating," analyze cultural artifacts, and use personal experience (p. 154). In each of these instances, an object (or Adams's artifact) can serve as the central node of analysis, allowing for a multiplicity of narratives to emerge. The object-oriented autoethnography functions much like the metaphor of the rhizome. Shoemaker (2013) notes, "embodying principles of nonhierarchical connection and heterogeneity, the rhizome recalls a queer aesthetic that conjures various horizons" (p. 531). As the rhizome moves in multiple directions, so does the story of the object. Solanas seemed to be on the right track then, orienting human as object. Orienting humans as scum. What does it mean to be objectified? To be turned into object?

As a theoretical framework, object-oriented feminism is political as it frames "objecthood as a situational orientation, so as to apprehend and alter objects' intersectional prospects for self-determination, solidarity, and resistance" (Behar, 2016, p. 24). Well, then, as method, what can an object-oriented autoethnography offer? Perhaps a positioning of objects as subjects of autoethnography? Or a framing of self as object? Object-oriented feminism offers a theoretical frame for autoethnography. The methodological roots of autoethnography rest in the exploration of self and story-telling and is poised to be an emergent pairing with object-oriented feminism.

* * *

The story has always been about my scalp. The thin membrane on top of my head. I think there are gnats living in my head. Not *inside* my head, in that existentialist Gregor Samsa way. But in a scab that is bleeding and sometimes green that is on the top of my head—on my scalp. Whenever I sit in this very spot on this very couch there is always a single gnat flitting about my head. I've looked for rotten food, dropped long ago and forgotten. Nothing. It's me. I'm rotting. My head is the object. It's attracted to the green sticky goo that flows between the scabs. This gnat is living inside my head.

Four months ago, I was told I have cancer and now my scalp is decomposing. Four months is a long time to wait to die. That's dramatic. Let's try again. There were 17 days between the time I was told I had eccrine carcinoma and the date of my surgery. This was the bad kind of cancer, I was told. Spoken to as if I was only capable of operating within the binary. I still worried why there were 17 days.

"Oh, so what do you profess?" The oncologist from Long Island laughs. "Failure and negativity." I respond as he pulls stitch number 32 out of my scalp. I try not to lose count. 33. 34.

I feel him laying eggs in the pus. Dragging his back legs just a bit so he has to fly lower. Into my field of vision as I, motionless on the same spot on the green couch, swat at him again.

REFERENCES

Adams, T. E. (2011). *Narrating the closet: An autoethnography of same-sex attraction.* Walnut Creek, CA: Left Coast Press.

Behar, K. (Ed.). (2016). *Object oriented feminism.* Minneapolis: University of Minnesota Press.

Berry, K. (2013). Spinning autoethnographic reflexivity, cultural critique, and negotiating selves. In S. Holman Jones, T. E. Adams, & C. Ellis (Eds.), *The handbook of autoethnography* (pp. 209–227). Walnut Creek, CA: Left Coast Press

Bogost, I., & Schaberg, C. (2017, March 23). Object lessons. Retrieved from objectsobjectsobjects.com.

Brown, B. (2001). Thing theory. *Critical inquiry, 21,* 1–22.

Kinney, A. (2016). *Hood.* New York, NY: Bloomsbury Publishing.

Shoemaker, D. B. (2013). Autoethnographic journeys: Performing possibilities/utopias/futures. In S. Holman Jones, T. E. Adams, & C. Ellis (Eds.), *The handbook of autoethnography* (pp. 513–537). Walnut Creek, CA: Left Coast Press.

Wiegman, R. (2012). *Object lessons.* Durham, NC: Duke University Press.

Desireé D. Rowe
Department of Mass Communication & Communication Studies
Towson University

Lightning Source UK Ltd.
Milton Keynes UK
UKHW02f0731071117
312328UK00005B/645/P